Happy Mothers Day, and Birthday
Sweetheart. your loving Huzzy
May 12-14 1989

SHANSI MI... [barcode] W9-ASV-214 ...RD.

Feu Chofu, China.
May 27. 1898.

~ Home Folks:—

Yesterday brought us
good letters, and the ones
father mother and Wallie among
. They were dated Mar. 20-21.
as the very best letter from
I ever had. I have read
ore than once already, and
ead it again more than once.
d me so much good to have
write such a funny letter,
washing, mopping and
y under the Porch"! The letters
Every one of them full of love
good cheer. There was one
one from Alice Price, or
Dot," telling how well th
heir new home, and here
worrying for fear the dear
would not have room to
her wings. I had a so

Feu Chofu, Shansi, China. Aug. 12 18
Dear Home Folks:—

Here it is time
another mail to go out. Our com
are all getting the ague, or alrea
have it in fact, so the mail bu
has become somewhat uncertai
This has been an unusually co
season and there is considerabl
ague in the country; so far w
been well since the siege in
in the early spring. Charlie
us a week ago to-day to visi
other stations. In vacation tim
isn't much to do ex---
service. Yo---

Feu Chofu, China.
Aug. 1st 19

Dear Dear Home Folks:—

During the past six weeks m
letters from the manifold
and us. Our lives
red and we hav
day expecting i
on earth. Two of
our nearest nei
church and Miss.
tally killed by a
hered in their c
the 28th of Jun
ed not go nea
n any particul
red stir out of o
All we know

Denver Col.
Thurs. 8. A. M.

~ur home folks:—

Will here we are in
wonderful city of the plains.
had a good rest in the
per—though the dust was pretty
. I heard one lady say it
w on her feet so she could n't
her shoes on! but I think
must have been like Charlie's
THE UNION DEPOT & RAILROAD CO. DENVER, COLO. WAITING ROOM.

CHINA JOURNAL

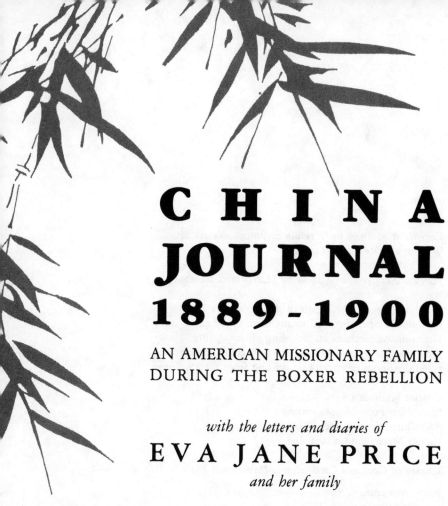

C H I N A
JOURNAL
1889-1900

AN AMERICAN MISSIONARY FAMILY
DURING THE BOXER REBELLION

with the letters and diaries of

EVA JANE PRICE
and her family

Foreword by

HARRISON E. SALISBURY

Introductory Notes and Annotations by

ROBERT H. FELSING, PH.D.

CHARLES SCRIBNER'S SONS
New York

Copyright © 1989 by Virginia E. Phipps, Verna L.
Wilson, and Velma A. Caruth

Foreword copyright © 1989 by Harrison E. Salisbury

All rights reserved. No part of this book may be
reproduced or transmitted in any form or by any means,
electronic or mechanical, including photocopying,
recording, or by any information storage and retrieval
system, without permission in writing from the Publisher.

Charles Scribner's Sons
Macmillan Publishing Company
866 Third Avenue, New York, NY 10022
Collier Macmillan Canada, Inc.

Library of Congress Cataloging-in-Publication Data

Price, Eva Jane, d. 1900.
    China journal.

    1. China—History—Boxer Rebellion, 1899–1901,
Personal narratives, American. 2. Missions—China.
3. Price, Eva Jane, d. 1900. I. Title.
DS771.P75 1988 951'.03 [B] 88-18483
ISBN 0-684-18951-8

Macmillan books are available at special discounts for
bulk purchases for sales promotions, premiums,
fund-raising, or educational use. For details, contact:

        Special Sales Director
        Macmillan Publishing Company
        866 Third Avenue
        New York, NY 10022

10 9 8 7 6 5 4 3 2 1

Printed in the United States of America

LETTERS COMPILED BY

Virginia Phipps
Lucille Wilson
Arlene Caruth

Grandnieces of Eva Jane Price, 1855–1900

CONTENTS

Contents

FOREWORD

In the spring of 1988 I spent a few days in Pingyuan county of Shandong province in central China, a distant place backed up against the Yellow River, almost as remote and secluded as you could find. I knew nothing about Pingyuan county other than that it was the birthplace of a friend of mine, the Chinese writer Deng Youmei, who had invited me to see what "the real China is like."

I had no notion that this pleasant rural country, rather upbeat in the glow of the Deng Xiaoping reforms, had a dark and deadly past. Hardly one hundred years ago it had given birth to one of the most violent, chauvinistic, antiforeign movements among those which have periodically swept China in recent centuries.

Pingyuan, I was astonished to find, was where the Boxer movement arose just before 1900, sweeping China like a prairie fire, only to die away under the merciless gunfire of foreign troops and the vacillating policies of the dying Manchu dynasty.

I was even more startled to discover that one of the original Boxers was still alive, although in extraordinarily poor health at an age of more than one hundred years, and to realize from the talk of villagers that the sentiments which had given birth to the Boxers had not entirely vanished. To not a few Pingyuan countrymen the Boxers are still heroes.

In talking with one man who has dedicated himself to the history of the Boxers and written several books, I suggested that people seemed to regard the Boxers as patriots—misguided patriots. "Not misguided," he said with great firmness.

The stories which the Boxers spread to fuel their movement— tales of Christian missionaries who sold baby Chinese girls into slavery and prostitution, tales of debauchery, cruelty, connivance of Christians with local landlords and gentry to keep the peasants in poverty and destitution, of missionaries conspiring with criminal Chinese elements to feather their nests—were, I was stunned to find, still accepted as gospel in this remote area.

I took this persistence of belief in the legends of the Boxers as evidence of the extraordinary power of the Boxer myth and a measure of the strength of feelings which the movement had stirred among ordinary Chinese people.

It is still hard for outsiders to fully comprehend the hurricane of emotion which the Boxers stirred up in China, and it was harder yet in the sudden whirlwind of their uprising. It would be impossible to find two environments, two cultures, more divergent than those of backwater China in the 1890s and Oberlin College in Ohio, the epitome of the Western ethic and a cradle of the powerful American missionary movement of those times.

Oberlin is where two idealistic young people from Iowa, Eva and Charles Price, went to study and from where, in 1889, they embarked on a missionary career. The Prices were sent to Fenzhou, an isolated mission in Shanxi province not far from Pingyuan county in Shandong where the Boxers began. They knew the town as Fen Cho fu. The post was south of Taiyuan, the capital of Shanxi. Their nearest mission neighbors were four days' travel distant.

The geographical distance between Fenzhou and Oberlin verges on 15,000 miles (almost three months' travel time in the 1890s). But the geographical difference is nothing compared to the historical and cultural differences. No amount of training at Oberlin could have enabled the Prices to understand what lay beneath the pleasant, often smiling, countenance of the Chinese world in which they were immersed. Nor was there any way in which the Chinese could understand this dedicated pair of young Americans.

Three or four centuries before Columbus, Shanxi boasted one of the highest cultures in the world. It was the heart of Chinese civilization. But by 1890 it—and all of China—was a shambles. There was no way in which Eva and Charles Price could penetrate the emotional and spiritual chaos with which China approached the end of the nineteenth century. China had been the proudest of

nations, its traditions, philosophy, technology the most advanced
on the globe. Now, in a fashion which no Chinese could understand, all that China valued had become dross. The barbarians of
the west and the east (Japan) displayed contempt for her. No Great
Wall or Imperial edict could contain them. Every nation in the
world, so it seemed, vented its will on China, spat on her shrines,
looted her treasure, addicted tens of millions of Chinese to opium,
marched across her domain, laying waste, robbing, raping as they
willed. Nothing Chinese was sacred. The throne was corrupt and
sordid. Society was for sale. China had become a nation of prosti-
tutes, pimps, beggars, and lackeys.

For the better part of a century, the Chinese had been struggling to shake loose from this nightmare which was not a nightmare but reality. They had fought the Opium War against the
British—and lost. The Taipings had tried to take power in the
1850s—and lost. China was about to lose two more wars, against
Japan and against Russia. The Dowager Empress Ci Xi, vain, ig-
norant, superstitious, clung to the throne by deceit, intrigue, poison, and murder.

How could the devout, honest, able young Prices, come to
China via Oberlin, possibly grasp the human volcano which under-
lay the polite, submissive, indolent, backward, impoverished, igno-
rant society which they hoped to "save" by converting it to the
Christian faith? There was no chance that they could see within the
minds of the Chinese world and sense the frustration, anger, pas-
sion, hatred, suspicion, superstition and pride which resided there;
the belief in magic, the belief in conspiracy, the belief in inherent
Chinese superiority. Were the Chinese not, even the meanest coolies, princes of the Middle Kingdom? Was not the Middle Kingdom
sited above the lowly earth, somewhere close to heaven? Was it not
surrounded by crude barbarians, evil people with round eyes, vain
and boisterous, doomed forever to live outside China's charmed
circle?

It is this contrast in perceptions that constitutes the tapestry
against which this extraordinary narrative of the tragic fate of these
young Americans, possessed only of a will to bring good to China
and her people, pay with their lives at the hands of fanatics who

were possessed of the belief that these plain, simple Iowans were foreign devils who sought to pervert and possess all that was precious to China.

There was no way in which these discordant and distorted images might have been brought into single focus. There is in the lively warm letters of Eva Price a riveting quality, like that of a Greek tragedy. We know the terrible ending. We want to cry out, to halt the story before the Boxers raise their savage swords. But there is no escape. The seeds of the denouement were planted long before the Prices set foot in China and long before the Boxers rushed onto the stage.

The root of the problem lay in China's continental struggle to reenter the world, a struggle still in progress, and in the still uncompleted task of American—and world—understanding of the tensions which arise within a great society that falls from its exalted plane and fights to regain its historic status. The Prices and the Boxers of Shanxi are small human figures who capture in microcosm the essence of a great drama.

—HARRISON E. SALISBURY

PREFACE

When we first began to read Eva's letters, tucked away for many years after having been passed down in our family from one generation to another, we were only mildly interested and curious. Here was a wicker basket of dusty letters almost a hundred years old from an aunt we had barely heard of, for time evidently keeps the memories and heartache silently inside those left behind. Therefore, we knew little of the gripping dramatic story that was about to unfold. We randomly chose a letter here, a letter there, and soon we became so engrossed we could hardly wait to see the next one. Here was a loving letter from Eva to her father and mother, sisters, and brothers; a letter from her husband, Charlie, inquiring of the latest news back in America; a childish scrawl to Grandpa and Grandma from little Stewart or Florence; a steamship menu, a leaf from a fig tree, a slip of dress material. Here was the story of a living, loving family that had faced the hardships of traveling far from home and loved ones, across a giant ocean and into the interior of a strange and distant land, not to seek fortune, but to answer the call of ministering to a strange and alien people in far-off China.

We each took a handful of letters to our respective homes, and soon typed copies were flying back and forth as we assembled the correspondence in chronological order. How different from the 1890s, when these letters were carried hundreds of miles by hand and mule cart over the Chinese mountains, then by railroad and steamship, and on across the land. How anxiously the home folks must have awaited these dear letters, just as the small family in China awaited the courier for word from loved ones at home. It took months for the letters to reach their final destination, so much could have happened in the meantime. Still, eventually, the letters from the small city in the interior of China reached the little brown "cottage on the hill" at 25th and Clark streets in Des Moines, Iowa, in the center of America.

As the story of Eva's ten years in China gradually unfolded before us, we realized what a treasure we had discovered. We came to know and love dear Eva and Charles and their children, to feel their worry and concern and sadness, and to rejoice with them at their small accomplishments. We could visualize the missionary compound, the school for boys, and the opium refuge; we could feel the grit between our teeth as Eva, a scrupulous housekeeper, struggled to keep her home clean in the ferocious dust storms; we could imagine Charlie waiting for the mail to keep abreast of the political doings at home and news of the war with Spain; and the children, surely lonely with few playmates and no school to attend. We could even see the little Chinese ladies tippy-toeing around on their tiny, bound feet. What a struggle the Prices must have had in this strange land, trying to learn the difficult language, and trying to help people of a distinctly different culture, many of whom rejected foreign ideas outright.

Through the letters we became acquainted with the other workers in the field, the missionaries, doctors, and visitors, and with the Chinese people Eva came to know and care so much about.

To include all the letters in their entirety would make this too lengthy a story, for Eva had many interesting things to tell and messages of love to brothers and sisters, relatives and friends. So, out of necessity, some letters and repetitive passages have been shortened or omitted.

Eva once wrote to her parents: "If you have not thrown away my letters to you, will you please keep them, for I have not kept any journal since we came to China and I may need them when I 'write my book.' " When we read that, we immediately knew we must publish her journal and letters. Her story, both happy and tragic, is as moving and inspiring today as when it was written almost a hundred years ago.

This book has been a joy and a labor of love, and we hope if

Eva is looking down on us, she is happy knowing that she has at last "been published."

VIRGINIA PHIPPS, Des Moines, Iowa
LUCILLE WILSON, Woodward, Iowa
ARLENE CARUTH, Tucson, Arizona
—Grandnieces of Eva Jane Price

ACKNOWLEDGMENTS

Material from the Price journal is used by permission of the Houghton Library, Harvard University, Cambridge, Massachusetts; the United Church Board for World Ministries, New York; and Research Publications, Inc., of Woodbridge, Connecticut. The compilers wish to thank the Oberlin College Archives and the Oberlin Shansi Memorial Association, Oberlin, Ohio, for the use of photographs and for other material that has greatly enhanced *China Journal*.

INTRODUCTION

The American and European Christian missionaries to China had a collective purpose awesome in its ambition, that of attempting to convert to their Western religion the vast, illiterate masses of Chinese, a people superstitious and distrustful of foreigners and steeped in Eastern traditions. The Protestant and Roman Catholic missionaries followed the soldiers and traders who had opened up China in the early to mid–nineteenth century, spreading out across the country to establish missions. For years the foreigners did much as they pleased, but then, quite unexpectedly, came a bizarre and savage retribution. A spark first struck in the mountain stronghold of Shan Tung* set all North China ablaze. There followed a summer of madness, catastrophic for the Chinese empire and disastrous for many foreigners, especially the missionaries, whom the Chinese authorities saw as a dangerous arm of outside advance.

Among the Christian missionaries to China were Charles Wesley and Eva Jane Price, who, with their young children, set out for the Christian mission at Fen Cho fu in the province of Shansi in the late summer of 1889. Shansi lies west of the Taihang Mountains in the loess highlands between the Mongolian steppes and the agricultural regions of China. Its area is about 60,393 square miles, with Tai Yuen (Taiyuan) the capital. The Great Wall forms its northern boundary, and it is separated from Shensi province, to the west, by the Yellow River.

*The reader should refer to Appendix D, A Word on the Transliteration of Chinese Words.

The China that the Price family was to encounter was still the empire of the Manchus, but it was an empire on the brink of upheaval, with dramatic political and cultural changes soon to come. China considered itself a self-sufficient nation with a distinct culture of its own, even under the rule of aliens like the Manchus. But China could not continually resist the commercial ambitions of the Europeans. During the greater part of the nineteenth century, a series of limited wars took place, each ending with China being defeated and forced to sign treaties granting the West increasingly extensive commercial and political concessions. These commercial privileges were deeply resented by the Chinese.

In the 1890s, the Manchu empire was to approach collapse in war with Japan, and China was to find itself for a time increasingly vulnerable to Western ideas and to the economic incursions of Western imperialism. Foreign merchants and financiers were to take firm hold of China's trade. Native-born reformers, influenced by Westerners, including missionaries, were seeking constitutional reforms and a modern interpretation of Confucius. The eventual violent backlash against foreign influence did not leave the lives of those at the Fen Cho fu mission untouched. Charles Wesley and Eva Jane Price devoted ten years of their lives to their Christian mission, struggling to communicate with the people in their difficult language, nursing the sick and opium-enslaved, teaching Western ways by example and Christianity by the gospel. Ultimately, however, this teaching by deed and by word became the vortex of tragedy. In the summer of 1900 the Price family was sucked into the antiforeign maelstrom known as the Boxer Rebellion.

The violence of the Boxer Rebellion resulted in hundreds of missionaries and thousands of Chinese Christians being put to death and the ransacking and burning of Protestant and Catholic churches and homes. It was quelled at last by a force known as the International Relief Expedition, made up of Japanese, Austrians, Italians, Russians, British, French, Germans, and Americans.

When Eva and Charles Price left Des Moines, Iowa, in the winter of 1883, their goal seemed simple enough. Charles would study at Oberlin College, become an ordained minister, and go to work saving heathen souls from eternal darkness. Reality, however, was not so simple. The journey from Iowa to Oberlin, Ohio, was the beginning of a greater journey whose consequences Eva and Charles could never have imagined.

The decision to launch a new life was a choice that demanded courage and determination. Eva Price, at age twenty-eight, and Charles Price, at almost thirty-six, were not typical Oberlin freshmen. Age was a factor, often a liability, that conditioned Eva and Charles's future.

To some extent, family was a liability. Never spoken but nonetheless evident was the lack of sympathy and understanding on the part of Eva's parents for their daughter and son-in-law's new calling. Neither of the elder Keaseys seemed strongly oriented toward evangelical Christianity, and both Charles and Eva were, apparently, conscious of the fact. At the other end of the spectrum was Frank Price, Charles's brother, who was already something of a missionary celebrity. Frank, who had graduated from Oberlin College in 1883, was a truly tough act for Charles to follow. Frank was the master of seven (soon to be eight) languages, and he and his wife, Jennie, were assigned to Shansi province, China, as pioneer missionaries. As if these family pressures were not enough, college was an economic hardship for Eva and Charles. They would see a reasonably comfortable life slip away and their savings disappear under the burden of educational expenses. The Oberlin years undoubtedly also represented a spiritual watershed in the life of Eva Jane Price. They provided a theological and ideological system for an otherwise raw faith.

The decision by the Board of Foreign Missions to assign Charles and Eva Price to Shansi was somewhat surprising in view of previously expressed concern over the age of the Prices. Frank and Jennie Price undoubtedly lobbied on behalf of their kin, but in retrospect the maturity and stability of Eva and Charles may even have assured them the China assignment. The tiny Shansi mission was in very serious trouble. For some time, highly divisive and destructive debates over questions of doctrine had split the mission (and, ultimately, one of the missionaries had rejected the divinity of Christ and had to be removed). Of equal destructiveness was the discovery of a domestic scandal that was especially grave since it was feared that the Chinese knew what had happened. The sudden departure of a missionary wife brought an immediate solution to this problem, but the viability of the Shansi mission was problematic. Under the circumstances, the assignment of Eva and Charles Price to Shansi was a wise decision.

On May 5, 1889, five and a half years after entering Oberlin College, Charles graduated from the Theological Seminary. The Reverend Martin Luther Stimson, who had started the Shansi mission seven years earlier, was in Oberlin at that time, and he persuaded Charles to apply to the Board of Foreign Missions for a foreign appointment. Eva wrote: "I know we had very little encouragement when we came here to Oberlin, but Charlie has done nobly and has the respect and recommendation of the entire faculty and will be able to work more for the good of the world than he could have done had we not come here. It is an honor to be permitted to be in the active work of spreading the gospel, especially in heathen lands."

On July 9, 1889, Charles and Eva received a telegram announcing their assignment to Shansi. Charles, now age forty-one, and Eva, age thirty-three, with their two young sons, Stewart, four and a half, and the baby, Donald, seven months old, left their home in Oberlin and began their journey to California, across the vast Pacific, and into the interior of China.

Eva's sister, Mary Eltha, wrote: "So you and Charlie have decided to go to China. Well, I wish for our sakes and your children's that you would stay in the United States. But then, 'a prophet is not without honor, save in his own country' and I suppose honor is a great thing, even if we do have to go to the antipodes to get it. Well, you know your calling and if you are determined to go so far all we can do is pray hopefully your lives will be watched over with care and your work rewarding. Just keep well and write to Pa and Mother as often as you can."

Eva did write. With the occasional assistance of husband Charles and the children, her journal grew to include a remarkable range of experiences and emotions. As a Westerner and as a missionary, but most of all as a woman and as a mother, she was destined to a uniquely personal China experience. Her bittersweet story is remarkably Chinese-like, and a testimony to the simple human qualities that dispel the cultural differences between East and West.

—ROBERT H. FELSING, PH.D.

"Thank God, this darkness and earthquake and fire and storm do pass by, and with rapt face and eager soul we listen for the still small voice 'Fear not, it is all right. God is watching and waiting. The Lord executeth righteousness and good judgment for all that are oppressed.' "

If we die we die in peace!

—Women's Board Calendar
June 29, 1900

Spelling on this map is that used by Eva Price in her letters. For more current usage, see Appendix D, page 279.

PART ONE
The Journey
SEPTEMBER 1889–MARCH 1891

Steamship *Oceanic*
September 15, 1889

Dear Home Folks,

Here we are 1,200 miles out in the Pacific Ocean and rushing along toward Honolulu at good speed. It is a larger lake than the one we ate supper near that last evening. I will often think of the pleasant time we had. After leaving Des Moines we jounced along all that night and didn't rest very well, but from Grand Island, Nebraska, we had a pleasant section in the sleeper and a kind porter and enjoyed the ride until we came to the desert or sandy plains. For two days we rode over such a dreary waste of land. Nothing but sand! A low range of mountains (or sand hills) were off in the distance on each side of the track, so far off that it did not break the monotony of our ride any as we seemed to keep about so far from them all the time. I always supposed Cheyenne to be surrounded with mountains and in a rough, broken country, but so far as I could judge by moonlight it is built right on the plains. After we passed Cheyenne we rode all the next day across plains, dreary and desolate, and finally came into some rougher country. The railroad would run between high cliffs where we could scarcely see the top in some places, but on one I noticed some enterprising beauty destroyer had painted in big white letters SOLZODENT so I suppose they can be climbed.*

We changed sleepers at Ogden, Utah, and had just as pleasant

---

*What Eva Price saw from the train was most probably the word "Sozodont," the brand name of a tooth powder popular in the late nineteenth century.

accommodations and a fat, jolly porter who called himself "Uncle William" to the children. We were a little unfortunate in that we passed the fine scenery in the night and had the dusty plains by day. The mountains generally were a disappointment as they only seemed like immense piles of sand without vegetation of any kind until we came to the Sierra Nevadas, which was at night (of course), so we had to sit out on the steps and get as good views by moonlight as we could, and it was just grand! Only I got awfully tired and sleepy and this overcame all my sentimentality and I went to bed while we passed beauty after beauty, I presume. I snoozed while we passed the Grand Canyon but I couldn't help it. There were forty-eight miles of continuous snowsheds in one place, and planks were left off occasionally to afford glimpses of the grandeur.

Thursday was the important day as we were to reach San Francisco, so we were up early and got our traps together so as to look out at the country. I rather expected to see oranges growing wild along the track like willows or hazelbrush. But not an orange did we see in all our stay in San Francisco. When we came to Sacramento it was hard to realize that we were in a city I had not thought of since I learned the "capitals." When we came to the bay we left the cars and crossed on a ferry, our first boat ride. We stayed at the Occidental Hotel while in San Francisco and had a good time there, taking several rides on the cable cars to see the city. We saw some fine residences and took a trip out to the Cliff House, where everyone goes, and here we got our first look at this old ocean over which we are riding tonight.

We got your letter before we left, which was a help to us and I ought to have sent one from there but waited to write until we should get aboard the ship. It (she) was close up to the docks so that a temporary bridge was thrown across for passengers and to carry the freight aboard. It was a queer sensation when we saw them untying the large ropes which held the ship fast to the docks and felt the old ship starting out on what was to be our long ocean trip.

Well, I am free to confess that before two hours I was sick, awfully sick! And while I was dumped down in a heap, Charlie came into the stateroom telling me to "brace up," and I thought at the time he needed to "brace up" too. Sure enough, in less than half

4

an hour he was sick as he could be. I rolled onto my berth without undressing myself or Donnie, and if we hadn't had a kind stewardess I don't know how we would have got along. She helped us all she could, but we were sick all night and all day and all night again. I managed to undress the first day by degrees, but it was hard to hold my head up long enough to do anything. Stewart and Donnie were neither of them sick, for which I was thankful.

I could not get to the dining room to meals until the third day. We sit at the Captain's table, an oval one in the center of the large dining room, and there are two long tables on each side. This is in the lower story with kitchen, larder, and seventeen staterooms on the same floor. The deck below ours is the steerage deck and there are nearly 500 steerage passengers, 450 of them Chinese. There are about sixty cabin passengers. From our stateroom, No. 13, we come out into a little hallway, through the dining room and up two winding stairways (not the narrow dark things I had imagined but broad nice stairs.), where we land in the saloon, or sitting room. From there we go up another short winding stairway to the upper deck, where we spend most of our time now that we are able to get there. There is a safe railing around the outside of these decks and I don't think Stewart is in any danger. Only four other American children are on board.

Our boat is 420 feet long, 38 feet wide, and is said to be the fastest sailer out here. The boat crew so far as we have seen are very kind and well-mannered. We are going by way of Honolulu (which is nearly three days out of our way) to take on about 400 more Chinese. It will be pleasant, however, to see the Hawaiian Islands and if we keep well it won't matter—a few days or five or six weeks. For two days and nights now it has been very smooth sailing and the boat has not rocked much. But oh dear! The first two days it was rock, rock, rock, this way then that way, then dip and tip endwise for a change, then up and down until it was small wonder nearly all on board were sick. I didn't like the water at all the first few days but am beginning to enjoy it now. It is overwhelming to stand at the railing and look, look, look at nothing but water, water, and to think we have been out only four and a half days and have weeks of water before us yet. We reach Honolulu Wednesday so that will be a pleasant change.

I will write more as we travel on our way to Honolulu. This has been Sunday at sea and there were services in the dining room.

The Hawaiian Islands are in sight! It is hard to realize that the dim, irregular line we see in the distance is a mountain. We have seen the flying fish, "Mother Carey's chickens," and some flying white sea gulls. The sea was rough again yesterday and I did not feel very well, but it is pleasanter today. We have nice meals (quite formal), and they have nearly everything on the bill of fare—fresh strawberries, melons, ice cream, sweet and Irish potatoes, half a dozen kinds of meat, and a host of other things. We stay on deck all we can for the lower part is very warm, especially when the sea is rough and the portholes have to be closed. But you would be surprised to see how comfortable we are and how little there is to fret about. They have two or three deck games to play including quoits and shuffleboard, and we sit and watch the waves, the clouds, and flying fish. If we could step off ship once in a while on terra firma it would be a little pleasanter, but I haven't been afraid yet—not even the first night when the ship was rolling and pitching so. It was comical too, for I saw our camp chair slide across the stateroom, bring up against the couch, and tip back gracefully on its back with its legs sticking up in the air. Our basket of fruit fell over, the cover came unfastened, and away rolled peaches, grapes, apples, and pears, first this side then the other, which they kept up at intervals all night.

We will get to Honolulu some time this afternoon. The ship will not go in but will anchor out some distance and all who go ashore will be taken in a tug. It is warm here as we are about the twentieth degree. After we leave Honolulu we will go northwest again to Yokohama and then to Shanghai, I presume. I am enclosing some pieces of seaweed I picked up on the beach at the Cliff House in San Francisco. Don't fret about us for we are doing nicely.

Your loving daughter and sister,
Eva

I remember the glimpse of Father at the train that night when he waved his hat and I waved mine and wished the boys would go—so I could cry, cry! Good-bye.

....

Yokohama, Japan
October 5, 1889

My Dearest Family,

We are here in this exceedingly interesting place and as we leave next Tuesday for Kobe I will send a short letter. We had a very pleasant sea voyage aside from the sea sickness, which lasted most of the way across. We were very glad to get ashore and have been having a fine time since we came last Wednesday. We have a very pleasant place to live while we stay here and have been riding about the streets in jinrikishas sightseeing. It is a comfortable way of getting about, but I can't get used to seeing the coolies act as horses. They start off at a dog trot, then faster if you care to have them, and will keep it up for hours if need be. We pay the men each ten sen an hour, which is about eight cents. Picture me in one holding Donnie, and Charlie in another with Stewart, going single file. Many of the coolies here go with but little in the way of clothing and we are getting used to sights that would make us blush in America.

We went to Tokio on Thursday, and as there were nine in our party each with a jinrikisha it made a long procession. We saw some streetcars and electric lights and visited the University of the Empire, and went "driving" around a beautiful piece of scenery including "Mississippi Bay."

There are a great many foreigners here in Yokohama and one can see stores and homes that seem like our own land, but a few steps away will be the native Japanese way of living, which makes quite a medley. I will send you a native shop scene and you can imagine it as being about fourteen feet square, not more than ten or twelve feet high, with a partition between it and another just like it. The fronts are all open and one may be a fish shop, the next a candy shop, the next eggs—all mixed up helter-skelter. The streets are usually narrow and crooked. But the sight which I enjoy most is "Fujiyama," the great mountain of Japan of which they are very proud. It is one hundred miles to the north but we could see it in the distance for hours before we landed and it can be seen from

7

nearly all parts of the city. It has snow perpetually on its peak—has been extinct for years. The harbor here is a beautiful one, said to be the finest in the world, and is full of shipping from all over the globe. It is a beautiful sight.

This morning we got our steamer tickets for Kobe and took a boat out to our steamer, the *Tokio*, to see what she was like. We have a very comfortable-looking stateroom, though I presume we can be just as good and sick there as anywhere. It will only be thirty-six to forty-eight hours to Kobe, however, and we will skirt along the shore all the time. We will stay there several days and will visit Kiota [Kyoto] and other points and will leave for Tientsin, China, on the twelfth I think.

We think of you so often and hope you are well.

Love to all from Eva

....

Yokohama, Japan
October 7, 1889

Dear Father,

I have only time to write a few lines, but that is all that is necessary as Eva tells all there is to tell. We are going on a little trip into the country today, taking our dinner with us. We will probably be gone all day and anticipate a good time. I wish you could be where we are this morning. It is a beautiful day! The door at which I am sitting opens onto a veranda from which there is a very fine view of little Japanese houses and cultivated fields small as gardens, and in the distance little clusters of trees. To the left we have a view of the bay where we see great numbers of little sailing vessels. I had the pleasure of seeing a whale as we came up the bay when we arrived here, the only one of our party so fortunate. I called Eva to take a look but she was too late.

We start for Kobe by steamer tomorrow and leave from there for Tientsin next Saturday. It will take us about two weeks to reach there and after that comes the inland journey of fifteen days. So we have about one month of travel yet. They tell us the route from here winds through different groups of islands and is considered the most beautiful in the world. We expect to enjoy the trip very much if we are not too sick.

We of course have not heard from home yet but hope to by the first mail.

Love to you all,
C. W. Price

....

Tientsin, China
October 25, 1889

Dear Loved Ones,

It is hard to realize we are finally in China! We are stopping at Mr. Stanley's home for a day or so.* We met the family in Oberlin so feel quite at home with them and they have everything pleasant and comfortable, and have American food.

We have been having very pleasant times and you must not think of us as having continuous travel all the time for we were in Japan about ten days in all. We left Yokohama Tuesday, the eighth of October, and came by way of the Inland Sea instead of Shanghai, being out only twenty-four hours when we reached Kobe where we stayed until Saturday noon. We went ashore on Thursday and took dinner with friends in missionary work. In the afternoon we took a railroad train to Kiota where the Dosecha School is located, about a three-hour trip.† After staying at a hotel Thursday night we were up early to walk about visiting the temple and other interesting things. Later we had a nice long ride of about two miles in jinriki-shas to the school and then took dinner with Dr. and Mrs. Davis whom we had met in Oberlin.‡ Their children are in school in Oberlin and we are well acquainted with them. We returned to Kobe that night.

*Charles A. and Mrs. Stanley were, in 1862, the first missionaries from the American Board of Commissioners for Foreign Missions (ABCFM) to be assigned to North China.
†Doshisha University, founded in 1875, was notable for its emphasis on Christian learning.
‡Reverend and Mrs. F. W. Davis were also China-bound; indeed, their destination was the Taiku Station in Shansi, not far from Fen Cho fu, to which the Prices had been assigned.

Saturday at noon our steamer, the *Omari Maru,* left for Tientsin, but made about four stops on the way so it was quite an interesting journey. We stopped a few hours at Shemasaku [Shimonoseki], then went on to Nagasaka [sic] where we anchored twenty-four hours, so we went ashore and spent a few hours riding about in jinrikishas. Our next stop was at Pusan in Korea to take on a great deal of freight but we did not go ashore. We anchored next at Chemulpa [Inchŏn] in Korea, a very dreary, desolate spot. The mountains were brown and bare, and the huts were built of mud mostly. The Koreans dress in white—long baggy breeches and queer hats.

While waiting at Chemulpa six of us took a boat and visited the *Omaha,* a United States "Man of War" and it was a very interesting experience. It, with the *Marion,* another of our warships, was anchored out about two miles. The Captain's and Admiral's rooms were very fine indeed. Lieutenant Miller, who was our very good host, gave us cups of tea and crackers and showed us the many curious things he is collecting to take home. When we were ready to go back to our ship he ordered up one of his boats, manned by ten sailors, to row us back. It was sunset, the water was calm, and it reminded Charlie and me of the sunset at Bronco Lake. It was such a comfort to see our dear old flag floating in the breeze from these ships and boats!

The next day we left for Chee-foo, port city in the province of Chihli,* and reached there Sunday afternoon in quite a storm of wind and rain. When the barometer indicated a severe storm the anchor was lifted and we pulled to a more sheltered place in the bay where we had to stay until Tuesday. We left then for this place, Tientsin, which I had supposed was a port city but it is about sixty miles up a river, so we had to leave our steamer and take to the cars again. This afternoon we start inland by riverboat to Paoting fu, about five days' travel. The season is following us and the weather seems much like our own October at home. Charlie is out this morning buying some necessary things for our trip. We have to do our own cooking, but the boats are quite comfortable they tell us,

*Now Hebei province. Chihli was abolished in 1928.

so we will not suffer. At Paoting fu we will leave the river and travel over the mountains in litters.

We are often wondering about you and hoping you are well. It is time now to finish picking up our traps so I will close with a heart full of love for you all. Stewart says, "Send to Grandma for me for a little cookie."

Good-bye from daughter and sister,

Eva

....

Fen Cho fu, China

November 25, 1889

Dear Pa and Mother,

We have safely arrived here in Fen Cho fu, China, and have had a pleasant journey! I especially enjoyed the trip across the mountains, the part I had most dreaded. If you would only have come along with us and have seen the comfort with which we traveled you would not be worrying about us. There were no dangers on the way that made us fear, and the weather has been fine.

We left Tientsin Saturday, October 26, and did not get very far until we ran ashore for the Sabbath. That night a cold wind came up from the north so we had to lie there in the rushes all day Monday too, which was not very enjoyable. We had food with us for the journey, which Mr. Sheffield's cook prepared on their boat where we gathered for our meals.* The boats are called "house boats," and are about fifty feet long and ten feet wide. Each boat had three little rooms and as we had our trunks, bedding, chairs, and food it made quite a home.

We were six days going up the river to Paoting fu. The river is narrow, sluggish, and shallow much of the way and we came along at a snail's pace for the wind was contrary so the sails were

---

*Devello Z. Sheffield (1841–1913) founded the North China College at Tung Cho in this year, 1889. North China College was one of the earliest missionary colleges in China.

not of much use. There were four boats in the party, one for the Davises, one for Dr. Murdock,* one for our family, and one for Mr. Sheffield, our escort, so we were quite a fleet. There were four men to each boat, one to steer and three to pole the boat along by sticking the poles in the dirt in the bottom of the river and running along the narrow planks by the side of the boat. So you can see it was not a fast way of "sailing." We left the boats at Paoting fu and were glad to know we were done with water travel.

Then we had to wait a week in the city for arrangements to be made for litters in which to cross the mountains. Dr. Merritt, at whose home we stayed, took charge of our party here and Mr. Sheffield went back to his school work in Tung Cho.† We were quite a party as we left for Shansi with four litters and about thirteen pack mules to carry our trunks and boxes. Each litter was strung between two mules, one in front and one in back. Don and I rode in one, Charlie and Stewart in another, one for the Davises and one for Dr. Murdick, and they were not nearly so uncomfortable as I expected, except that my mules did not keep in step so it was "jerkity jerk" much of the way. Donnie slept a great deal of the time. We would stop at an inn for dinner, which would take an hour or so as we did our own cooking, then go on till late when we would stop at another inn for the night. The Chinese inns are cheerless things as they have nothing in them but a chair or so, a small table, and the k'ang, which is a brick platform about eight feet by six feet and two feet high on which we made our beds. There were two or three adjoining rooms so we were not all piled in together. We would get our suppers and "bunk down" for the night and sleep like tops—no fire to keep warm by, excepting a small charcoal stove which we carried with us for cooking. We usually were up and off by half past six in the morning, having to waken the children and wash and dress them after a fashion.

It took fourteen days to travel from Paoting fu to Fen Cho fu. Brother Frank met us at Taiku. He and Jennie are delighted to have

---

*Dr. V. C. Murdock, a female physician, who arrived in China in 1881.
†M. D. Merritt and his wife were assigned to Paoting fu in 1887. Like Dr. Murdock, the Meritts were ABCFM missionaries.

us come here to them and it is a joy to us having them here to welcome us in this strange land. When we are settled we will have a teacher and begin to study the language. We feel very thankful that this long journey has been safely accomplished and we are all well. I only wish I could describe all the queer things we have seen.

Stewart is having a good time after being kept close for such a long time. Donnie is creeping everywhere and pulling himself up to chairs. His sixth tooth is almost through and, excepting a cold, he is very well.

We are very anxious to hear from you and can hardly wait for a letter to come. It has been such a long time. They are waiting now to take the letters to the courier so I must close, with a great deal of love to you all.

Your daughter and sister,
Eva

....

December 21, 1889

Dear Home Folks,

Last evening Frank stepped up to the window and shouted, "The fast mail arrived!" He then came in, opened the sack, and dumped the contents on the carpet—papers, letters, and packages, with two bread tins as part of the lot. It did not take long to sort it and I was very happy when Charlie handed me a letter from Des Moines, for we had not had a word from you since we left San Francisco in September. It fairly made me cry with joy when I read of Father's army pension and his getting work at good wages, and of your comfortable house with beautiful trees. It is so pleasant to think of you there where the other children can visit. I was telling Stewart all about your letter this morning before we got up and when I said, "And the house has trees around it," he said, "Oh, isn't that nice, Mamma?" And when I told him about Aunt Dell and Uncle Edgar and the children visiting you, he said, "Oh, wasn't it nice for them to go there and comfort Grandma!" So you can see how delighted we all are.

We are very comfortably fixed ourselves and are all well and busy. When I write that I have two Chinese "boys" to do my work you will wonder what I have to do. But I take care of the children, study with the teacher an hour each day, do my sewing, and oversee the place in general. Fen Cho fu is not a large city, has crooked narrow streets, and the walls of the compounds where people live line both sides of the street. We have a large outer gate or door in our street wall which is kept shut and fastened except when we go in and out. The gatekeeper has a little room near the gate and the rest of the servants sleep there too. We have a small court about fifty feet square, paved with brick and walled in with our rooms so that all the outdoors we get is the sky and air and dust. The rooms are not all together but are built around other little courts and connected by little gateways and it is quite like a little village. Some of the places look spooky after dark. The whole premises cover about two acres but many of the rooms need repairs and are not used now. It is all enclosed by a high wall with only the one outer gate, so we are pretty well shut in. I have been outside the gate only three times since we came.

Our place consists of a large sitting-dining room, which we use for church services and prayer meetings, and a smaller room for our beds. The kitchen is quite a ways off and the "boy" has to carry the food and dishes to a little door in our wall which opens into a small cupboard. Then he comes around to our front (and only) door and has to walk across the room to get the things to set the table. So doing the kitchen work is not the most convenient thing in the world. His kitchen is about twelve feet square and has a brick stove built along one side which has three holes to cook on and two large ones with iron kettles for water, so we have plenty of hot water at all times. The stove does not warm the room very much but will keep things from freezing. The "boy" gets along well with his work of cooking, dishwashing, table setting, and marketing, and is quite clean and economical. He is busy most of the time for he gets his own meals about the middle of each forenoon and afternoon. We pay him about $3 per month and he boards himself, which is said to cost about $1 per month. The other "boy" makes the beds, sweeps and dusts, takes care of the fire, and washes and irons and gets $3 per month also. They like to work for us as the wages are much higher than what the Chinese pay.

We can get more of the necessities of life here than I supposed. The flour is dark but makes fairly good bread. The sweet and Irish potatoes are good and we can get sugar, tea, rice, squash, pears, grapes, cabbage, turnips, good mutton, a red fruit that makes a sauce something like cranberries, good nuts like the English walnuts, and various other things. We get good stone crocks, and Charlie has had the carpenter make Stewart a bed, a desk for himself and one for me, clothes bars, two tubs, a kitchen table, a pail, a breadboard, and a set of blocks for Stewart's Christmas present. Aunt Jennie is going to give him a doll so the carpenter made him a cradle. The children are looking forward with much pleasure to Christmas.

We have very pleasant times here. Our children have nice times playing together. Mr. and Mrs. Davis, who came when we did, live about a half mile away and Mr. Thompson, the single man in the mission, lives with them. We are the only foreigners in the city and get together about three times a week. Our church services are on Sabbath evening and our prayer meeting on Thursday evening, with one evening for social times. Charlie led the prayer meeting and preached on Sunday night as Frank has a bad throat and the doctor has said he must save it all he can this winter. Mr. Thompson leads the Sunday morning Chinese service, which is held at the chapel over there. Charlie and Mr. Davis are both studying and will take their turn preaching in Chinese as soon as they can. The Annual Meeting will be held here in February and Dr. and Mrs. Goldsbury and Mr. and Mrs. Clapp will come down from Taiku. It is about two days' travel and they will come in a cart which is a cumberous, awkward, two-wheeled affair drawn by a mule.

Our trip over the mountains was a very pleasant part of our journey and it was wonderful to see the way the Chinese cultivate the mountainside. They level a strip, even if it is not more than an acre or so, and sow wheat or something on it. The fields were all bare and brown when we crossed as the fall seeding had lately been done. The mountains usually were sand and rocks with only one or two places having pine trees. We had some dangerous places to cross but had no accident.

The people seem industrious and very saving though oftentimes their savings go for opium. It was amusing to see the way in which they watched every little scrap of anything that would make fertilizer for their fields. Little boys and old men made a business of getting on the road as soon as it was light enough to see to pick up the droppings of the mules and oxen, following along for miles and scraping up refuse of all sorts, which they put in a basket and dumped in heaps, finally gathering it all up for their fields. And where the mountains were the rockiest they would put straw, dirt, and all sorts of trash in the road to be tramped into a mass by the mules, oxen, horses, and camels. We passed long lines of camels carrying coal over the mountains. The great unwieldy animals looked comical with a small load of coal on each side of their humps. The teams we saw were often a queer mingling—one time a mule, an ox, and a pony; other times two mules and an ox or some other combination.

The people here do not look like those we saw in America, as those come from the south of China and are smaller and more yellow. These men are larger and look some like our Indians, being a brown-skinned people with black hair, black eyes, and rather high cheekbones. They wear "queues" of course, and are very proud of them. The women I have seen all have the small bound feet and usually paint their faces if they are young, pasting on the white and red until their faces look ghastly while their necks are left brown and dirty.

It is more comfortable living here, so far, than I expected to find it, and it is a great help having Frank and Jennie so near. You would laugh to hear me spouting my few Chinese words at my "boys," such as "juggu jow shenima" ("what do you call this"), or "jugga bu-shing" ("this is not right"), "ging tien tso momo bu" ("do you make bread or not"). *Momo* is bread, *bu* is negative, *tso* is to make. I have learned several words and a few sentences in the three weeks we have been keeping house. If you hear me go to the door and yell "Eshin! Cashsway," I am just telling the "boy" to bring some hot water. The "boys" names are Eshin and Gnagen and Jennie's cook is Ding San. The gatekeeper is called Lou Hau. We will be glad when we get enough of the language to do missionary work but I expect it will be some time. The missionaries (the men) all wear Chinese clothes when they go on the street. Charlie had a time getting shoes made big enough for him.

We have four hens and a rooster which I feed and take care of, which seems quite countrified, don't you think? We are all well at present and want to hear from you every mail.

With lots of love to you all,

Eva

....

February 19, 1890

This is wash day and I have a "boy" I am teaching and he needs close watching lest he boil the flannels or do some other awkward thing. Our Eshin was light-fingered and took a fancy to some of our money and napkins so we invited him to leave and we took a boy who has never been with foreigners. I have put him to making beds, sweeping, dusting, washing, and ironing and he is doing nicely. It would take away your appetite I expect to see them strapping about in their clumsy clothes—wide sleeves dangling, greasy queue hanging, quite untidy in all their general appearance and ways. But you can get used to it and they are kind and willing, which covers a multitude of defects.

We are busy nearly all the time—Charlie studying with might and main, and I oversee everything, which is about as much trouble as to do it all in the first place. My cook got sick and wanted to go home, which is about fifty li away [one li is approximately one-third mile], so I have walked about seventy-five miles since then trotting out to the kitchen and back. We have relished our food extremely well, however, and have the satisfaction of knowing how it is prepared. People of fastidious tastes who make up their minds to live in China had better leave such tastes at home. Good housekeepers have very much to try their grace in this land. We are getting nice grapes for about three cents a pound now. I have seen no apples but they have apricots and peaches in their season and very small inferior oranges are shipped here from other parts. The pears are good only for stewing and baking.

We have had quite a number of callers. If I hear a jumble of chattering out in the court I know we are to be invaded. They go in Jennie's room first and look at her things, the sewing machine and organ being the greatest curiosities. After they have seen all they care to there, they come in here to "open their eyes" as they call seeing our foreign things. The baseburner and the platform rockers are the wonderful things here, excepting always the baby. He was the center of attraction all the way across the country last fall. They will jabber and chatter about him, and Jennie will interpret that they think he is well fed and pretty and fat. They think boys are the nicest things in the world. When we stopped in Taiku we had to get out of our litters in the street and when Frank lifted out the baby the crowd that had gathered gave a great cheer. They were delighted to see a foreign baby and that baby a boy!

Last Monday we took a jolting ride out to a pagoda about three miles from home. It was thirteen stories high and looked very smooth and easy of ascent, but with the baby to carry and Stewart to watch we concluded to postpone the climb until some future day. A pagoda is a place for idols and for worship, I presume.

It has been so pleasant this winter with brother Frank here, and we dread to think of what it will be when they are away. They expect to start for the coast in May or June. We had word yesterday from Boston that there are two young ladies coming out this year and another evangelist.

....

Fen Cho fu, China
March 1, 1890

Dear Father,

Eva has been writing you all the news so there is not much for me to say. Brother Thompson and I are going out to a village this afternoon in a cart to look at some places for summer residence. The village is about five miles from here in a beautiful valley with high mountains on each side and with a stream lined with trees. Eva will like that if we get a place there, for trees in China are scarce. There are scarcely any on the plain where we live and the outlook is rather dreary. I hope we will be able to get the place for it is quite unpleasant living in the city during the hot weather. There is so much filth in the streets the odor is not the most pleasant. They are the general dumping ground and everything not useful is thrown into them from a dead dog to spoiled cabbage. It is bad enough now and we can imagine what it will be during the summer.

The streets here are very narrow, generally room for but one cart and if two happen to meet there must be a good deal of backing and loud talk before they can pass. The Chinese are a noisy class of people at best and when anything excites them they lift their voices to a very high pitch. It is amusing to see two of them quarreling on the streets. They can be heard much farther than they can be seen. However, they are very kind to us and usually treat us as though they are glad we have come to live among them. They treat us much better than Chinamen are sometimes treated in America.

Now Father, I want you to write us a letter. Do not think we will be satisfied by your letting Mother do all the writing. Give our love to the boys.

Your son,
C. W. Price

....

Fen Cho fu, China
March 16, 1890

Dear Home Folks,

This is a beautiful Sunday morning with us though it seems very queer to think it is Saturday night with you and you are doubtless in bed and asleep. You are often in my thoughts and it would be a comfort to know that you are all well and happy.

Charlie and Mr. Thompson are going to start for Taiku tomorrow to be gone until next Saturday. Charlie is going to get some things for Frank as he does not like to risk going about in the cold. The winter has been very open and pleasant and our coldest weather was last week when it seemed like winter. We are in the same latitude that you are but are up so much higher that the climate is very dry and we do not feel the cold so much.

We are having an experience now with Chinese workmen and

it would make Father open his eyes if he could see the carpenters and masons work. Nearly all the woodwork is glued and dovetailed together as they have no nails to amount to anything. They work so slowly that a dozen men do not accomplish what two good workmen at home could get done. They are putting new windows and doors in some of the rooms and we are quite torn up and unsettled.

Frank and Jennie and the girls were here for supper this evening. They live just a few steps from our door but it is nice to have company occasionally and we sang songs afterward, then put the babies to bed and we older ones played Parcheesi.

Last Wednesday afternoon we took a cart and went outside the city for some three miles to visit a temple. A Chinese cart is an abominable heavy cumbersome vehicle—two big wheels, no springs, covered like a "movers" wagon, no seat except the floor, and will hold one person very comfortably but was a tight squeeze for the baby, Helen, Alice, and Stewart, with Charlie getting on in front occasionally. The Chinese roads fit the carts admirably—narrow, crooked, full of deep ruts into which the cart wheels drop, and it is jostle, jounce, jerk all the way. All in all I believe this way of getting about causes some of the ill health of the missionary women who are thought to break down from overwork. The temple we visited was quite an interesting place. It did not appear to be well patronized as a place of worship and there are strong indications of indifference to these supposedly sacred places. The sides of the room in which an image representing Confucius was sitting were covered with large coral-shaped branches made of mud mostly and painted to represent wood. In the crevices and nooks formed by the branches were images of all sorts—animals, men, women, pagodas, temples in miniature, and priests and idols in all sorts of posture. There must have been a thousand of them all told and I presume they were supposed to indicate the crowds honoring Confucius.

I must close now with much love to you all. Ever your affectionate daughter and sister,

Eva

....

March 28, 1890

The courier came last night and we were made happy by receiving a letter from you. It does seem a little like "angels' visits" though to only have two letters from you since last September. Your letter finds us all well at this time. The children are better now than they have been for two months, as I think we must have had "la grippe" and it held on the children so long it made me very uneasy. So we have stayed very close to home.

There is a stone stairway leading to the roofs where we can walk and look off over the walls to get a view of the city and mountains. But the city is so depressing with everything so woefully dilapidated that I get down again very quickly and am glad to get back inside our rooms. If the surroundings were all we came here for we might well wish we were away, for it is not a very inviting home so far as beauty and pleasantness goes. But when we think that we are entirely surrounded by people who know nothing at all about the One, True, and Living God and never heard of Jesus their friend and Savior and that we came here to learn their language in order to teach them as best we can, we get above the feeling of loneliness and homesickness and only long for the time when it will be easy for us to talk to them, though it seems almost hopeless at times. However, I have been advised against having a Chinese woman to help care for the children in order to have more time for study. I do read with the teacher a short time every morning. Some women give their children almost entirely to the care of a Chinese nurse but I do not feel that it is best. There will be plenty of opportunity for "preaching" when they are older.

The Chinese Inland Mission has about thirty workers in this province and the Catholics have been here for many years. Our mission has worked here about three years, but the number of converts is very small. In this city of about 100,000 there is one native helper who with his wife are the only reliable Christians we have. Several others have united with the Church but have not been very faithful. Lately, however, we have rented a room on one of the chief streets—the great street—and the native helper preaches there every day. At the Sunday services, where Mr. Thompson preaches, quite a crowd usually gathers, but as much out of curiosity as anything else for the earnest inquirers are very few. China is the result of heathenism and is a fair specimen of what a country's development will be without the civilization that grows out of a Christian gospel. A person traveling cannot help but be struck with the progress and advancement of Christian lands in contrast with these lands which have grown so little in all these years.

Stewart has a rage now for asking all manner of questions. "Mamma, how do bees sting?" "Why, with a stinger, a little sharp thing behind," I answer. "Where is the behind to a bee, Mamma?" "Well, Mamma, how many bones have I got in me?" "Where does my food go to when I crowd it down in my throat?" So you see by this he is waking up to the fact of knowing something as he goes through the world. Donald is such a comfort. He toddles about from daylight till dark except when he takes his naps, busy as a bee from one piece of mischief into another. Stewart and he have good times playing together.

I have encouraged the patriotism of the house lately by making a good-sized flag, a regular regulation flag too—thirteen stripes and thirteen stars.* It created quite a sensation when it was first finished.

I want to ask you, Mother, to send me some flower seeds this fall if you please. You can send a small box of seeds to Langdon S. Ward, No. 2 Somerset Street, Boston, to be sent out in the November shipment and we will get it before spring. I do want a flower bed like the ones we have always had at home. Then when I look at their beauty I will think of everyone that is so dear to me and you won't seem so far away.

We are taking *Scribners Magazine, North American Review, Congregationalist, The Household,* and *Wide Awake* besides a paper from Oberlin, so we are not losing track of your doings at home.

Good-bye, and all my love.

....

*There were thirty-nine states by March 1890. It is not known why Eva chose to put only thirteen stars on her flag.

May 26, 1890

Dear Sister Dell and "all e-tokes" (All the folks),

We are alone in this city now that Frank has gone* (except for Mr. Thompson but he is a bachelor), as the Davises have gone also to Li Man to spend the summer with Taiku friends. We are sixty miles from a doctor and I am the only white woman in all that distance.

I will be so glad when we get the language well enough to help in the work here. Mr. Thompson is the only one here who can work and he is not very energetic. Charlie is studying very hard but they say it will be a year or more before a man can do anything after coming here, and most of them, Frank excepted, were here longer than that.

Our goods came through pretty well when we came here—the glass lamp Mother gave me on my twenty-eighth birthday came through fine but a glass fruit dish, a plate or so, other lampshades, and a few things were smashed. The green leaf dish you gave me was broken but I got it mended. The Chinese mend things very nicely, cementing the pieces in and then riveting with brass rivets, and it costs less than fifteen cents of our money. We brought but little in the way of furniture so bought several things in the mission and had a few things made, and bought some things from brother Frank when they left. The other missionaries who came out with us had a good deal of fine furniture, one outfit came to more than $1,000, but we are very comfortable and yet have nothing too nice for the people around us. They envy my sewing machine.

Edgar has asked about the market here. I think there is very little shipped away from here as all the way of shipping is by carts, mules, or camels. We burn coal, a medium between hard and soft, and it is about $2.25 per ton. The flour we get here is good now, and we pay about sixty-five cents for fifty pounds. There are a good many sheep raised here and some of the wool is taken away. Pigs are very common—seen in all corners nosing about in the filth of the streets—a black, pot-bellied animal of which the sight alone is

*Frank and Jennie had returned to the United States because of Frank's poor health.

fully enough. They are called "jew" by the Chinese and I don't wonder the Jews don't eat hog meat if they had such-looking things as these. We have not had any kind of meat excepting mutton (so far as we know). The cook buys all the meat.

There is a large quantity of opium grown in this province and most Shansi people use it in large quantities. They do not raise much corn and it is said to be a small variety although I have not seen any. They made some meal for us once this winter and wanted it to be especially nice so they ground it and ground it until it was as fine as flour and of course was not good at all. We fed it to the chickens.

The wants of the average Chinaman are very few. Our servants are a fair sample. Their bedding is a mattress about six feet by two and a half feet and is not very thick. This is spread on the k'ang, a brick platform under which the fire passes from the fireplace in the front end where they cook their food. The k'ang is said to get very hot sometimes. This is the only way they have of heating their rooms, which of course in cold weather are very cold every place but on the k'ang. They have a comforter of some sort but no sheets or pillows so far as I know, and I don't think their bedding is ever washed. They are said to strip off all their clothing when going to bed, but that isn't much. They may wear a shirt made of unbleached cotton, often worn out without being changed or washed. In winter they wear a wadded garment (which I know my cook wore all winter without changing) made of coarse blue cloth and belted down with a long strip of cloth that is wound around the waist two or three times. The wadded garment comes halfway to the knees and under this is a pair of comical-looking wadded trousers which is tied about the ankles with other long straps wound round and round. The seat of these trousers is very baggy coming down below the outer garment. This is all my cook wore all winter, except shoes and stockings without which a Chinaman never goes. You do not see bare feet in China except on very small children.

When my cook dressed up he put on a pair of half pants over his wadded ones, tied in at the ankle and hitched up by strings to the waist underneath. They look very comical to us. The better class, however, teachers and merchants and wealthy men, wear a long garment coming nearly to the ankles which covers up the uncouth breeches. This is often made of very nice material and over this is worn the *canjenza,* which is exactly like the vests our men wear only a great deal larger. It looks queer to see the vest worn outside of all other clothing. Charlie wears his own clothes about home but when he goes on the street he puts on the *takoos* or half pants over his foreign pants and wears the long garment and the *canjenza.* He wears their caps, shoes, and stockings all the time, at home or abroad. On Sundays for church he wears a black cap, a red satin *canjenza,* a gray pongee [silk] long garment, gray pongee *takoos,* white stockings, and black shoes.

The women look very much as the men do only their garment is not belted and their shoes of course differ. They do not wear the cap nor *canjenza,* just a band across the forehead brought around to the back at the neck and tied—no bonnets, no hats, no bustles, no corsets, no fine underclothes, no gloves. But they do wear the wadded breeches—it is not often you see a woman with skirts. Hurrah for China! A place where the women can wear the breeches and be fashionable! I have had some of their outer garments made for my own use though the sleeves are a nuisance. The style of clothing is the same all over China they say, but the material may be cotton, silk, or satin. Pongee is worn a good deal by those who can afford it. The lower class all wear the heavy blue cotton, or in summer for mourning wear the white coarse unbleached cotton.

Their food here is very simple. Rice is not raised here and is considered a luxury as it has to be shipped in from the south. Their substitute is *show mea,* which is our millet and is really very good. We cook it as you would cornmeal mush, let it cool overnight, then slice and roll in flour and fry and that is what we have nearly every morning for breakfast. The "boys" use a great deal of it simply boiled in water. They also mix flour and water, like pie crust but without shortening, and cut it in strips and boil in water. They are supplied with all necessary things if they have what I have mentioned plus a bowl and chopsticks, and an iron kettle and ladle. But then it saves an awful sight of clutter—few dishes to wash, no washing and ironing, no bed making (just roll up your bedding, you know), no carpets to make dust, just brick floors which get little attention, and a chair or so which is never used as they squat about generally or sit on the *k'ang.* This is all the average Chinaman wants excepting his pipe tobacco and opium, with wine when he can get it.

Mr. Stimson, who belongs in this station, is at home in America now and it is somewhat doubtful whether he will come back. He has been in the work eight years, which is the age of the work in the mission. The China Inland missionaries, with Hudson Taylor at the head, are scattered over the province in different directions and there are some English Baptists. The C.I.M.s are mostly Scottish and English and are doing much good. It is very slow work, for the Chinese are superstitious and egotistical and are afraid of us and think their own Confucianism is as good as our religion. And then one can't go about forcing them into a belief of our doctrine. We have to work slowly, here a little and there a little. The knowledge of our purpose in coming here is widely known, that is, they speak of us as foreigners who have one God and are come to teach a new doctrine, but there are comparatively few who come to the chapel service and then it is out of curiosity. All we can do is to scatter the truth as much as possible in preaching and distributing tracts and leaflets, in selling books, in conversation, and in the medical work. Brother and Sister Clapp in Taiku have a school of fifteen or eighteen boys and this is a very encouraging feature.

Yet we do not feel discouraged at the outlook. We can live here, and in safety, and have the liberty of doing all these things without being molested. The magistrates of the cities usually favor our coming in to settle, but sometimes they will not allow us to buy property, and a few years ago many places could not even be rented. Even now it is hard to get property in some desirable places, but on the whole we are treated with a good deal of respect by the better classes. It is the common thing for us to be yelled at by children and sometimes stones are thrown and "foreign devil" is often heard. But it is no worse than a certain class of our people would do at home if a strange people were to come in their way. We hope to live before them uprightly, and quietly gain their confidence and esteem. They regard us as truthful and honest in business, which is a great deal. In time the truth of Christ's gospel will prevail here through the missionaries, which seems to be God's way of spreading His kingdom, though why so slowly and laboriously is mysterious.

We have a pleasant place to live here, quiet and safe for the children. They have not played with any of the Chinese children yet because there have not been any come here except once or twice with their mothers, and they are afraid of us. As we walked out one afternoon we came suddenly upon some little fellows and they ran screaming at the top of their voices, crying and yelling as though we were going to take their heads off. And you must remember too that we are shut and locked in a compound that is surrounded by a wall fifteen feet high. This is the way everyone lives in China if they can afford a wall.

I hope you will enjoy reading this and that you will pass it on to some of the rest to read. Remember us always. Kiss the children for us.

With love to you all,
Sister Eva

....

June 9, 1890

It does not seem possible that it is June and nearly a year has passed since we left Oberlin. Mother, what do you think I wanted the other day? Well, I'll tell you if you'll promise never, never to tell—one of your big aprons so I could put my head in it and cry and imagine it was your lap! Now you may think that exceedingly foolish and that I was homesick and all that, but I couldn't help it, that was what I wanted.

It is much prettier here now than it looked to be in the winter and we do see a lot of trees scattered over the plains after all, but there is nothing like the woods at home. The nearest we come to seeing woods is when we go out about fifteen li to a village in the foothills. The river there is divided into little streams which irrigate a good deal of country before coming together again as a full-fledged river. There are quite a lot of trees all along the streams and it was so pleasant to walk along them two weeks ago.

You would have laughed to see us hunting for a spot to eat our dinner that day where we would be away from the gaze of the Chinese, but there is no such thing I don't believe in all China. It is so thickly populated that if you were to go on top of a mountain, a crowd would gather in less than five minutes. We are such a curiosity and especially if they get to see the "foreign devils" eat. There must have been as many as a dozen men, women, and children standing around in solemn silence watching our performances, and only the fact of a fair being in progress a few li away kept more than that number away. I presume they had never seen silver knives and forks, napkins, or tablecloth. As soon as we had eaten our dinner we took up the line of march and went up the stream quite a distance, leaving the cook on guard, otherwise we would not have had anything left, for some are inveterate thieves.

It is only about thirty li there and back, but oh dear, if you had to bump along in one of these carts for ten miles you would say it was the worst ride you ever took. We have only had two rains since we came here and the dust was terrible. I was so tired when I got home that I was tempted to declare I would never go again. Part of the way is over an old deserted riverbed full of stones and ruts and you may imagine what discomfort it is to sit cross-legged on the floor of a bumpy cart holding a baby! And the children were both sick afterward. Stewart had a high fever and diarrhea which gave us some anxiety for a time, but we gave him aconite and then several doses of quinine, which seems to have helped him a great deal. Do you wonder I like to stay at home?

We are quite anxiously expecting our order from San Francisco now, for we are out of milk and about out of butter. We have no cow as yet so are using Eagle Brand condensed milk. It is very sweet and Charlie does not like it in coffee, but Don drinks a teaspoon in a cup of water three times a day. Our butter is Top O' Can brand, which is put up in cans of one, two, or five pounds. We have to send about two orders a year to keep things going.

We have put a shade made of poles and mats over the court and have put netting in the door and windows to keep out the flies, so I think we will be quite comfortable this summer. It is too hot to be outside until about four o'clock. Mr. Thompson comes over nearly every evening to play croquet. Charlie is in his study nearly all the time pegging away. We have to conduct the Chinese prayers every morning now that Frank is gone. Charlie can read John's gospel and has several hymns and a prayer he uses, so he gets along very well. He helps me with my verses for the reading lesson, and both servants read and we feel that we are not standing entirely still.

I will close with a heart full of love to you all and best wishes for your prosperity and happiness.

....

July 9, 1890

We have actually had company lately. A Mr. Hoste of the China Inland Mission came in last Saturday evening. He was quite ill Sunday night and all day Monday but was able to leave us Tuesday evening. We enjoyed his visit so much as visitors are so rare. I haven't seen a foreign lady for over two months and only one or two other foreign gentlemen, but I have not been nearly so lonely here as I expected to be when we decided to remain in the city.

We are buying some very nice apricots now. We seldom can buy mutton now, but we bought a good many chickens some time ago and are getting our fill of them and have plenty of fresh eggs. My cook does not understand a clock very well and when I told him to boil the eggs three minutes and showed him the time with the long hand of the clock I thought they would be all right. But when they came on the table they were as hard as could be and when I spoke to him about it he said he only boiled them three minutes, and to prove it showed me by the clock. But alas, he had used the short hand, which had to be about three-fourths of an hour! However, I have read that an egg boiled long is healthful.

This courier brought word of the appointment of two young ladies and possibly another gentleman to the work in Shansi, which is good news. And we hope Dr. Atwood, who was formerly in the mission, will return also this fall. We get some encouraging word about the work in some other parts of China but there does not seem to be much of that nature here at present. We realize, however, that there must be a sowing time before a harvest. It makes one long more than ever for the time when all the nations shall know the Lord. I am overwhelmed oftentimes when I read and hear of all the forces of evil that are at work against us, but then again I think it has always been so and yet the Lord will finally triumph. It makes one realize more than ever what wonderful patience God has and is expressing now in his dealings with us poor mortals.

Still our San Francisco goods come not and we have about given them up until fall. It is trying but can be endured. Donnie is getting some more teeth but is feeling pretty well. Stewart is learning lessons and is making good progress. Good-bye with a heart full of prayers and love to you all.

....

July 24, 1890

Our patience is being tried now since the rains have set in and the courier is a week behind and our goods that were in Tientsin in May have not put in an appearance yet. We are out of milk and butter but the rains have kept the dust down and everything is so much nicer, excepting the smell in the streets, which has not improved any. Our own compound, walled in as it is and kept clean, is quite free from all unpleasant odors, but when we go outside we wonder that there isn't cholera or something else as a result of the vile smells. Physicians would be amazed at the way all rules and laws of health are trespassed and transgressed and yet no epidemic follows.

Well, I was just this far when the cook very excitedly cried out "Boxes have come!" (in Chinese of course). And sure enough, here were our long-lost boxes and glad we were to get them. Charlie immediately stopped work in the study and began opening them— three cases of kerosene, three of condensed milk, one big one of canned butter, washboards, brooms, groceries—everything was in pretty good shape considering distance and the recent heavy rains. The servants think we have very many things. We had two clocks in this order, one that strikes, the first I have heard for months. We sent for shades for the lamp you gave me but they were smashed *de lehigh,* which is Chinese for something very emphatic. The children were greatly excited you may believe, but there is something disgusting about sending so far for our things. I sent for shoes for Don but couldn't tell how big he would be in eight months so of course they are all too small. I don't think he can wear a single pair. The children are wearing Chinese shoes, however, and I don't believe I will send home for any more.

We took another ride out to the country village the other day as I wanted to see how the country and roads looked after heavy rains. It took two mules to pull us. (I walked a good part of the way.) We could see the mountains, and Stewart asked if God made the mountains for the clouds to rest on, which is quite a pleasing thought, isn't it?

This morning I was washing the dried currants that came with the goods and it made me homesick. I had thoughts of the times there on the farm when I spent so much time and used so much water getting them fit to eat. I sent home for yeast and the renowned "magic" proved to raise the bread about as quickly here as though it had not come thousands of miles and been months on the way. I've got five pounds of hops too and feel quite independent.

I must confess I misjudged this country when we came through last fall for it looked then so barren, but the springtime had the same resurrecting powers here as elsewhere. The birds, however, have been disappointing for there seem to be none of our sweet home birds and I miss the bluebirds and robins most of all.

We are all well as usual at this writing. Stewart is getting along very well with his studies—has had nearly twenty-five lessons in *Appleton's Reader*. When we were out riding the other day and he noticed the beautiful growing things, he said, "Who do they think makes these things grow? Do they think it is their idols?" I thought it was a good idea for a little fellow, it showed he was doing some solid thinking. He and Donnie have some good times playing together. I do hope they will be spared to each other and to us as long as we are here. It would be terribly lonely without them.

....

Fen Cho fu, China

August 11, 1890

Dear Grandpa, Grandma and Uncles, [written by Eva]

Mamma says I may send a little letter to you. We had a big scare the other day. You know Papa bought Uncle Frank's revolver for sometimes the wolves are bad outside the city. Well, he put the revolver in one of the trunks and Mamma made him take out the load first as she is awful afraid of guns. When she came across it the other day she thought she would be brave and see if she dared to cock it and draw the trigger. Don and I were sitting on the floor close by playing and the first thing I knew— Bang!!! I looked up and there sat Mamma pale and frightened almost out of her wits. She called, "Papa, Papa! I thought you said this was not loaded!" And then she cried for she might have killed us or shot herself or something and she was awful scared. The noise made her deaf for an hour. She did shoot a hole through one end of the till to the trunk and then the ball hit some cakes of soap. Mamma had another scare the same day for Don choked on a plum pit till he could hardly see but finally got it swallowed.

We go outside our gate (the big door you know is called a gate) nearly every evening and walk up and down in front for a while and if Mamma is there too it won't be but a few minutes until lots of women gather around her and she will sit down on the stones and they look at each other and try to talk. They bring their little babies too (there are lots of babies in China), and these warm days some don't have any clothes on or just a piece of cloth over their stomachs with a string tied around the neck. Some big boys, eight or ten years old, go without any clothes on. It is pretty hot here but I wouldn't like to go that way. I like to get my clean clothes on and go where they can see how nice I look for they are quite dirty. Don and I get dirty when we make mud pies and biscuits in the dirt. We go barefooted most of the time.

I hope you are all well and will live lots of years for I want to see you when I come back there to school. If we don't get sick we will stay here eight or ten years. I can talk some Chinese talk but I like "Oberlin talk" best. We have a nice black rabbit and we call it "Bunny."

With lots of love to you all,
Stewart Leland Price

Fen Cho fu, China
September 28, 1890

We are waiting again for the courier as we have so often done this summer. Heavy rains east of us in Chihli province have done a great deal of damage as the lowlands are mostly under water. As a consequence the roads between here and Paoting fu are very bad and carts as well as foot travelers have a hard time getting through.

Yesterday was quite an eventful day as Mr. and Mrs. Davis, the friends who have been spending the summer at Li Man, came back to this city and were here to supper last night. I had not seen a foreign woman since last May, and I realized all at once that I was a little homesick to see the face of a friend. Her stories of the fleas, mud, and robbers makes me think we were fully as comfortable here as we would have been there. The summer has not been as severe in heat as I expected and I think, considering this is our first summer here, we have been greatly blessed.

We have had word from Frank and Jennie that they had a very pleasant voyage home and were in our own dear native land about three months after leaving us here. The doctor, a specialist in San Francisco, said Frank would be well in less than a year if he gave his throat absolute rest for six months. They were very much elated and I am sure we of Shansi are hoping they may come back.

You will be glad to learn that we are to have Dr. Atwood, a homeopathist, and family with us here in Fen Cho fu this fall. He has the language well as he has been in China seven years or more and will be of great value to the work here besides a help to us personally. Charlie and I have done a little medical work this summer for we have given medicine and directions in several cases of very sore eyes that have been cured in a marvelously short time. My theory is that as the Chinese have never been treated medically by anything outside their own nearly useless stuff, our really efficacious medicines take hold of their troubles sooner than they do with us. Charlie has treated several cases of cuts and sores, which he has helped in every case. The most distressing case we have seen was a young fellow who came to see if we could take a needle out of his stomach which he had swallowed the day before. It was not an ordinary needle but one of a curved shape such as they sew mats with, curved and flat and about four inches long. And how do you think he swallowed it? He had been trying to stick it up his nose and make it come out of his mouth! I judge it has been done, perhaps he had succeeded before, but this time it went on down his throat instead of coming out of his mouth, and I don't know what the result has been for we told him we could do nothing. It will probably kill him for I don't see how that crooked thing can go through his stomach and intestines.

We are busy studying again with the teacher, and Charlie says he has preached his first sermon. He was out to a village distributing tracts and one old man who was reading one turned to him and said, "Jesus, who is Jesus?" Charlie said he told him as best he could and talked for a few minutes to the crowd that had gathered. They may not have understood a thing he said, but this only proves their ignorance and the very great need for work being done.

Good-bye and love to you all.

....

October 20, 1890

Every week here is just about like the one before—no place to go, no friends to visit, no callers coming in (only our Chinese friends occasionally); one day so much like another that we hardly know them apart. Except since Mr. and Mrs. Davis are back in the city we have our prayer meeting Thursday nights and Sunday night a service is held, sermon read, hymns sung, and prayer similar to regular church service, which is a very precious time. Charlie spends every forenoon in his study and every other afternoon goes out to adjoining villages to distribute tracts and invitations. He is working hard and Mr. Thompson says he is getting on well with the language.

I bought some chrysanthemums which I set up on the window ledge outside the sitting room and they are refreshing. If we stay here another year I am going to have some flowers if possible. By tearing up some of the brick pavements I think I can have quite a flower garden. The old stone stairway by which we climbed to the roofs to walk and get a view of the city and mountains fell down with a crash one night and since then I can't get a squint at the rest of the world unless we go outside the compound.

The weather is fine now and the children are out in the court tearing around and making noise enough for ten boys. Our last postage stamps which we got from Tientsin are red, white, and blue. Hurrah! The cook is making mincemeat. Come over and take Thanksgiving dinner with us.

....

Shansi, China
October 20, 1890

Dear Father,

Eva has told you all about our home so there is not much for me to write. I have been doing something in the medical line, such as treating men for sore eyes or cuts or bruises. No doubt you will say it is grand work to help these poor people, but if you could see the patient in all his filth and "live animals," you would think him a hard-looking customer. There was a man in yesterday though, whom it was a pleasure to help. He was, for a wonder, almost clean. He had a sore that had been with him twelve years. I hope to be able to cure him, and if I do he will in all probability be my friend.

Truly I do like to do such work. It is all I can do at present and I am glad to be able to do even this small thing. Perhaps the people may grow to have some confidence in us if we succeed in doing good to them and it will be after long patient work of this kind that we will make them believe we are honest in our profession of interest in them. At present they have various theories as to why we are here. They think their country so much better than ours that we prefer living here. They do not seem to be able to comprehend or accept the idea of any country being better than theirs. Or the most common idea is, we have come here as agents of the American government—it may be to see how strong the military force of the country is or to see how rich the soil is in minerals as productive qualities. They can't grasp the idea of self-sacrifice for the sake of Christ. Tell them we have come to tell them of Christ that they by him may be saved and they merely laugh.

Hence, it will take a long time, perhaps years, to convince them of the sincerity of our purpose. Of course, they will not believe the gospel so long as they are suspicious of us, but their suspicion is being overcome in other parts of the empire and in time it will give way here. But the time of waiting is long. If one is working, he wishes to see some result of his labor, but we ought to be willing to abide the time of the Lord. We know that our work shall tell in the future if we are faithful. I often think of the Apostles preaching with untiring zeal from city to city. Yet although inspired men, their preaching had no effect. If men of such power could see their efforts so unfruitful of results, why should we complain if our very weak work should fail of immediate result? I am not discouraged. The work is being carried on in God's own way in His time. When He speaks the people shall hear.

Love to you all,
Your son, C. W. Price

....

Fen Cho fu, China
December 10, 1890

Well, we are about done with 1890 and by the time you read this it will be 1891—March perhaps. Dr. Atwood and family came about a month ago and boarded with us until after Christmas, more than three weeks in all, which made a good deal of extra work. But we got along nicely and the friends said I had a good cook! They didn't know just how much I did. My experience in cooking for harvest hands and threshers is not forgotten yet, so I know how to take hold.

Besides boarders I was over to Mrs. Davis's most of one week as her little baby was born on the fourteenth but only lived a few days. Dr. Atwood said he thought it had la grippe. We have all been sick with it this winter, but it did not seem sick at all until just the day before it died. It was very sad to have to put the little body away so soon and was a great sorrow to the mother. This is her first baby. We had the Chinese carpenters make a coffin and a great, uncouth box they made. Mrs. Atwood and I lined it with cotton and white cloth and the gentlemen painted the outside. It is in our croquet ground now with a little brick vault built over it. There is no place for us foreigners except on our own property. The foreigners have a ground at Tai Yuen fu but that is four days' travel from here.

As I am writing this I hear the servants in the gatehouse singing "He Leadeth Me." Whether they sing in the spirit or not it sounds good. Since Dr. Atwood came, we have quite a number of "boys," as they have two and we have two plus the gatekeeper. The gatekeeper is a church member and their cook is also. Just how genuine they are is not for us to say. Sometimes they profess a good deal to see if they can't make some money out of it. One of our couriers had to be discharged as he got to stealing books, and he was a church member! He had ten he had brought from Taiku and some of them were foreign medical books and he couldn't read a word of them.

Well, I will close for this time and let Stewart write a few lines. He and Don are both asleep but that doesn't matter.

....

Fen Cho fu, China

Dear Grandpa and Grandma, [written by Eva]

Maybe you think we can't have any Christmas way out here but we can. Don and I hung up our stockings and got lots of presents. Papa rented a little evergreen bush from one of the temples here and they brought it in a big dish so Mama put it on a stand. After we went to bed she hung some little bags of popcorn and candy on the branches and had two pretty little dolls sitting underneath and there was a little hairy dog between them. Around on the edge of the stand were books and toys and an iron train of cars—engine, coal car, two other cars, and two iron men! I like them very much. And two clapper things the peddlers use here on the street that make a nice noise. Maybe I can send you one some day. And there were some little rubber dollies that squeak when you squeeze them and two rubber balls, one for Don and one for me, and some nice books with pictures and stories. I was very delighted.

Dr. Atwood's live in this same court now and they have two

boys. Paul is twelve and Edward is three. Paul has two canary birds and a dog and a gray goat. I have a black rabbit and a black goat. The goats climb way up on the top of the house sometimes. When Paul was coming here from Tientsin his dog was stolen three times. The last time was in Taiku and they couldn't find it and had to come here without it. After it had been gone about a month one of the servants saw it on the street in Taiku and he got it and sent it down to Paul for Christmas. Wasn't that nice? And the dog was so glad to see the family again he was about wild. He wiggled all over and jumped around and ran from one of them to the other.

Mamma made me new cotton flannel night drawers and they are awful big and baggy—like Chinese breeches Papa said and he laughed and laughed. I want Mamma to fix them.

Well I must kiss you all goodnight and go to bed. I hope you are all well and having a good time.

With love to you all from,
Stewart Leland Price

....

Fen Cho fu, China
February 2, 1891

Tomorrow is the first day of spring and it is hard to realize the winter is over. Next week our Annual Meeting begins, to last a week. The Taiku friends were all expected but they write now that only the gentlemen, Dr. Goldsbury and Mr. Clapp, will come. We have not seen the two young ladies, Miss Bird and Miss Hewett, since they came out last fall. The secretary writes that we are to have another gentleman and wife come out this year, so if no one has to go home we will soon have a good working force.

I sent Jennie a sketch of one of our gateways with a dragon's head and Frank writes that he thinks I have "talent" and wants me to do something for the good of China! I wish I could have taken more drawing lessons but I am afraid my natural talent is hardly big enough to warrant anything very important. I will send you the drawing like I sent Frank. The gateway is between the first court and the court in which we live and is rather pretty. The tile roofs

The Gateway

which cover all the buildings and gateways are very pretty too, some of them so old they are covered with lichens and graylike moss. The eaves are very wide. You may imagine what a picture these roofs make with one of those hideous dragon heads on each corner. They are also on each corner of the gateways. Two horrid stone dogs guard the entrances to the courts, one on each side of the gate.

Mrs. Atwood and I called on one of our near neighbors the other day and were treated well. They gave us tea to drink and showed us about the place and asked our ages and all sorts of polite things. We came home with flowers in our hair—the Chinese women usually wear something stuck in the hair for ornament, usually bright paper flowers. These are real flowers, however, something like our sweet currant and are strung on a small piece of bamboo.

I wish you could see the children. They are such a comfort to me. Donny is plump and so sweet. He and Stewart play camel now.

Stewart lies flat on his stomach on the floor and Don gets astride his back with a firm grab on the coat collar and then Stewart raises up on his hands and knees and prances about. Don rolls off once in a while but that is fun too.

Stewart and Donald and Charlie and I send lots of love to "all e tokes."

....

March 17, 1891

I was most discouraged about home letters but Mother's came last week and cheered me up not a little. It had been three couriers since we had heard from home.

We now have the luxury of really, truly cow's milk! We bought a cow, a pretty shorthorn, and she gives a whole gallon of milk a day! She has a calf a few months old and if she were a Christian cow would be giving lots of milk, but as she is a heathen cow we have to put up with her. It is one of the characteristics of a Chinese cow that they won't give down their milk unless the calf is right with her and helps do the milking. It milks awhile and then we milk awhile. I wonder if it couldn't be changed but they all say a cow will dry right up if the calf is taken away and we are only too glad to have plenty of milk and cream.

We had a treat last month as we all went to Taiku to Annual Meeting and stayed eight days besides four days going and coming. We have to hire these pokey old mules besides carrying our food and bedding so it seems quite like moving to go on even a little journey. The morning we started we were ready at 7:30 and waited around until 9:30 before the cart came and then found out, before we were a mile away, that the innkeeper had given us a no-account mule that couldn't make the trip in three days. The children and I were in a litter, the cook and Charlie in the cart. There was nothing to do but get out and have a big fuss with the old innkeeper who had followed us out of town intending (we found out later) to sponge a free ride to Taiku as he had business there. Mr. and Mrs. Davis were along with their cart and Mr. Thompson had another, so Charlie unloaded the traps out of his cart and put them on Mr. Thompson's cart. Then you ought to have heard the old fellow storm! He declared if the cart didn't go the litter shouldn't go. I said, "All right I'll go back home." We put Mr. Thompson in as spokesman and there we stood and fussed for two hours more until finally Mr. Thompson told him to take his old rig and go.

We sent the cook back into the city to hire another and it was only after handling the bedding five different times and fussing around till about noon that we were able at last to go on our way! We were afraid after such a delay it would be impossible to get through in two days so we pushed on till 8:00 P.M. only stopping long enough to eat dinner. When we came to the place where we were to stop overnight we hoped our troubles were over. But alas and alack! It was New Year's time, which here in China is a month or more later than our New Year's and is the holiday lasting two or three weeks! Well, they were having some sort of celebration or feast and had all the streets blockaded and we wandered around for a full hour trying to find a place to get in. Finally, when our patience was about exhausted, we found a little back street that was clear and it was not long before we were in our inn getting supper and making beds.

We started out again early the next morning and it was late afternoon when we finally got to our friends' home in Taiku and glad we were to get to a civilized place. We spent a very pleasant time there, only there came a big snowstorm which kept us two days longer than we had planned. We had good meetings, there were seventeen of us counting the four children, and one evening we had entertainment with readings, music and recitations, and my "paper." Stewart spoke his piece like a little man. Mr. Liu, the Chinese teacher in the boys' school in Taiku, was baptized and publicly confessed his belief in God. He is a very large, fine-looking man and a good scholar. We hope he will be a great help to the work there.

When Dr. Atwood came back to Fen Cho fu after the meeting he brought with him nine men, including a son and some other relatives of Mr. Liu, for treatment of their opium habit. A fourteen-year-old boy has used opium since he was seven years old and is now using more than any man. It is going pretty hard with him, poor fellow, and the doctor has thought he wouldn't live through it.

There is a beggar staying in one of the *yaos* * here who has a sore leg that Dr. Atwood is treating. He had a good many lice and they bothered him so much that Dr. Atwood gave him some carbolic acid and told him to have the barber put a little in some water and wash his hair with it. So when he went out to have his queue fixed he took it along but the barber said he couldn't have that nasty-smelling stuff in his dish as it would drive all his customers off. So what did he do but douse the acid right on the poor fellow's head and when he came back he said, "It burnt holes in my head—but it killed the bugs!" The doctor said, "Well, if you use foreign medicine you must do as you are told."

We have saved more than $200 this last year which we will send to Oberlin to be put on interest for the boys' schooling.

---

*A unique feature of Shansi province was the use of cave dwellings, houses literally carved into loess hills. These houses or rooms are called *yaodong* or *yao*.

PART TWO
Peeking Place
MAY 1891–MAY 1892

Yu Tao Ho, China
"Peeking Place," China
May 31, 1891

Dear Home Folks,

That is "peeking" you will notice and not Peking, which is the capital of this famous land. I will tell you why I call it "Peeking." We are out here in a valley in the foothills of the mountains expecting to stay three or four months. We are living in an old mill and the buildings form three sides of the compound with no other outside wall. We ventured on cutting a small window through the wall of the room we occupy, which gives us an opportunity to look on the outside world, the first chance of that kind we have had in China. To be sure the window is small, but it lets us look out on the hills and higher mountains as well as the trees, grass, and running water without the tiresome walls. This window is low from the outside too and while it furnishes us with this chance of outside beauties, it furnishes as well a fine opportunity for the "outside beauties" to look in. What if my view is suddenly shut off by half a dozen black heads with their black eyes and dusky faces? They only look and look until they are satisfied and then are gone maybe for a half hour and in the meantime I can look out. However, it is a little disconcerting to encounter instead of my glimpse of the mountain the steady stare of a curious Chinaman, or maybe half a dozen, but I go on with what I am doing pretending not to see them and after gazing their fill and commenting in an undertone about what they have seen, they go off as suddenly and quietly as they came.

....

That the China missionaries required special summer quarters may seem extravagant to the reader, as it did to the Board headquarters in Boston. While comfort and the need to get away from the frustrating business of converting uncaring heathens no doubt played an important role in the missionaries' requests for summer quarters, summer retreats were a very real necessity to the survival of many China missionaries. Casualty statistics clearly show that the heat and disease of summer in urban China had a deadly impact upon foreigners (especially children).—R.F.

....

And so they keep it up day after day seeming never to tire of the luxury of watching the "foreign devils" at close range. It disturbed me a good deal the first day or so. We have our table placed in full view of the window so have an uninvited audience for nearly every meal. I sit with my back next to the window, however, and let the others face the music. They are so quiet and peaceful that we put up with the annoyance hoping it will do good to let them see us and how we live. The people were opposed to letting us come here and it was only after several attempts that property could be rented. I am the first foreign woman most of them have ever seen and I seem to be a great curiosity. So I hope their suspicion and animosity will be allayed this summer and we will make friends with them. They are greatly taken with the children and make a great deal over them.

It is such a luxury, after living in the close courts in Fen Cho fu, to be able to step at once outdoors and saunter and stroll in the shade beside the stream. We may be tempted to stay here all winter. The "boys" (our two Chinese servants) are afraid. They say these people are *pu hao,* or bad folks, and will steal all our things, but we don't feel afraid although there are certain rude forts up on the hilltops to which the inhabitants of the valley are said to flee when robbers come down like wolves on the fold.

We are about ten miles from Fen Cho fu and yet when we climb to the tablelands back of us we can see away off across the plains beyond the city. We can see the pagoda, which is so high that it is seen for miles and miles, and the whole view is very enchanting. We walked way up the river one day and drank some excellent water from a spring. The Chinese utilize this river for all its worth and irrigate a large scope of country until very little water is allowed to run in the natural bed. There must be nearly a hundred mills all along the way a few rods apart and a large share of the flour for the province must come from these mills. The water plunges down underneath the mill on a sideshot wheel which C.W. says he has never seen before. They make a very good quality of flour but, because of something in the climate, bread two days old is not fit to eat in hot weather. Break off a piece and you can see fine hairs of mold and it will have a spoiled taste.

The room we are living in is about sixty feet by twenty feet and is built of brick but has a board floor. We put a curtain across one end for a bedroom and use the other for a dining and sitting room. We did not bring many things out here with us and it is quite like a picnic. The "boy" cooks in a side room. Mr. and Mrs. Davis expect to live in the rooms on one side of the court.

There is quite a variety of wild birds but none I recognize except we hear mourning doves and another that sounds like the wren, but I would like to hear a bluebird. The land about here is mostly in the white poppy which makes the opium that so many of these poor people are slaves to. Since we came here I saw one man who was on our place in Fen Cho fu for two weeks breaking off opium. He looks real well and said he is not using it at all. He remembered the children and seemed glad to see them again.

Donnie is not very well today but as he is getting some more teeth it may be it is that. We brought your pictures along and he talked to you this morning. Charlie will go to Fen Cho fu tomorrow and will carry this letter to send with the courier.

Love to you all and many wishes for your best prosperity, from your loving daughter and sister,

Eva

June 16, 1891

We are enjoying our summer home very much. Mr. and Mrs. Davis, Miss Hewett, and ourselves took an eight-mile walk last Saturday afternoon. We all sauntered out and kept going on just a little farther until we came to the source of the river. Stewart walked all the way and Donnie walked over two miles I am sure. Charlie carried him the rest of the way. It is so pleasant to take these walks along the stream and we have fine rock views. A temple is built over the spring which furnishes the largest amount of water at the source of the river and has been a large, important place in past years. But now it is falling into decay and does not have the appearance of being used or very cared for. The images in most of these Buddhist temples are in ruins or so covered with dust and cobwebs that they look fully as neglected.

The people here so far have been friendly and pleasant. They wonder, no doubt, what we want to find when they see us on these strolling expeditions, for the Chinese never seem to walk for the pleasure of it, the women especially, for their little feet are so crippled that it is a great effort for them to get about. They usually have a cane of some sort to help them. The women seem willing to admit that our feet are best—they never hurt and we can get about so fast and comfortably.

But our way of wearing our hair is a constant distress to them. One woman said yesterday, "Your hair doesn't look well, why don't you wear it like we do?" They wear a stiff contrivance on the back of the head which is awkward to lie down with and you can't even lean back in a chair with any comfort. However, the fashion was not intended for lazy folks who take naps in the daytime or who loll back in rocking chairs. The Chinese women have no rocking chairs, are in fact afraid of them. And when they sleep they have a blocklike sort of pillow which allows that stiff apparatus to stick over it. There is not much individuality about the fashion for every woman looks nearly exactly like all others, except the faces—some of them look bright and pretty, others look almost stupid. They look so disgusted when they admit they cannot read. I have not met one yet that can read even a little. The older missionaries say it is something accomplished when you get an idea into a Chinese woman's head. They cannot take in more than one thing at a time and then you are not certain that they have it right. One woman, after weeks of training, insisted that Adam was the mother of Jesus.

We had a good rain here last week which revived the thirsty ground. It was quite local though and the wheat fields on the uplands are pretty yellow. They have begun harvesting but I think the crop is unusually light. There are no big fields of grain here, it is mostly in small patches and cut by hand.

We saw some men in a poppy patch near us at work so we went to see what they were doing. Each man had a small tin cup and a knifelike instrument. After the blossom has fallen off and the seedpod has reached a certain maturity they make incisions around the pod and a creamlike juice exudes which the men, with their dirty fingers, "swipe" off into their cups. I smelled it and it was like old, rotten potatoes. I don't know how many times they take the juice from a single pod, but the work lasts for about two months. Every single pod in a patch is visited and revisited, so you can see it requires tedious work. They are planting more and more of it every year and a workman can earn more than he can in a wheat field. We understand it is against the law now for it to be grown.

If it were not for wolves and robbers I would like to live here all winter. Dr. Atwood thinks there is no doubt but their new house will be ready for them before winter, in which case we will move back in the old rooms.

I would like to see you all but that will come some day maybe. In the meantime let us hope and pray that our lives may not be spent here in vain.

....

June 29, 1891

The enclosed flower with leaves came from an acacia tree which we saw when we went to a nearby village last week, although this blossom has faded so you cannot tell it was once bright crimson hairs, as strange a looking flower as I ever saw. But what a beautiful sight! The tree was larger than an ordinary-sized apple tree and covered with bright blossoms. I am also enclosing a little paper flag we found stuck in the ground. It is the custom here to put these along the road at intervals to mark the way to a grave.

We are carrying our drinking water from a cold spring a mile up the river and that is the first water we have had in China that was not first boiled. We have had a little experience that has been annoying to say the least. The first spring we tried was in a riverbed a half mile from here and for a time all went well. One evening when we walked down to get the usual supply we found that someone with a small heart had polluted it and so we had to resort to another spring a mile up the river. This spring came from under a bank so was not easily polluted. We have carried water from there for two weeks without trouble, but last evening when we got up there, lo, someone had carried stones and dirt and had dammed it all up. Mr. Davis wanted to throw some of the fellows who were sitting around to see the fun headfirst into the stream, but we urged him not to for maybe he wouldn't get the right one and we have to go slow here and not make enemies if we can help it. So Charlie "fell to" and cleaned out the rubbish and in a few minutes the water was beautifully clean again. They have gone after water now and I am expecting to hear of something else when they come back.

"Yes, there was a piece of paper in the bottom of the spring weighted down with a stone," they said. What it was they did not know but it was taken out and the spring cleaned out and then they waited again for the water to run clear and got their pails full. The people generally seem friendly, and I am sure if two families of Chinese were at the mercy of some neighborhoods in the U.S. as we are here at their mercy, they would be made to suffer far more than we do. Boys at home, yes even grown men, would delight in playing jokes on them if nothing worse. We are truly "pioneers" in this part of the province, for foreigners never lived here before.

The village where Mrs. Davis and I went last week is about a mile from here and the people there are said to be very much opposed to foreigners. We called on some women, three of whom had been to see us, and they seemed very glad to see us and we had a pleasant time. We sat on the *k'angs* and drank tea while the people crowded around us to examine our clothing and comment on our hands and faces and way of wearing the hair. We talked to them

The *K'ang*

as best we could. They were all very poor apparently, and the one little room which was the general living room for the family did not smell very good and by the time the people had crowded in, men with their pipes and all with not very clean bodies and apparel, the odor was decidedly sickening. We visited five homes in all. Many of the homes here are built in the hillside with only a door and paper window in the front. A cloth is hung over the doorway in the summer time. The room will be maybe thirty feet by twelve feet. The *k'ang* is built along the side under the window and there is a chimney in the wall at the opposite end and as it often does not draw well there is a good deal of smoke and gas* in the room. You can readily see the poor man's home is a cheerless place.

The *k'ang* is the all-important thing—sleeping place, sitting place, and general catchall. The fireplace is in the end of the *k'ang*, you know, and poor people use it to cook their food on. They may have a bench, and if they should have a chair it is usually a high awkward thing, almost too heavy to lift. A *kuei tzu* (pronounced gwā zä) is a tall wardrobe that nearly everyone has at some price. The rich have them in pairs and often they are very beautiful and expensive. The lower part does not open but things are piled in from the top. The *kuei tzus* are next to the *k'ang* in importance and hold the wardrobe for the family. The Chinese clothing all folds up and nothing is hung, so their wardrobes are made to fit the clothes. The garments are slit up from the bottom like a man's shirt and are comfortable to wear. The women walk with their arms extended as they use their arms for balance and sometimes look like they are flying. They usually carry a long stick or cane, or sometimes a long brass pipe, which does double duty. It is a poor woman who cannot afford large brass or glass earrings. They sometimes have hung their

*Eva probably was referring to fumes caused by burning peat, charcoal, or twigs.

rings over my ears to see how I would look, then they laugh and say "Hao kau" ("That looks nice").

If you have not thrown away my letters to you, will you please keep them, for I have not kept any journal since we came to China and I may need them when I "write my book."

....

July 23, 1891

We are all well and are enjoying this place so much. I never tire of being outdoors or of looking out the little window at the scenery. The carts loaded with bags of wheat or flour and the lines of donkeys we so often see with bags or baskets strapped on their backs, plus the quaintly dressed people who walk along the stream, lend life to the scene and add to the interest. Last week I painted a picture of an old mill with side wheel, water, snow, and moonlight and friends say it is good. Just now some children have come up and are looking in the window and they are talking quietly to one another and I wish you might take a peep at them.

Last Sunday we had quite a crowd come to our room, about seventy-five I think, for Mr. Thompson had come out to visit and we thought it a good opportunity to have them hear the gospel. Miss Hewett was also here and she played the baby organ, which attracted them greatly. We could not furnish seats for so many so the men generally sat or squatted on the floor. The Chinese, women especially, are childish, and as they had never been to church before they made some little disturbance by their talking aloud. And one or two got up and meant to investigate the places behind the curtains which we have hung to divide the rooms. They had to be spoken to as little children would and made to sit down and keep quiet. Some behaved very well indeed, but how much they understood or how much good was done we cannot tell. When one realizes that most of such an audience as we had Sunday, with their many dark superstitions clouding their minds, had never heard of Jesus or the True God, and that perhaps they would never hear again, it seems a stupendous work to "convert China." But God has chosen this slow way to perfect His kingdom and if it is not accomplished then the Church of Christ in the world has not done her duty because she has sent so few laborers into the harvest field. What can a few Christians do to evangelize such a vast, vast country as China?

We all went on an excursion last Monday going up the river seven or eight miles. We had three donkeys, one with baskets for the children to ride in, another with baskets for the lunch boxes, and the third with side saddle to give the ladies an occasional lift. As the baskets are not strapped on, it does not look to be a very safe way to carry the children but that is the regulation way here. I walked all the way. Our own family with Mr. and Mrs. Davis, Mr. Thompson, and Miss Hewett made up the party. We ate our dinner up in the mountains on a rocky table and then took naps on a rocky bed, but we all enjoyed the trip very much. We reached home before dark and I gave the children bread and milk and they tumbled into bed asleep before they knew it.

I stepped outside the compound the other evening and found a woman out there doing her washing. She was sitting on the ground near where a stepping-stone is laid across the stream and there she rubbed and rubbed back and forth on this stone, dipping the garment in the water occasionally and rubbing again. They use no soap and the water is cold and there is no boiling or blueing and it was not particularly clean when she got through. This woman had a pile of old-looking duds—no tablecloths, bedding, and things we think so necessary.

Stewart and Charlie went into the city today and got back about two o'clock. Stewart wishes we could take the brook to Fen Cho fu with us.

....

August 24, 1891

We are having delightful weather. I wish you could visit us once at this pleasant place; you would feel better about our being here. You wouldn't think the house very fine for the roof is not ceiled and you can see the bare poles and heavy beams, and we have no window sash either, only cheesecloth and mosquito netting. The board floor is rough and the Chinese doors are awkward things, but then we can live without fine houses if we can see outdoors.

We have been having services here in our room for several Sundays but Mr. Thompson is going away tomorrow so it will be up to Charlie and Mr. Davis. It has been very pleasant to see the people gather in from different directions and meet here. They have no Sabbath but go on with their business and work seven days a week. There are so many children come in. I wish I could send you a picture of the crowd that comes in just as we see them—some men half naked, children nearly nude, women nursing their babies with not even a handkerchief to cover their breasts, an occasional boy with a hen or basket of eggs to sell (which we do not buy of course on Sunday), some dirty, lousy fellows but with souls to be saved.

We had such a treat two weeks ago. Mr. Liu, the Chinese teacher in the boys' school in Taiku who was baptized at the Annual Meeting in February, was visiting Dr. Atwood in Fen Cho fu and we invited him out here to stay over Sunday. He is such a fine, large, noble-looking man and, I believe, an earnest Christian, and we were anxious to have the people here in the valley see one of their countrymen who had accepted the foreign religion. He preached to over 200 who crowded into this room, and his talk was a good one. Of course I couldn't understand nearly all of it but I got enough to know he was urging the people to accept Jesus as their Savior and God instead of the gods they pray to. It made me feel very solemn to feel that perhaps that was the very first time most of them had heard the gospel in their own language by one of their own people. Mr. Liu stayed over Sunday and ate at our table using knife and fork very successfully and apparently enjoyed his food. It was the first time we ever had a Chinaman eat with us and I felt it was a real honor that we had the privilege of entertaining such a "nature's nobleman" as Mr. Liu, the true gospel to their people. We must expect the chief work of preaching and saving souls will be done by converted Chinamen.

Charlie goes out nearly every day to distribute tracts and cate-chisms. He gave an old man one of the books with questions and answers a few weeks ago. The other day as Charlie was in a mill a few li up the river trying to talk to the men there, this man came in and at once and with considerable earnestness began to tell them of the doctrine as he had read it in this little book. Charlie understood enough to know he was explaining to them about the One God and Jesus dying on the cross and other points which showed he had intelligently read the book.

We have some visible effects of the services on Sunday as we have about 400 fleas, though they are not seen as often as they are felt!

....

September 22, 1891

The courier leaves in the morning so, although it is late and I have had a jolty time today, I will write a short letter to you. We went into the city today and were late getting back. We had the pokiest old white mule and I thought we would never get through. I poked her once when the driver wasn't looking and she kicked up with both hind feet so I didn't try that plan any more. The morning was a beautiful one, so cool and fine, and Stewart and I walked down the valley about three miles of the way. The path was good and the trees and water made it very pleasant. Charlie sat in the cart with Don. But after we got out of this immediate neighborhood to where the people were not acquainted with us, any little fellows who happened to see us would race away as though the evil one himself were after them. Today more than ever before it seemed to me we heard the cry on all sides, "Yang kneitzu" (Yäng gwāza)—"Foreign devils!"

One day when some people came here to call on us, instead of first coming to the gate, they came around to the little outside window and called out that they wanted to come in. When I paid no attention to such uncivil manners, one of the children called out "Yang kneitzu!" Finally they went around to the gate and knocked and one of the servants came in and said there were people at the gate wanting to come in. I told him to go out and ask them if they were acquainted with our name. If so, I wanted them to call us by it, that our name is Chia (Jä) and not "foreign devil," and that he must not let the children in who called us that. When they did come in I told them very emphatically, "Our name is Chia and not foreign devil. We don't like that!"

Sunday, Stewart had to be spoken to a number of times and didn't pay much attention, so when it came time to go up to the spring after water I told him he couldn't go: he must stay here by himself while we went. This of course was quite a punishment for a little fellow not seven years old. Don and I did not go very far, but we went out of sight of the little window where Stewart stood watching us (and crying some too he told me afterward). I was a little afraid to go off a mile away and leave him alone, so pretty soon Don and I turned back and Charlie went on. Stewart had shut the window by putting in the board so he did not see us come back. I waited around awhile and then knocked at the gate and he ran to open it, first asking. "Who is there?" in Chinese. When he found out it was Mamma he was delighted and rattled on about being so happy and how he felt while we were gone. So I asked him what he resolved in his heart while I was gone. He said "Iniquity." "What?" said I. "I resolved iniquity in my heart" was his answer. I thought if the punishment had made him "resolve iniquity in his heart" that I would have to try something else the next time.

The children were both so good today. They are well and enjoy living out here very much. We have a black-and-white kitty like "Maria Jane" we had on the farm. I am very tired so must say goodnight.

....

October 20, 1891

It will not do for the courier to leave without a letter for you and so I will hasten to write one. I wonder if you realize that our letters are carried over 500 miles "by hand" before they get to the coast where they are put on the steamer? This mission has two couriers—one going, one coming—every two weeks. They carry our outgoing mail over 300 miles to Paoting fu, then come back again with the incoming mail. The Paoting fu couriers for the North China mission carry it on to Tientsin. One of our men makes the trip very quickly as he is gone only about eighteen days. When they come back it is an event I can tell you, and we can hardly wait for the bags to be unlocked and opened.

There are five Chinese children in the room playing with the hammock and a woman and a boy leaning over the table watching me write. That is one thing we have to get used to for I am afraid always of doing something that will drive them away. There were over thirty in to services Sunday and I hope some of these people who are so friendly to us will get some knowledge of the truth while we are here.

We have been having a good many callers lately as we have brought the sewing machine out here and it is a wonderful curiosity. I usually take time to show them the machine for they come sometimes several li to see it. I will soon have to charge the Board for muslin as I have used quite a piece as I hem, ruffle, and run every day so as to show what the machine can do, and they all want a sample to take home with them. There were about fifty different ones in last Thursday but that is an exception as there was a fair in a little village across the valley from us and we came in for our share of attention.

Charlie has done a good deal of visiting villages this summer and thinks he has made more advancement in the language than in all the time before. He has services every Sunday and I can't say how well they understand him but there has to be a beginning some time.

I overheard Stewart telling Donald what a birthday is and his explanation was something like this: "Why a birthday is—a birthday is—when you get older and older and someone gives you a present—maybe a blanket shawl." I wondered at this idea of a present and if Don was anxious for a birthday after such an inducement. Stewart is drumming on the baby organ now and Don is walking on his hands and feet playing he is a camel. We saw quite a number of camels the other day when we were out in a cart and the children were delighted. The camels were lying down resting when we went and when we came back they were up eating so we had a good sight of them. They travel a good deal by night and rest in the middle of the day.

Callers here in China are not very ceremonious for when they come in they usually go from one end of the house to the other and as they are supposed to be light-fingered we have to follow them so as to watch them while they "open their eyes" as they call seeing things. I went on with my ironing, however, when these people came in and they were interested in the performance. Then I had to show off on the sewing machine and organ and then saw that if this letter is to be finished in time I would have to write with them looking on. The people here are so friendly to us and seem so childlike and cordial that I usually don't mind their coming. Now, however, this Chinese woman is tipping about on her little feet, fussing about the stove and peeking into things in general and I have to keep an eye on her.

I must close now for the courier has to walk back to Fen Cho fu and it is nearly night.

....

Fen Cho fu, China
November 30, 1891

We moved back to the city the fifth of this month and the next week after we came, the Atwoods moved out of our rooms and into their new house across the alley. Since then we have had workmen repairing and cleaning and hope to get settled this week. We will have lots of room now, more than we really need, but as long as the rooms are here we might as well have them arranged conveniently. We are living in the side rooms until the others are ready and I have to go outdoors and across the court to the room where we cook and eat. The back court is all cleared now as the old *yaos* and walls are all torn down and carted off, so we have a fine large open court there and we hope we can get grass to grow on it. We can see lots of sky and it is a fine playground for the children and we can have tennis and croquet too. There is one nice tree and four smaller ones, which is refreshing.

Some of the better class people here seem quite anxious for us to have a school similar to the one in Taiku and promise to furnish the pupils if one can be started. Mrs. Davis and Charlie would do what they can toward teaching them and a Chinese teacher would also be hired to take them afternoons.

There is a good deal of sickness about now—diphtheria and some other diseases. I hope our children will be well this winter for we had such a siege with la grippe last winter. I feel thankful we have a doctor in the city.

We brought the old man in with us from Yu Tao Ho and he takes hold very well. He has learned to wash dishes very nicely, peels potatoes, does the marketing, runs the washing machine, tends the gate, carries water, and makes himself generally useful.

There was a goodly number in to service last Sunday. It is held now in one of the new rooms on the doctor's place. He preaches to them as he knows the language, having been in China nearly ten years. He has several opium patients but they are not a very hopeful lot. There are two who have been coming to service every Sunday this summer and claim they are converted and want to join the church. Such are kept on probation a year before they are baptized. If at the end of that time they bear a good record they are taken in the church.

Charlie and Stewart went to Taiku last week. Charlie had to go to take an examination in his Chinese. Mr. Morgan, an Englishman of the Baptist mission in Tai Yuen fu, was the examiner and after Charlie had finished reading his chapter in John's Gospel in Chinese said, "Well, it would have been better for some of us, perhaps, if we had come to China when we were past forty years of age."

....

December 30, 1891

At long last your letters reached us! One was dated way back in August, but wherever they have been made them none the less welcome.

We have had a Christmas, and Santa Claus came again and brought us some presents. Stewart enjoys a box of watercolor paints as much as anything. Mr. Thompson gave Donnie a little toy which he enjoys too. It is a man on a velocipede that runs around over the floor when we wind it. I gave Charlie a pair of slippers but as he saw them before Christmas (while we were moving), he was not very astonished, and he gave me several little presents he bought here. Mrs. Atwood invited us for dinner and what a feast we had— roast duck with all the trimmings and ending with fruits, nuts, cake, and coffee. Last evening I had them all in to take supper with us. It was partly in honor of C.W.'s birthday so I had to make a birthday cake.

We have had company for a week. About twenty miles from here are some Swedes and Norwegians who came out last spring as associate members of Hudson Taylor's mission.* We have met several of them (there were sixty-five in all, about half being women), and we like them very much. We invited four of them to spend Christmas week with us but only two came. They had their guitars and played and sang for us. We enjoyed them so much and they seemed very happy indeed. Hudson Taylor has his mission- aries live as the Chinese do and adopt many of their customs.† These friends who have visited us said, "No place but in Fen Cho fu do we get treated dis way. You shake hands wid us and your lady friends eat wid us at de same table. We tink we not lif long if we lif as de Chinese do." It is a real treat for them to come to our American homes and to be treated as brothers indeed. One of our guests, Mr. Gulbrauson, lived four and a half years in America before coming here, and Mr. Tornvall was there one and a half years. They think a great deal of America and Americans. These friends said, "We never thought to haf such a good Christmas as dis in China. We tank de Lord for dese homes where we can come once in a while." They are such earnest, pious boys that it does us much good to meet them. They are all unmarried and have made a sort of pledge not to marry for three years, so they will have a lonely time. The women are sent to one city or village and the men to another. Some are in the south and some here in Shansi. There are twelve or more over in Kiai Hsiu (ger-shu), and we hope to have them all here during our Annual Meeting, which will be the first week in February.

*J. Hudson Taylor was from England and was the legendary founder of the China Inland Mission. A Protestant, his mission was nondenominational.
†Adopting Chinese dress and customs was seen as a means of reducing the distance between Chinese and Westerners and thereby facilitating conversions.

I have had several callers lately. One was a *Tai Tai* (tĭ tĭ; a lady whose husband is some high official).* She came with her servant and I treated them as well as I knew how, but the lower class of people are usually more friendly to us than the better classes.

There are three families here in Fen Cho fu, Dr. Atwood's, Mr. and Mrs. Davis, and ourselves, with Miss Hewett living with Mrs. Davis this winter. Once a year the Taiku friends (Mr. and Mrs. Clapp, Dr. and Mrs. Goldsbury, and Miss Bird, and also Mr. Thompson, who is living in a large village about fifty li from Taiku), and our station all get together. Mr. Thompson is alone in his village and is meeting with some opposition from the people who do not want foreigners in there. He says he has had showers of brickbats come down in his court and the people now threaten to burn him out.

There are rumors of a general insurrection against the present ruler but whether it will affect us or not remains to be seen. There is a great deal of opposition to the foreigner in most places, but so far we have had no cause for fear and do not anticipate any serious trouble here in Fen Cho fu as the people are quite friendly to us.

We have been having very pleasant weather for some weeks but it is much colder today with high winds. Write, write, write and your letters will get to us after a while. I have your pictures hung where you have a good view of our sitting room.

....

February 3, 1892

Mother's letter of September 24 came by courier yesterday. Where has it been all this time? "Wo pu chih tao," which meaneth "I don't know." We were out to a Chinese dinner when the mail came and found it waiting for us when we got home.

Two weeks ago I gave a dinner in Chinese style to sixteen of our Chinese friends and this dinner was a return of the compliment. I will tell you about my dinner first. We have a poor family out a few li from the city that are interested in the doctrine. One little girl is a cripple being hunchback and having hip disease. Their home is a

Tai Tai is the Chinese word for Mrs. or lady or wife.

dreary place to us but is like most of the other homes about us, and I thought it would be pleasant to invite them to spend the day with us. Our present gatekeeper is a good Chinese cook, so I gave him full swing to get up a good dinner. He bought a good many things and was all day the day before boiling, frying, and fussing. In China, as far as our experience goes, the host and hostess do not sit down with the guests but stand around and wait on them. Charlie was not sorry for it gave him an excuse to avoid eating Chinese food. The fashion here is to not have any tablecloth on the table and to eat the dessert first, so when they sat down there were grapes, nuts, red fruit, and fancy cakes, which quickly disappeared. Then these dishes were taken away and some small saucers given to each one into which was poured a little vinegar. The dinner then came in by bowls full, two at a time, and was made up mostly of pork in different styles with other things which I did not recognize, but the bowls looked very pretty as the food was nicely arranged. Here the amount is counted by the number of bowls and we had eight, I believe, or eight different courses with bowls of rice at the last.

And how they did eat! The food disappeared like frost before a summer's sun. When the bowls were brought in, two of the friends with their chopsticks fished out to the others a portion which went into the vinegar in the saucers. Such a sloppy, mussy time! I congratulated myself more than once that there was no tablecloth to be mussed up. The chopsticks are awkward things for us to handle but they have no trouble. What can't be picked up is shoved in and sucked down, and such a smacking and swallowing noise followed that it surely sounded as though the food was good and they enjoyed it. When they went away Stewart gave the little lame girl a doll that opens and shuts her eyes and Donnie gave her a scrapbook of bright pictures.

Well, yesterday we were invited to eat at their house and they said we were not to call a cart for they had carts and would come for us and bring us back. You would have smiled if you could have seen us on the way. A big, bony ox was our "prancing steed," which poked along like going to a funeral. The cart was one of the freight carts the farmers use, a clumsy two-wheeled affair without any top such as the passenger carts have. But we enjoyed the ride rather more than the rest. I sat on the *k'ang* for four hours with my feet crossed tailor fashion. Oh, how I ached! Mrs. Davis, Miss Hewett, T'sui Tao,* and I sat on the *k'ang* even when we ate our dinner as they brought in a low table and placed it in front of us. It was not an overly clean table and it was swiped off with a rag which we would think dirty for a dustcloth. Is it any wonder if we had very little appetite?

Mr. Davis, Charlie, Stewart, Paul Atwood, and T'sui Chiao Yo ate at another table, for the men and women seldom eat together. We used chopsticks and I got along much better than ever before. Some of the things they had were boiled chestnuts, fried English walnuts, stewed pork and Chiao tzu (pronounced jow za). This dish is one very much used by the people at New Year's time and is made thus: flour and water to make a crust from which are made little balls and these are rolled out very thin and round into which chopped meat or vegetables or both are placed, then it is pinched in a shape something like a fried oyster and then boiled in clear water. Last Saturday was the first day of their new year, and they make these tiny dumplings by the hundreds at this time of the year. I managed to eat several with vinegar but I was glad when the food was all taken away.

After dinner T'sui Chiao Yo talked to the people who came in about our religion, using Matthew 4:12 as a basis for his remarks. He has been a Christian for several years and has a good knowledge of the doctrine. His name is pronounced Swā jow yo, and his wife, who ate at our table, is Swā da sow. They have two little children, the older a girl whose feet have not been bound, which is a great step for Chinese parents to take, for large feet with women here is a drawback and they lose caste and are not so marketable as a wife. Then we sang a hymn and came away, glad the day was over and hoping some good would come of it.

Charlie has visited several villages since we came in from Yu Tao Ho but now at New Year's time it is useless to go out as everyone is busy.

---

*Wife of T'sui Chiao Yo, one of the Christian converts.

....

March 7, 1892

It has been so long since we had a letter from any of you that I can imagine almost anything has happened. I wish I could see you all long enough to know if you are well, but that is part of our life out here and a part that is hard to get used to. Our mail has been somewhat uncertain this winter as the steamers leave all mail for Tientsin in Shanghai and it has to be carried overland until the winter is past when steamers come again up to that port. From Tientsin our mail comes all the way overland, with two places where it is overhauled before it reaches us so letters may easily get mislaid.

I wonder if you are made uneasy by reports of the rebellion in China? We do not know anything much ourselves, except as we get the news from American papers. Sometimes these reports seem exaggerated, but yet our sources of information are so meager that the condition of affairs may be worse than we think. Shansi is known as a quiet province and the people are peaceful compared to many other provinces. We have had no cause for alarm except from these occasional rumors and so far we do not feel unsafe or afraid. How soon the trouble may develop into something really alarming we have no way of finding out and all we can do is to go on as though nothing was the matter. I believe matters are approaching a crisis and that the present ruling power may be overthrown, but it may or may not affect the missionaries. It is only fair to add that there is a great opposition to foreigners, and missionaries particularly, in a few of the most disturbed provinces. We are not anticipating any trouble and hope the work may go on unmolested.

We have recently held our Annual Meeting, the third since we came here, and the report is encouraging. There were seventeen persons in Taiku who professed a belief in Christianity and three men are on the books as inquirers here. The new hospital buildings and consequent advantage in the medical work is going well here. Yesterday in the chapel there were about seventy-five who paid quiet attention to the preaching of the word. Dr. Edwards of the China Inland Mission, who lives in a city three days' travel northeast of here, was at Dr. Atwood's for a few days and preached for us yesterday.* The work seems to move slowly but we can only trust it will be of permanent value and will bring forth fruit. Our Annual Meeting was held with many drawbacks. La grippe attacked us right and left. The smallpox broke out on the place where Mr. and Mrs. Davis are living and for a while we feared it would spread amongst us, but as we were all vaccinated before we left America and used caution it has not been taken by any of us foreigners. Smallpox is nearly as certain here as measles is at home and nearly all Chinese have it sooner or later.

Miss Bird, who came down from Taiku to attend the Annual Meeting, has been visiting with me since then, and we have been trying to teach Wang Ta Sao (Wäng dä sou) and Teh Teh the Commandments, explaining them as best we can. Miss Bird has only been here some over a year but she is doing very well indeed, and I think between us we got the woman and little girl to understand pretty well. Wang Ta Sao is the wife of our second "boy" and Teh Teh is their little girl, twelve years old, who are living in a small court here and I like them very much. Wang Ta Sao says, "Before you came here I didn't know anything about these things." I hope she will truly come to believe in the truths of the gospel. The father says he believes the doctrine and before we came away from Yu Tao Ho he spoke in one of the meetings. The family name is Wang and comes first when speaking their name. Thus, Wang Ta Sao is "Wang elder sister." Our name is Chia (Jä), and the Tai Tai, which we foreign ladies are called, means "Lady." So instead of saying "Tai Tai Ja" or "Lady Price" they say "Ja Tai Tai" or "Price Lady." The Chinese call the head "tou" (toe), which is changing things about, isn't it?

We have a little school started now and there are seven boys from ten to sixteen years old. Our Chinese teacher takes charge of

---

*E. H. Edwards, a medical missionary assigned to the Shou Yang station, was to write a book in 1903 that incorporated portions of diaries written by Charles and Eva. *Fire and Sword in Shansi* is probably the best-known book on the missionary effort in Shansi province. The Prices did not belong to the China Inland Mission; they were affiliated with the American Board of Commissioners for Foreign Missions (ABCFM), which was affiliated, in turn, with the Congregational Church.

them afternoons and Charlie has them an hour or more in the mornings. They live, eat, and sleep here and pay 500 cash* per month each, which is about thirty-five cents, not half of what it costs to keep them, but the rest of the expense comes from the Board. We have a cook to take care of their meals, bathe and look after them. They come in to prayers every morning and attend chapel on Sundays and are taught the catechism with their other studies. It is a small beginning but we hope it will be the source of something greater.

Our place is pleasant now since we have it finally repaired. Wish you'd come visit us. I do wish you could see the children. The other morning Don said, "Would I were in Mer'i'kuk to see Granma." Donnie gets his Chinese and English mixed up pretty badly sometimes and it is very amusing.

....

Shansi, China
March 8, 1892

Dear Father,

We are pleasantly situated in good rooms with large courts for the children to play in. I wonder what you would think if I were to tell you how much I play at tennis and croquet. There are not many days that I do not play one or the other, but it seems to be more of a necessity here than at home. The doctors think a tennis court is almost as necessary as a bedroom, and it is a great help. Outside our compound there is so much dust and filth that we seldom go out except as our work calls us. Most of our work is done on the home place, so to relieve the monotony we have our games.

I suppose Eva has told you about our school. We have seven boys on the place and will have one more in a day or two. Also we have promise of enough to make eleven within a month. That seems a small school when we think of the hundreds in our American schools but it is quite as many as I care to take charge of. They

---

*Cash was the term applied to the small copper coins, of variable value, that served as the major medium of exchange in China.

are bright boys and we hope to see good results from the start we have made. I teach them in the forenoon using our own Chinese books. We now are using a catechism on God and Jesus, Creation and Redemption. They have learned the Lord's Prayer, which they repeat very well. I am also teaching them our system of numbers, which they are very much pleased with and learn very fast. All this teaching is of course in their own language, the numerals being ours called by Chinese names, as: 1 is *yi,* 2 is *erh,* and so on. During the afternoon the Chinese teacher teaches them using their own books. We also have a Chinese family on the place and Eva is teaching the woman and little girl. They are now learning the Ten Commandments. We had them come here to live chiefly because we wanted to get their bright, agile little girl where we could teach her. She is very quick to learn and for this country, very pretty. Stewart and Donnie like to play with her very much and she seems just as pleasant with them as our American children. I am glad they can have her to play with.

I don't remember whether I told you about my village work or not. I go outside the city quite often and visit the neighboring villages, distributing tracts and trying to talk to the people. I usually can get an audience of fifteen or twenty. I like such work very much, but now that the school is started I will not be able to do much else but teach the boys aside from my regular studies.

We are a little alarmed at the prospect of a famine in this province as we had very little rain last year and so far this winter no snow to amount to anything. If we do not have rain soon there will be no wheat except near the river where they can irrigate. It is said that three years without good rains brings a famine as there will be no crops, and bringing grain in from other parts of the empire is impossible for lack of transportation facilities. However, we will hope for the best and if it comes to the worst we will be obliged to leave the province for a time.

We are always thinking of you and look anxiously for your letters. We send our love to you all and pray that your blessings may be multiplied.

Ever your son,
C. W. Price

Fen Cho fu, China
April 22, 1892

I am not entirely rested yet from a week's trip but will try to send some account of our journey. You would have laughed to see our rig! A mule took the lead and then came a bony horse followed by the awkward two-wheeled *peng* cart. As the cart was covered with rough-looking mats you may imagine we presented quite a novel appearance. This cart was so much larger than the passenger carts that we had enough room to be quite comfortable. We have to carry our own bedding and enough food for two days so it is no small undertaking to leave home on such a journey. Think of being nearly two days going sixty miles! We had the pleasure of once more seeing the telegraph poles and wire which the children, as well as we older ones, enjoyed. This line was put up about two years ago, the first one to go through this part of the empire and it truly seemed a connecting link with the homeland. The telegraph and these slow-moving carts do not match very well, but it will be a good many years before the railroads come.

I dislike the inns the most of anything else about traveling here and you would not wonder if you could have a glimpse at one. You must not imagine anything like a hotel but picture to yourself a rough inn yard into which we ride to find donkeys, mules, carts, dogs, and people. People always crowd in to see the "foreign devils." We have always been fortunate in being able to get a vacant room so we have never had to sleep in the same room with the Chinese. The last time Mr. Thompson went on this trip he had to sleep on a *k'ang* with eight Chinamen and they smoked opium and tobacco, which must have made the room awful—not to mention the lice. The door has a ragged curtain hung before it and the one window is covered with paper, which the Chinese sometimes stick their fingers through in order to see what is going on inside. The floor is brick, the walls are very dingy and black with dirt, and the furniture is the brick *k'ang* and an old rickety table and a chair to match. All this and nothing more but a greasy old Chinese lamp which is like our old-fashioned "dips" and makes about as much light as a lightning bug.

We carry a candle, wash dish, soap, towels, and tea as well as other bedding and food. The bedding has to be carried in from the cart and the beds made up on the *k'ang,* then we stand around and eat our cold victuals. It is so horrid because everything is so dirty and there is generally a big manure pile just outside the door into which everything nasty and bad smelling is thrown. When the animals are not out of hearing we can hear their munching, braying, and stamping all night. We get up as soon as we can in the morning, wash, pack the bedding, eat a cold breakfast, and start out as soon as the carter will go. We jolt along slowly until lunchtime when we stop at another dirty inn where the carter feeds his team and we eat and rest about an hour, then jog on again. We got to Taiku the evening of the second day and were very glad to see our friends and have a bath and good supper, as well as a comfortable bed.

The next morning, after breakfast, we started on for Tientsin, where Mr. Thompson lives. We were about six hours on the road. He keeps "bachelor hall" and his cook does not know much about cooking but I helped some and we had a pleasant time. He is living on a fine large place with trees and many flowering shrubs. We went back to Taiku on Saturday and spent Sunday with Mr. and Mrs. Clapp who have charge of the boys' school there. It was a pleasure to see them gathered for Sunday service and Sunday school. Mr. Liu explained the lesson to the men. He is a gift from God truly and seems to be in sincere earnest.

We had to sleep at another wretched inn on the way home and some of the days on the road were terribly windy and as we had had no rain for nearly a year you can imagine how dusty it was! We have hardly got clean now and this is Friday. So when I write that the rain has been falling for three hours this afternoon you will know how glad we are to have the dust laid and the air clean again. We have celebrated the day and the rain by setting out seven evergreen trees. They are small but if they grow it will make a famous green spot for our eyes winter and summer. Stewart stood watching the rain and the new trees and said, "Oh Mamma! See the rainbuds on the trees." Five of them are the flat-leafed kind like arborvitae, and the other two are pine trees. We planted the two pine and one of the other kind in the back court not far from our bedroom window and planted the four little trees in the dirt circles left in the brick pavement. I am having a raised flower bed made in the middle of this court with a very large crock in the middle that will hold about a barrel of water for sprinkling the court and the flowers.

I am glad you liked the dishes and things we sent for Christmas as it gave us as much pleasure to send them as for you to receive them. We wanted our faraway loved ones to know we do not forget them. Our expenses are less in some ways here than at home for there is no place to go—no lectures, no concerts, and I haven't bought a new hat since we came and Charlie wears some Chinese clothes, partly because we do not want to appear extravagant to the people.

Your kind presents of the *Youth's Companion* and *Household* are coming now and I appreciate your thoughtfulness very, very much.

I am at a loss sometimes to know just what I ought to do about the children. If we have the Chinese around us in our homes there is danger of the children catching diseases as well as learning things we don't want them to. Don got "lousy" a while ago but that can be gotten rid of quicker than other things. Just now he has a bad sore on his face similar to the sores so many Chinese children have and it worries me for fear it will spread and spread. With the school on this place it is about impossible to keep the children away from them as our children have always been a great attraction to the Chinese. We do not like to shut ourselves away from the people with only the men preaching and going out to villages. Yet all the while I feel it is a great risk to have the children even so much as touched by the strangers that come about us. I am tempted sometimes to take the children home and leave Charlie here to do what he can, but then other people have lived on the mission field and had families too.

Teh Teh, the little Chinese girl, has done so well in learning to read and is keeping up with the boys. The Chinese teacher teaches her the Chinese classics just as he does the boys and he says she is very bright. It is so unusual for women and girls to be able to read that we have been glad to give her and her mother this chance. But it was from the little girl that Don got his lice and maybe his sores too, so it is hard to know what to do. I get almost frantic sometimes, but then again I feel thankful we are here and are doing what otherwise would never have been done.

Cold weather has hung on unusually late this spring and we have had so much high wind and the earth is so dry that the dust was a quarter of an inch thick all over everything when we got home from our trip. I have become discouraged over keeping the house clean. This rain will help to lay the dust but it will take a lot more to ensure the crops. If the crop fails this year, as it almost did last year, there will be much trouble and suffering for the poor people. Seventeen years ago there was a terrible famine here and the people died by the thousands. They even ate one another! I trust they will be spared another such calamity.

The "boy" has "chimed" me to dinner so I must close. Don't imagine I am blue because I have grumbled in this letter, for I am not. I only think I don't amount to enough to pay for the Board keeping me here and wish we could have come out fifteen years sooner when we were both younger and could have studied better.

....

May 16, 1892

Dear Sister Eltha, John, and Babies,

We were pleased when the last courier came in to find a letter from you. I am glad you got your Christmas present all right and glad you had a place for it. Think of Eva and Charlie when you sleep on your new bed! Dream too of us.

C.W. has a backache and is generally debilitated today so is not up but I think it is not anything serious. Don had a very bad sore on his face which gave me much uneasiness for a time, but it is healed now and he looks like my sweet-faced baby again. I got discouraged for a time over it and wished I was in America, but now it is well again I do not feel so blue.

We have done considerable in the way of improvement this spring and I wish you could see our place here. If you were to wall in about two acres of land with a brick wall fifteen or twenty feet high you would have a place about as large as our compound, and that is divided into about eight courts by other walls. Originally this place had ever so many courts and higher walls but we have torn some down. The houses or rooms are built of the same gray brick that the courts are paved with, which makes it seem like being walled in top and bottom. If there was a roof over the whole compound it would finish the job for certain. However, the largest court is not paved and we have tennis and croquet back there and the well is in one corner. There are six trees in this court including the new evergreens we have just set out. Mrs. Davis's little baby is buried back here and I had a little brick wall built around the grave. There is a pretty little tree in the enclosure. A picturesque old gateway with a bench in it makes a good place to sit and watch the games. Some of the morning glory seeds are up and I hope to train them over this gateway. In the house court I had a large raised flower bed made with bricks and filled with dirt with a big water gong sunk in the middle which holds about three barrels of water. Some of the nasturtiums, zinnias, lady's slippers, and morning glories have come up, but I am afraid the rest of the flower seeds are too old. I have pots of roses, oleander, geranium, day lilies, and some mosslike stuff and it is very pretty. The doves and sparrows, bees and wasps come to my "lake" to drink.

We lately heard that a rebellion was breaking out in Shensi, the province west of us, and that 500 li of telegraph poles were destroyed. So far we have not been molested.

Thank you for your good long letter. Kiss the babies for Aunt Eva.

....

May 27, 1892

Dear Loved Ones,

You can still remember when God called for little Harris and how he brought a great blessing to your souls through the affliction. And now when I am called to write to you that He wanted our little Donnie too and we gave him back to Him with joy even, you must not grieve for us nor think of us as stricken and suffering but as looking up into the Heavenly Father's face with trust, peace, and gladness that He has enabled us to so willingly give back this precious, precious little one we had for three and a half years. His sickness was only for a week and he did not appear to suffer greatly. He was so patient and gentle all the time and was conscious to the last minute and went away so quietly that it comforted us greatly. It is all right. Don't think either that it was because we are in China that caused his sickness. Are not the sick, the suffering, the stricken, and sorrowing all about you in the homeland? No! It was God's time and He called him home. We gave him every care and attention in our power and Dr. Atwood was very kind, as well as all the other friends. We were not alone. Our dear English sisters came over from Hsiao-I and comforted us so much by their presence and helpful words. Mr. and Mrs. Davis and Miss Hewett as well as Dr. and Mrs. Atwood were all so kind and helpful. We had a very pretty little coffin which the Chinese carpenters made with great care and everything was as nice as we would have wanted in the homeland. The blow was made just as light and easy for us as the kind Father could make it and He has enabled us to rejoice even in the midst of this our first real sorrow.

Everyone who knew Donnie loved him. He was so winning, so kind and beautiful in his little life. The Chinese thought so much of him and about thirty of them came in to the service. It may be this "little child will lead them" to the heavenly land, and that we can do more for China by giving this precious baby back to the Savior than in any other way. Our servants all loved him and when they see that our religion does give us a hope that they have never had, it may be one of God's ways of drawing them to Himself. The little body is placed near the baby of Mrs. Davis on this place. It is a beautiful little spot under a pretty tree and is safe and quiet. Oh, how safe, how happy our little one is; how free from all sin, all suffering and sorrow. God is greatly helping us to bear this affliction he had to send to us for His own wise purpose, and we feel that our heavenly mansion is nearer and more real than ever before.

It is such a comfort that you saw our little one and will meet him again on the other shore. Oh, we must all hold fast this hope and faith in Christ's love and mercy. Give our love to all the dear brothers and sisters and tell them of our peace and hope. We have been the first of all your children to pass through these deep waters but God is blessing us. Pray for us that we may get all out of this lesson what the Father had in mind when He sent it.

Donnie was taken sick Monday night and the next week, Tuesday night, he "was not, for God took him"—the night of the twenty-fourth of this month. His fourth birthday would have been the second of this coming December. What a precious beautiful little angel he is for the heavenly home!

May God bless and comfort you all and bring us all nearer together by this another anchor within the vail. With much love for you all everyone.

Your affectionate daughter and sister,
Eva

....

Shansi Mission of the American Board
P.O. Address: Tientsin, China
Shansi, China
May 31, 1892

Dear Father and Mother,

Eva has written you of the sorrow that has come to us and I will only add a word. You must not think of us as being overwhelmed by the sorrow, for we have been able to find many things which cause us to rejoice in the midst of our trouble. We think of the goodness of God in that when he takes from us that which we love, he softens the blow by the peace which he sends into the heart. Death is not the terrible thing it was to me even two weeks ago. We can realize what it is to have a hope of eternal life and can rest in that hope more than ever before. Our Donnie boy was the joy of our life, but he will still be our great joy in the pleasant memories which we have of him. It has already become a pleasure to me to see all his looks, his smiling face as he would come stepping into my study to ask me to do some little thing for him. Isn't it a great blessing that we can have these pleasant things to think about?

When I first saw that he must leave us I thought at once of Eva. He was so much to her in our lonely life here. How could she bear the separation. How thankful I am, and I know it will comfort your hearts when I write that she has been able to rest in the love of our Heavenly Father. Our boy has not lived in vain. If you could have seen how very sorry our servants and the boys in the school were to see him go you would feel sure as we do that their hearts have been touched. There were about thirty of the Chinese at the funeral service and I am sure they must have been impressed. God can make his short life and his leaving this world glorify His name.

In our sorrow we praise God for the sympathy of friends. I wish you could see some of the helpful letters we received. Let us praise God that we have another light guiding us to our Father's home.

Our best love to you all,
C. W. Price

PART THREE
The Interim
JULY 1892–FEBRUARY 1897

Dear Mother, Father, and All,

I have thought of you all very often lately. We are all quite well
now and I feel much stronger. We miss our dear Donnie boy
constantly, but God has strengthened us wonderfully and given us
grace and a strong faith that looks away from this life to the one
beyond where we will be together again forever.

We are quiet enough here now. There are reports enough
flying about to stir us up but there have been several good rains
lately, which will quiet people a good deal. It seems so strange to
us that they will plant so much of their ground to opium whether
they expect a famine or not, and then afterward risk sowing millet
or buckwheat. Dr. Atwood says that when their bodies are so
saturated with opium they cannot digest much food. It makes them
lie and steal, but use it they will. There are two women in the
hospital now who cannot walk and seem to suffer a great deal. The
older of the two is only thirty-six years old and they are quite
attractive. It seems hard to see them in such a condition and to know
they have no hope beyond this world. The shut-ins at home have
much that is very hard to bear, but think of the poor shut-ins here
in China that cannot read and know so very little of the world
around them and no knowledge of God or hope for a future life.
When they spoke of Donnie yesterday I could tell them something
of our hope and that if they believed Jesus and trusted him they
would go to heaven where they can walk and never have any more
pain. Until they came here they probably never heard of God or
His plan for them.

One of the women who took dinner with us last winter and lives out of town about three miles is here to call on me. She has been sick a good deal lately and her daughter died some time ago. She gave us a pomegranate tree because she was too poor to buy water for it. It is in a big crock and sets out in the court and is nearly one hundred years old, but they grow so slowly it is not more than ten feet high. It has double crimson blossoms on it larger than a double lady's slipper. She had two other trees, which she gave to Mrs. Atwood and Mrs. Davis. She did not ask anything for them but as she is so poor and sick and is trying to be a Christian we did not want them for nothing so we each gave her 1,000 cash. Today she said, "I thanked God for what you gave me."

We had a call the other evening from a Mr. Lutley, an Englishman who is preaching in the south of this province. He had a native evangelist with him who had been a Christian for ten years. Pastor Hsi (shē) seems to be a devoted·man and is doing a great deal of good. He has been persecuted on account of his belief in Christianity—has been beaten twice but he is earnest and his faith is very strong. Mr. Lutley said all the Chinese like Pastor Hsi and have confidence in him. The work is more than twenty years old there in the south of this province and they are now beginning to reap what others have sown. It only proves that we cannot say what good will come of work faithfully done.

Dear Grandpa and Grandma.
It is Sunday, and has been raining. I hope you are all well We miss our dear Donnie but he is happy.
With much love to you.
Stewart L. Price.

....

July 26, 1892

I will be glad when I know you have received our letters about Donnie. It seems so far and so long when we are waiting for such letters. All these weeks Donnie has been in Heaven and we have been very lonely without him. We went out to Yü Tao Ho last week and we missed him out there even more than here, for we could not step outside but it reminded us of the pleasant days we spent last summer when we were all together. I will be glad when the time comes for us all to be together never to part again. If we are only God's children it will not be any calamity when we are called away.

What do these poor people do without this hope of a better hereafter? They are so perfectly heathen in many ways that one is led to wonder if they can appreciate the difference there is between our lives. For instance, the Chinese look on their children as being worth so much to them from a money point of view. Daughters are not welcome or loved because they will cost them a great deal and will not bring in very much. Sons are worth more because it is the son's duty to take care of his parents when they grow old. When their sons die, especially while they are young, they have lost all their value and are worth nothing at all to the parents, so in very many cases they throw the bodies outside the wall or any place convenient where dogs and wolves will save them the expense of a coffin and funeral. Not long ago a man with his wife and little baby came to Dr. Atwood to get his wife's eyes treated. While they were here the baby was very sick and on their way home it died. They threw the body outside the cart and went on, not caring what became of it. How can such parents appreciate the pleasure and blessing of the Christian's hope that some day we will meet our little ones again?

In another case the eight-year-old son of one of our workmen met with an accident while playing about a pile of heavy boards and his foot was so badly crushed that Dr. Atwood thinks he will have to amputate it. At the time of the accident the father was so angry because the boy was hurt and would be a bother and expense that he sent out for a coffin intending to bury the child alive rather than be troubled with it. The grandmother rescued him and others have taken charge of him.

We have a caller now, a Swedish brother who came in afoot yesterday on his way to the extreme south of the province. He has come from beyond the Great Wall in Mongolia, over 1,200 li from here. He has been in China a year and a half and perhaps in all that time has not sat at a table with tablecloth and other foreign ways. He lives with the Chinese, eats Chinese food using chopsticks, and seems a very devoted consecrated man. He thinks many of the late inventions are from the devil and that higher education is assuredly from his satanic majesty. He seems to enjoy his stay with us though I presume he thinks we are very wicked to live as comfortably as we do. He does not believe in medicine, even objected to some Vaseline we offered him for a sore foot. When a fly fell in his cup of tea I insisted on throwing it away. "No, indeed," said he. "I would think it was very wicked to waste the blessings the Lord gives me." So I let him drink it.

We meet with many earnest Christians going up and down this province, living as the Chinese do, and denying themselves the comforts of a Christian land. Some of them think it is wrong to take a home paper or magazine. We have come out here, they say, to preach the gospel and ought to give up all for Christ's sake, and should cut loose from everything concerning politics and the world, but I believe perhaps God wants us to use our Christian home as a means of blessing to the people. This is not our abiding place and it does not really seem right to think too much of these earthly blessings for Heaven has something much better in store for us. Where our treasure is, our hearts will be.

I have been trying my camera some lately and will send you two pictures although they are not a perfect success. If you want to send me a little present some time I would appreciate a dozen or so sensitized plates four inches by five inches and some sensitized paper of the same size. If you do buy some you must be sure and not open the packages to look at the plates and paper for if a bit of white light gets at them they are spoiled.

Charlie opens his school again this week after a month's vacation. He is reading to Stewart now out of *Youth's Companion.*

September 7, 1892

We are still waiting for the courier to come in but we have had such heavy rains that the plain is flooded in many places and the roads are almost impassable. Our couriers say they have to wade water armpit deep part of the way between here and Paoting fu. Before the rains set in there had been such a drought that we did not suppose we could ever wish it would stop raining. You ought to see my pretty flower garden. I am going to try my camera on it this afternoon and if I get a good picture I will send it to you.

Charlie is in the schoolroom with his dirty little urchins and they make quite a racket. Stewart has just finished reciting his lessons to me and is writing on the slate. It is a pretty lonely life for him out here. The other day I heard him say, "If I had Aladdin's lamp I'd rub it and Uncle Frank would come back, or if I was dissatisfied with my position I would rub it and I would be back in America. Then I would rub it and would have a wife and child." At the table he said, "When I get back to America my first employment will be to get a glass of lemonade and a banana."

A special messenger has just come in from Taiku and brought word that Dr. Goldsbury is sick and wants Dr. Atwood to come at once. I hope it will not prove to be a serious illness for it takes nearly four days for word to come from Taiku and for a return, so if the illness is very serious it is almost useless to send so far for a doctor.

Two new families are on the way to join us this fall and will probably get to Taiku next month. Mr. and Mrs. Atwater with two little ones, and Mr. and Mrs. Williams who came last year but have been staying at the coast for several months.

I am going over to Hsiao-I (Shou-e) day after tomorrow to stay over Sunday with my English friends. These English sisters are doing good work there and they expect to have a baptismal service on Saturday for twenty or thirty Chinese. They came here to Fen Cho fu a few weeks ago and spent several days and went on out to Yu Tao Ho and spent a week with Mrs. Davis. We love these sisters very much and they were a great help to me spiritually after Donnie went away. They have been in China eight years and have such strong faith and are so zealous and helpful. Dr. Atwood and Charles bought a sedan chair in partnership this spring so now when I go, I go in style for it takes four men to carry me!

I invited a Chinese Christian woman with her three children to come and stay in our court a while and they have just gone home after being here nearly three weeks. She said when she went away, "You have wasted your heart and spent your money," but she thanked me very gratefully and seemed happy.

Mr. Tornvall, a Swedish brother who spent last Christmas with us, came yesterday and is quite sick today with high fever.

....

October 11, 1892

The next mail will surely bring letters in answer to the ones we wrote about Donnie. It takes so long and all these months since May we have been receiving letters with messages and kisses for the dear little one who went away from our home and left us so lonely. I long to touch him again, but I pray every day that the good Father will keep me patient and faithful. God is giving us another little baby that will come to us next spring and it will surely be a comfort. No one can ever fill Donnie's place, but my arms will not ache so with emptiness when the new baby comes.

Mrs. Davis and I walked out to a village about five li from the city yesterday afternoon and sat on the *k'ang* about two hours, and as a result last evening I felt something crawling on me and when I undressed I found it to be a louse! This is one of the trials of missionaries' lives and we have to expect to get them every time we go into a Chinese home.

Mr. Tornvall was just able to leave this morning after being here sick for five weeks. Another boy left this morning also after a three-week stay. Besides these we had two Swedish sisters visit us for a week who were from the China Inland Mission. About six months ago a party of ten young women came to a place about thirty-five miles from here. Most of them were Swedes who had lived some years in America. One girl from Des Moines was a

Captain in the Salvation Army and another was an Army Captain from Chicago. I met nine of these sisters when I was over to Hsiao-I a few weeks ago and found they had a very warm corner in their hearts for America and Americans and I invited them to visit "Little America" as they all call our Fen Cho fu and Taiku stations. The two who visited here seemed to have a fine time and we enjoyed their stay.

Miss Hewett is on her way to the coast in company with an English family, and Mr. Thompson, our bachelor, is to follow and they will be married after living in Tientsin three weeks. He is a British subject as his home is in Newfoundland, and the law is that one has to live three weeks in the place where his Consul resides before he can get license to marry. So you see how much trouble our young folks have before they can get spliced. All this long weary way to the coast and back just to have the sanction of the Consul when there are four ordained ministers right here!

Stewart is in the schoolroom now where the Chinese boys are reciting their lessons to Charlie. We are going to have him read Chinese with the teacher this winter if nothing happens. He is looking forward now to Christmas. One day when I found more buttons gone off his pants he said, "Yes, they just fly off like a gun does when you pull the trigger. If I just had 'spenders.'" The boxes will be here in a few weeks and I expect he will have "spenders" before long. Donnie's Christmas presents will have to make some little Chinese child happy.

....

December 2, 1892

Today is the birthday of our Donnie boy. He would have been four years old. I have been thinking of him so much today as I do every day. I was thinking how he used to mix his English and Chinese. If he wanted the hammer he would call to the old man, "Lao Han, Lao Han! Na ko hammer tsai na er?" "Hammer" is the only English word in it. Oh, how still and mysterious it seems when I try to think of what and where he is now. He is just "beyond" but we cannot see or know.

I invited the friends here for dinner Thanksgiving day and I did miss my baby so much.

You may be interested to know what good things we had for dinner. Not a *very* elaborate "Bill of Fare" but a great plenty:

> *Soup (mutton with macaroni)*
> *Roast goose (wild) with small fried sausages*
>
> | *Mashed potatoes* | *Squash* | *Chow Chow* |
> |---|---|---|
> | *Pickled peaches* | *Red fruit* | *Mince pie* |
> | *Pumpkin pie* | *White cake* | *Grapes* |
> | *Coffee* | *Nuts* | |

The red fruit makes a sauce very similar to cranberries in taste and color. The goose was *awful* tough but, as it couldn't be helped at that late hour, I didn't make a single apology. We had had a wild goose a short time before that cooked in two hours and was as tender as could be, but *this* one must have been a voter as *four* hours left it tough. We had a nice day, the weather was cold and clear and my dinner was pronounced very good. After dinner we had the Communion service, which Charlie led and talked very helpfully. A few of the fall boxes came in that night but only one for us and that had a few canned goods and was not very important. But Mrs. Atwood's baby carriage came, which had been about given up for lost as it had been on the way somewhere since March. The boxes are nailed, screwed, and wired up as though they were never to be opened and it takes lots of patience to wait so long when one is so anxious.

The other day at the table Stewart said something about what he would do when he had a wife. I said I hoped he would be good to her whatever happened. "Yes," he said, "I'll be better than Papa!" I asked him how he would improve on Papa. "Well, I'll say 'Elizabeth, do you want to take a nice walk?' If she would rather go in a cart or on a donkey I will not argue a word with her." So you see he is prepared to let Elizabeth have her own sweet way.

I must tell you a joke on us. The cook said some months ago that the butter was almost gone, that the box would soon be empty.

I thought it strange that we had used it up so fast but we had had a good deal of company and a good many waffles and cakes, and C.W. would eat butter on his cookies and fried cakes, so I thought it might be so. C.W. went to the box to look and he said there was lots of butter yet so I felt quite relieved. In a few weeks, however, the cook came in with two cans of butter and said that was all. So I went out and pawed around in the sawdust in the box and I couldn't find any more. So I sputtered to Charlie, "The idea of wasting butter eating it on cookies and now we will have to go without for two or three months! And you said there was lots in the box!" Well, he felt pretty cheap and took the remarks very meekly and I guess he wished he had not wasted so much butter. We went without butter two months and longed for the boxes to come. About two weeks ago C.W. was straightening things around and he came in the sitting room with his hands behind him and said, "Got a find—guess what it is?" But I couldn't guess and he showed me a can of butter and said, "There are twelve cans out there!" Then I felt cheap and couldn't see how I missed them. He said there was a layer of boards in the middle of the box and he lifted them out and there was another layer! Now three more of our boxes have come and the new butter was in one so we've got lots for sure! The boxes do come straggling in so aggravatingly lately and it is always the box we want worst that comes poking in last. Christmas is nearly here and Stewart begins to think maybe Santa Claus won't get here. Some of the things are for Donnie and oh, if he only could be here to help make us happy.

Dr. Atwood's horse was stolen but he recovered it two weeks later. We discharged the old gatekeeper and have another now and it remains to be seen what he will do. There are quite a number of Chinese living on our place—three servants, sixteen schoolboys, their teacher and cook in one court, and Wang Ta Sao and Teh Teh are living in a rented room now not far from here. They both come in every morning for Chinese prayers besides Teh Teh coming every day to recite.

An old woman who lives across the street from us is paying for her grandson who is in the school, a boy of about eleven years old, and I have lately been giving her sewing to do, which

Fen Chofu, China. Dec. 6. '92

Dear Grandpa and Grandma,

We are all very well
only, I have a cough.
We are looking forward to the
boxes coming. Every morning
I come to mamma's bed and
she says "I wonder if
the boxes will come to day".
I say I don't know but maybe
so. I will be very much
disappointed if they do not
come before Christmas.

From your loving
Grandson Stewart L. Price

118

helps her as well as myself. The boy's mother is blind. It costs the grandmother 500 cash a month, or about thirty-five cents, which is a good deal for her to make. The wages for a woman are 100 cash a day so it takes five days sewing to pay for a month's schooling. We give the boy his food as the 500 cash does not nearly pay for his schooling. Another boy is working for his board by setting the table and wiping the dishes three times a day. We don't need him at all as the cook could do this but it helps the boy and his widowed mother.

....

January 16, 1893

We are having the coldest weather we have known in China. I don't believe the thermometer has ever registered below zero until this past week when it fell twelve or fifteen degrees below. It seems like Iowa for certain! The snow came first, an inch or more, then the wind came down from the mountains north of us and blew and blew growing colder and colder, and now our windows are pretty well covered with frost and we have hard work to keep warm. Our sitting room stove too is of little account as the lining has all but given out and we will be obliged to buy a new one before another winter. This is a secondhand one we bought after we got here. To buy a stove in America and pay the freight here makes a pretty expensive stove.

Stewart is studying now after his Christmas vacation and has a new geography and writing book. Charlie is busy every day in the school and has Chinese prayer meetings Wednesday nights and Chinese services Sunday mornings, and a "sing" with the boys in the evening. You wouldn't think there was much music in their singing but they enjoy it. Four persons applied for baptism last Sunday and four more were taken on probation. In Taiku they baptized twelve a week ago. The work grows very slowly and it requires patience and perseverance.

Mrs. Russell and Miss Whitchurch have been here the past week and we have had a good helpful time. They are such spiritual women that it is a privilege to be with them. They said when they left this morning that it had been a real rest to them to be here.

Mrs. Davis has a nice boy baby two weeks old and they are getting along nicely. Their other little boy only lived four days.

We had a merry Christmas and are in the "New Year" now and hoping it will prove to be a happy one to you all.

....

April 25, 1893

My little daughter is some over five weeks old and has cried so much I have not had time or strength for letter writing. Charlie and I were alone when she was born as Dr. Atwood was in Taiku and when I come home I will tell you all about it—how near she came to strangling because the cord was around her neck and Charlie didn't know it and how I had to boss things until Mrs. Atwood could get here. Charlie twisted his hands some of the time 'cause he didn't know what to do, but when we once got started he was good as gold and took good care of me. Stewart is delighted with his sister and in fact we all are. However, I have been so nervous and worried as she has had a very bad cold for the past two weeks and I had to sit up with her a good deal in the nights for she couldn't breathe lying down. I greased her nose and her feet but it didn't seem to do one bit of good and I have had to tend her so much nights that I am quite tired, but I think we will pull through.

It makes me very happy that Florence looks so much like Donnie did when he was little. I have missed him so much! The other day when Stewart came in from outdoors he walked across the floor with quick, short steps and it sounded like Donnie. Dear, precious little boy! I hope in some way he can know about our dear little baby sister. I told Stewart perhaps God let Donnie pick out the little spirit that was to be in her body. Just about a year ago we went to Taiku and had such a time in the dust. I often think that was the beginning of Donnie's sickness. The dust storms are awful here and the dust is said to be full of disease. Last Sunday was about the worst day I have known in China. Oh, how the wind did make the dust fly and everything was covered in a short time as our houses are not tight by any means, and it nearly drove me wild. Pity us poor dirty, dusty heathen!

Charlie is busy with his schoolboys again. There are twenty-five this term and he has applied for an appropriation from the Board to build more suitable rooms for the school, but it will be some time before we can hear from it. If we had $500 we could get things in much better shape.

Our Annual Meeting was held in Taiku last week but we did not go. Dr. Atwood's family came back on Saturday and reported a good meeting. They held a memorial service for Dr. Goldsbury who died about a month ago. He was a fine man and was down here just a few weeks before he died. His wife and little Ned intended to leave Taiku yesterday for the coast on their way home. It is a sad time for her and she is expecting another baby. Dr. Goldsbury had typhus fever and was unconscious most of the time, could not even recognize Mrs. Goldsbury, which made it very hard for her. It was just such a short time ago that he was with us asking about Donnie and we had a good talk. Now he is there too, happy and safe forever.

Stewart recites his lessons to me again every day. Miss Bird wrote of him after he was in Taiku with Charlie not long ago, "Stewart has grown since I last saw him and how he has progressed in his reading! You would not find many boys eight years old who could read as well. He is getting along splendidly." Of course this made me feel proud. I sent for some young folk's histories and they came in the last boxes, so we will read them together this summer.

Thank you for that picture of us when we were children. How I laughed when I saw those funny looking little creatures.

....

May 23, 1893

Mother's little thin letters come in quite regularly and I find myself wishing they were three times as long, but perhaps she stays at home as closely as I do so has not much to write about. Florence and I have been over to Mrs. Davis's twice, which is the extent of our visiting. We went in the sedan chair with four men to carry us and we made them puff too. The Chinese men are not strong though, and two American men could lift more than any four of these. I think it is too bad, when I have such a fine baby girl that "all e tokes" can't see her. It would do your hearts good to cuddle her. If she lives to come home with us when our time is up she will be a big girl five years old. She looks and acts very much as Donnie did at her age. It is a whole year tomorrow since he went away. It is nearing four years since we started for China. I hope we have done some little good since we came here.

There is considerable typhus fever around us but so far we have kept well, schoolboys and all. It is some risk having so many Chinese as near us as they have to be now. The recitation room is not ten feet away from our sitting room and it is occupied every forenoon. It is hard to keep Stewart away from the boys as they have to come into this court and he is so lonely that he gets with them by some plan whenever he can.

My flower seeds are up—pansies, portulacas, zinnias, and others. Last year's pansy roots are in bloom now and the Chinese admire them very much as they have no pansies. We buy monthly roses and I have eight pots of them, four crimson and four pink, and they are double and very pretty. My one crimson geranium is in bloom now and I have five pots of day lilies that will bloom before long along with one pot of crimson and white sweet Williams that the Chinese admire. The pink oleander will soon bloom too, so you see I have some beauty even if I am surrounded by bricks.

The mail goes out tomorrow. You can drop your letters in a letter box and they go through by fast mail, but ours have to poke along 500 miles on the back of a slow mule.

....

August 1, 1893

The last mail brought a welcome letter from Mother. Don't be alarmed about our being driven out of here. We hardly think we will be troubled at all. The Secretary of our Board wrote for us to be prepared but he did not anticipate any real trouble from the

Restriction Act, or Exclusion Act,* for he thought it would become a dead letter very soon. News travels very slowly here in China and the people right around us have never heard of the Exclusion Act and probably never will. At any rate we will not borrow trouble.

Everything is moving on slowly as ever. Just now Charlie is busy overseeing the workmen who are building the new rooms for the schoolboys to replace the old *yaos.* They will be of brick with a door and glass window in each room. The Board granted $900 to buy the land and build the rooms.

Just now we have three guests: Miss Bird of our mission who lives in Taiku, and two of the Swedish sisters. We have had a lot of company this spring and summer and they all seem to enjoy themselves when they come here. I am not able to do much outside work, but I give the others a chance to come here and rest and have a change. Stewart enjoys having company as well as any of us.

I exposed a plate in my camera last week and am going to send it to the coast to be printed and mounted and will send you a picture as soon as they are finished. Mr. Thompson kindly developed for me and wrote, "A very pretty picture of the baby," for which I am very thankful. I can hardly wait to see them. I do wish you could see my dear little baby girl. She is so sweet and good.

My old cook "kicked" in the hottest weather so I did the cooking for a week until I could get another "boy." This "boy" is good-natured, though dirty.

....

August 15, 1893

This has been a very trying summer here on account of the great heat, by far the hottest summer we have had. We have kept well nevertheless, and feel thankful. I dreaded the month of May

*During the 1860s and 1870s California vigorously, at times almost hysterically, opposed the immigration of Chinese laborers into the state, and finally persuaded Congress to pass the Chinese Exclusion Act of 1882. Although Eva is referring to this Act, in the strict sense she means the Geary Act (May 5, 1892) that extended the original anti-Chinese legislation. This Act outraged the Chinese government and American Chinese communities, which took the fight against the legislation to the Supreme Court, which upheld the law in 1893.

somehow, for it brought back precious Donnie's sickness to our minds. I miss him so much and so often wish he could be with us long enough to love us a little at least and see his little baby sister. We cannot tell how such things are in the other world but I like to think he knows all about us and the baby the kind Father sent to comfort our hearts.

The courier came in on Sunday morning before we were stirring and I chanced to find it out and got the mail all sorted before anyone else knew it. We do not want our couriers to travel on Sunday at all but this man evidently could not make it in Saturday night. China is without any Sabbath and it takes a long time for the people to learn that we have a Sunday and do not transact business on that day. It isn't to be wondered at though for it is an entirely new idea to them and they evidently think it goes along with a lot of other queer things the foreigners do. It is depressing to realize that on Sunday all over the empire they are buying and selling just the same as on any other day. But even in the Christian lands many people forget or ignore the command, "Remember the Sabbath day to keep it holy."

This, however, is only one difference we feel between Christian surroundings and heathendom. It even becomes apparent by means of filth, for it is no mistake that "cleanliness is next to Godliness." Nor is it a small thing where the Lord promised Israel, "Then will I sprinkle clean water upon you, and ye shall be clean; from all your filthiness, and from all your idols will I cleanse you." It will be a blessed time for China, this vast cesspool morally and literally, when she is taken from among the heathen and cleansed. If it were not for the hope that inspires missionaries that in some way they will be the instruments used to help purify this vast dreary waste, I am sure every one of them would board the first steamer that could carry them away to more congenial surroundings. I feel discouraged sometimes because I do so little for the people.

There's a lot of tobacco used in China and it is quite the exception to find a man or woman who does not use it; they all smoke it. I have seen no tobacco chewing since we came here, and not one third the spitting we have seen in some churches at home. The Chinese, nearly all, drink wine too, and yet we have never seen a drunken man since we have been here. I judge those who drink enough to stagger would stay indoors somewhere and not be seen on the street. I think, however, that the staggering drunkards are very, very scarce. But the gamblers, opium users, thieves, liars, and mean men and women are on every street, one is almost tempted to think in every house. Because they don't get crazy drunk or chew tobacco is no sign that they don't do everything else that is low and mean. But their meanness seems to run to something that will not be so conspicuous as reeling along a street or spitting tobacco juice on one's parlor carpet and church floor. Difference in tastes!

The schoolboys have all gone excepting one, a nice little fellow about fifteen years old named Ch'iao Ko Ling. He takes care of the baby some, that is wheels her in the court, and she acts as though she likes him and he does her. I had him bring her to me the other day and he seemed very proud because he could take her in his arms. I don't as a rule let the Chinese hold her for they are dirty and usually lousy. Her Chinese name is Chia Nai Hua, or turned around it would be Love Blossom Price. One of the Chinese servants named her, for said he, "I know you all love her and she came in the spring so call her either Love Blossom or Spring Blossom." Stewart thinks a good deal of his sister. He is quite a big tall boy now, almost nine years old, and will soon have to be sent home to school. That will be the hardest part of living here. So long as we are well and all together our home here is not so different from homes in Christian lands except when we want to see somebody and would like to go to a regular church, or long for a sight of the "cars" and to see things rush. Then we realize that we are in slow old China. I miss the woods and open yards the most and if we could live here without the walls I could feel less that I am in a strange land. I will never get used to being walled in. It is like being in a prison. But dear me, we couldn't live here without the walls so what is the use of growling. Thieves are too many and the people, generally, too avaricious, and too many famished dogs and beggars to admit of tearing down our walls. There were two thieves beheaded in this city a few weeks ago.

There is a beggar at the big door now making his peculiar noise and if we can't stand it we give them some bread or cash, which will send them off. There are so many beggars in China and some of them get comfortably well off, for nearly everybody who has cash will throw it at them rather than hear the fuss.

Just now there are over fifty workmen on the place making lots of noise and doing lots of talking but getting less work done than twenty-five good American workmen would. This is a different climate, however, and American workmen would soon succumb to this hot, dangerous sun. The Chinese work right out in the heat with nothing on their heads and with very little on their bodies. There will be eight rooms for the schoolboys besides a cook room and the recitation room and the place will be far more healthful than the old *yaos*. I hope they will not get full of lice, bedbugs, fleas, centipedes, and scorpions. My second "boy" was stung by a scorpion the other morning and he was badly frightened and suffered a good deal of pain. Dr. Atwood applied a soap made of equal parts of ammonia and sweet oil and gave him a hypodermic injection of morphia to ease the intense pain. We have seen but few in our rooms since we came here, but the old walls and *yaos* have plenty of them. When they were tearing down the *yaos* the workmen found thirty before breakfast. Dr. Atwood asked them to preserve a few specimens for him and they took him a pint bottle half full. He covered them with alcohol and although they were in "good spirits," they could do no harm. We use flea powder in our beds and clothing as a remedy for fleas and bedbugs.

Our ex-teacher came in the other day from his home about twenty-five li from the city and he was fairly beaming as his wife had lately died and now he could be somebody. He said his wife used so much opium that he could not lay up any money. (While all the time he is or was using it himself.) He had on white shoes, the only sign of his heartbreaking grief, and he said it cost him ten liao (deon)* to bury her. It looks odd to see a long procession of mourners all dressed in white. If a father dies his sons will wear white caps, clothes, and shoes and not shave for a hundred days, but other relatives require less show.

*This may be a mistranslation of Eva's handwriting. The term is most likely *tiao* (which she may have spelled diao). Chinese cash were copper coins with a square hole in their centers. They could be hung on a string, and a *tiao* or "string" was generally considered to be 1,000 cash tied together.

Some of the schoolboys planted sunflower seeds and one looms high in each corner of my luxuriant garden this summer. The phlox, verbena, and portulaca are very pretty.

I wish you could spend a few weeks visiting us and you'd find out how precious Florence is.

....

September 19, 1893

Charlie and Dr. Atwood left today for Chia Ch'eng and Ch'ing Yuen and I got up bright and early to see them off. Charlie will only go as far as Chia Ch'eng and will be back tomorrow evening. He wants to see a man who Dr. Atwood thinks will be a good teacher for the school as the old teacher, Hau, has been dismissed because he used opium and made fun of our doctrine.

The buildings are about completed for the new quarters for the school. You would not think them very much perhaps, but they are well built of brick with a good roof, a foreign window of glass, and a foreign-style door in each room. The recitation room is on another side of the court and will accommodate all the boys we will be likely to have. It will have five glass windows and a door.

After dinner yesterday one of the shop men who had been here a few days ago with cloth came and said his wife wanted to come to "see things." I don't like callers who want nothing but to look us over as one would monkeys in a sideshow, but I told him to have her come in and she was a piece I tell you! Had her face powdered till it looked as though she had emptied the flour barrel while her neck was as scrawny and dirty and black as could be. She was dressed in her silks fine as a fiddle and looked at me in my gingham skirt as though I might do for a foreign devil but not much else. I tagged her around while she went through the dining room and kitchens and out the back door, but I left her there and she had a good time pegging around on her big toe looking at the washing out on the line and peeking at this and that. They wanted to get into the doctor's place and thought they could by coming through here but that plan fizzled as I told them they must go to the doctor's front door and the gatekeeper would tell them whether it was convenient

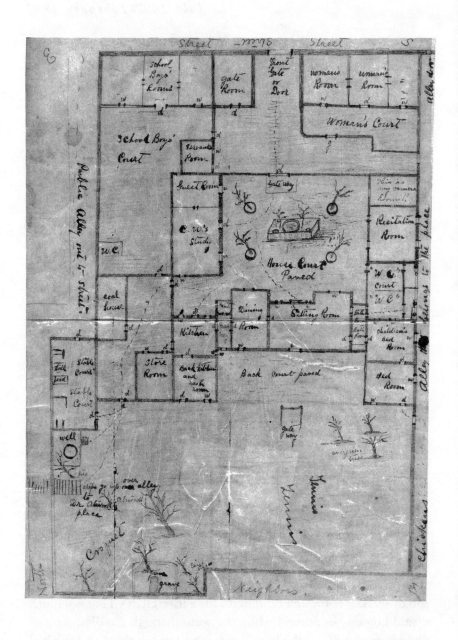

or not. Such people as this always make me so weary as they care nothing for us except to see how we look and live inside our homes. I feel just as though I am a sort of monstrosity, like a double-headed calf or something. Many of them have better manners than these however.

It is time now to hear Stewart's lessons. He has begun his fall term of study after a long vacation. The first morning he said with great gusto, "I'll pitch into my books headfirst and come out a doctor!"

....

Tuesday morning, September 26, 1893

Charlie came home last Wednesday night in time for supper. He enjoyed the trip, and the man he went to see is to come as teacher for the school. He claims to have taken down his idols and wants to learn more of Christianity. They were entertained in good Chinese style—slept on the *k'ang,* and Charlie found a louse on him after he got home.

Charlie and Stewart went up on the wall near here the other morning to see the soldiers drilling. The drill ground is just outside the city wall and they can get a good sight from the top of the wall. The soldiers drill nearly every morning for several months through the warm weather and make a horrid banging for an hour or so when one would rather sleep. They usually drill as early as 5:00 A.M. Stewart is delighted with the firing of the guns and goes about banging and making as much noise as half a dozen boys ought to make. The morning they were up there happened to be a time when two of the men had to be disciplined. Father would have laughed at the Chinese way of punishing soldiers, for they were not put in the guardhouse or made to do double duty, but had to be scolded by the magistrate and then had to lie flat on the ground on their stomachs while a man with a stick gave them a good spanking, one man had ninety strokes, the other had forty. They are very like children in their maneuvers. These soldiers are all cavalrymen and the horses are quite as well drilled as the men. Every "fu" city has its squad of soldiers, I believe. What they drill for is hard to say for their guns are old-fashioned and a few foreign shells would knock out the whole bunch.

There is a court not far from here where they make powder using a donkey to turn the grinder. There was an explosion the other day which killed the donkey, an old man, and two children. The shock jarred our windows and made me think of the earthquake.

Mother, I am going to risk sending a pair of shoes to you by this mail to let you see what kind of shoes we big-footed foreign women wear. They cost less than fifty cents a pair, but do not wear very long. I hope they will reach you and that you can wear them.

Your loving daughter and sister,

Eva

....

November 7, 1893

Such a time as you seem to be having in the U.S. with your Sunday closing, your panics, and your politics! It makes us content to live in slow-going old China where we can have quiet if nothing else. There isn't much stir here. Things have been as they are now for hundreds of years, I presume, except that the foreigners are gradually coming in and getting a foothold. In some parts, however, they are so actively opposed that no foreigner has ever been able to settle. Here in Shansi they seem to be more or less indifferent. The only thing in which they are not really indifferent is to get out of us all they can in the way of cash.

The last report we have of the Chinese bill is that this government will wait and see if the matter will be repealed, in which case they will make no trouble. But if there is no change in the present law then all foreigners, Americans at any rate, will be invited to leave the empire. Special word has been issued that foreigners shall not be molested, and until America has time to repeal the unjust act,* there shall nothing be done in regard to us. We would hate dreadfully to have to give up our home and work here, but if we are ordered out we will have to go or run all risk ourselves.

*Chinese Exclusion Act of 1882 opposing immigration of Chinese laborers.

The school is running again now with eighteen boys and we have a new teacher who seems able to govern the boys better than the other one, and we think he does not use opium. One trouble with him is that he has to go home for half a month twice a year to look after some farms besides the vacations. His wife is a nice little woman but is in a badly crippled condition and scarcely able to move so she will stay here in the hospital and be treated while he is away. Their name is Chang.

Yesterday a woman came in to see me who last year was in the hospital breaking off opium and getting her legs doctored. She is a pretty woman and more intelligent than the average and is now able to walk about. She and her husband want to unite with the Church. They live in Ching Tuan, two days travel from here. So many women are cripples, caused partly by the binding of the feet and partly by sitting cross-legged on the *k'angs* I believe, and when they go out in carts they have to sit cross-legged on the bottom of the cart. I have often wondered that the children are not born deformed.

So many of the people have eye troubles and skin diseases. Some come with cataracts in one or both eyes, some entirely blind, and very many with sore eyes. The doctor has had pretty good success with cataract cases. It is a grand way to get at the people for they can't help but be grateful if they were blind and regain their sight. The teacher said it was sleeping on hot *k'angs* that made so much eye trouble. Much of the skin trouble must be caused by the people being so filthy. The woman who is sewing for me now is a fearfully dirty woman, and today while I was out transplanting some sweet Williams the baby cried and she had picked her up and the baby was frightened. I told her she must not take the baby. I don't see how some women can give their sweet little babies up to the entire care of these dirty women. Some have been caught giving their nasty, dirty, dry breasts to a baby to keep it still.

We had Florence baptized last Sunday and her name is settled. It is Florence Muriel.

....

November 21, 1893

Mother's last letter written in September came last week and she was writing in the midst of a great heat. The fact that here it is cold and blustery now with flurries of snow only emphasizes the time and distance there is between us. Our big stove hasn't come yet from Boston though I presume it is on the way inland from Tientsin and will be here in a week or so.

The San Francisco boxes came in yesterday morning and Stewart fairly whooped around here for a time, partly because he thought the butter had come. We have been out of that luxury for some weeks although I have scraped around in the sawdust of the old boxes hoping to find a bonanza similar to that of last year. When he found it was not the Boston shipment he had to postpone his bread with butter. It is exciting when the boxes come.

Florence wasn't a bit well yesterday and it worried me a good deal. She sits alone and sputters and plays at a great rate. Don't I wish you could see her!

If I were to tell you what came in our boxes yesterday I expect you would think we were awfully extravagant folks. Well, we sent for canned fruits for there is no small fruit here and we get pretty hungry for some. Then there were a dozen brooms, salt, for salt is expensive here, pearl barley, farina, chloride of lime, carbolic powder, patty pans, cake cutters, dry goods, and last but not least, some Christmas presents—marbles, a Noah's ark, horns, and a big girl doll and a sailor boy doll. Some things are coming in the other boxes, and Charlie intends giving Stewart a "Waterbury" watch, which will be enough to make him wild. We will remember the other little children in the mission as far as we can. We make a good deal of Christmas out here in the way of presents because there is so very little for the children here.

It will soon be Thanksgiving day and I give thanks, which I do every day, for my precious girl baby. She is so much like Donnie was at that age, and yet my heart aches to think that she too may be called away from us. We cannot know God's plans, but I do pray that she may live to be a good woman.

It is very late now and Charlie wants to finish putting up the mail so I will close. This will not reach you until after Christmas and I'm afraid I forgot to wish you all a "Merry Christmas" in harvest time!

....

January 2, 1894

Happy New Year! We had a very busy day on Christmas as we had forty-seven Chinese to dinner. The chief cook and bottlewasher was also the leader of the band which made a horrid noise in our house court for a half hour or so. The schoolboys seemed to have a very happy time. Stewart was up bright and early and was surprised to find a small evergreen tree in the middle of the sitting room around and on which were his presents. He had too many as nearly everybody in the mission sent something, besides what we had provided—books, marbles, horns, a Chinese drum, Noah's ark, mouth organ, and the "Waterbury" watch! My, wasn't he delighted? He could scarcely eat his breakfast. And what do you think Santa Claus brought me? A nice, little gold watch! And someone else was delighted I can tell you. Florence got two dollies and she will sing "Ah, ah, ah" when I put one in her arms and will rock back and forth. We had a very pleasant day and each schoolboy got something. I had made thirty-eight bags of netting and crimson yarn and filled them with nuts, fruits, popcorn, and candy. Each one had a bright handkerchief too. The day cost us over $15 but we felt that it was well worth it. We hope another year to have more for the schoolboys. Nine of them said lately that they believe in Jesus and want to follow him.

I called on the women a day or so after they had been our guests on Christmas and they were very pleasant and cordial and gave me an urgent invitation to come once a week and teach them our doctrine. I do not know much of the language and what I have is not very correct, but I can tell them that God is our Father who loves us, that their gods are all false and cannot help them, and that we have a hope beyond this world. They have no knowledge of such a hope.

We had been waiting all fall for the new stove and it finally came in the last day of the old year. Charlie and Stewart celebrated New Year's day by opening the crate and getting the stove put together. My, it is a big one! So far we have had very little cold weather and only a little spit of snow now and then. Stewart runs to the window the first thing each morning to see if the ground is white.

Charlie was forty-six years old the twenty-eighth and is pretty white around the ears. He says when he comes home he will be introduced as "the venerable missionary to China, Mr. Price." He has to wear glasses most of the time and I do once in a while.

It is late so I will close. Goodnight with love to you all.

....

February 27, 1894

You may be wondering why there is such a gap between letters this time and perhaps are thinking they must be lost on the way. But we have been visiting. It is the first time since we've been in China that we have made such a long visit—three whole weeks! We went to visit the friends in Taiku and had such a good time. I have scarcely been out of the city for two years until we took this trip. There are three foreign families there besides the two young ladies.

It was the Chinese New Year's time and the first day in Taiku was made hideous by the incessant firing and banging of firecrackers. All day long they kept it up, in the streets and everywhere, and some of the big ones sounded as though they were in our courts as they make a noise almost like a cannon. The shopkeepers very early in the morning burnt a big bundle of straw in front of their shops and bowed down to the ashes afterward knocking their heads on the ground to secure the god of prosperity for their business through the year. Mr. and Mrs. Clapp expect to leave there for the homeland in less than three weeks and she has promised to visit you. We see the telegraph poles and wire when we go to Taiku for there is a line from the coast which runs past one of the cities we go through, and Stewart ran up to one of the poles and gave it a hug, which I felt like doing too. It seems to bring the homeland much nearer, but when we realize it would take months for us to get there it isn't much good after all.

When we came home last week we left our cook behind as he decided to go into business and not come back here. The past week has been busy I tell you, for it took me some time to get the kitchen and closet dug out so that I could go to work and it isn't done yet. But I can manage to hang on to the dishes, which were so greasy

I could hardly bear to touch them. My fingers and hands bear the marks of the lye I've used. I am tempted to never have another cook as long as we stay here. It doesn't sound much like missionary work to tell of baking bread, frying out fat, browning coffee, making fried cakes and custards, but when it's done I know it's clean and it is a relief to know things aren't being stolen. We have bought whole sheep several times, big fat fellows, but the fat went somewhere besides into our storeroom. We use mutton fat for about all our shortening. These Chinese servants slop about and smear around till it is enough to drive one wild! And it is such a source of anxiety to wonder if the water has been well boiled and if the milk things are clean. If you follow up all these things as you ought to you might as well do the work and be done with it.

School opens this week and a few of the boys are here now with more expected today. We would like to have about forty as the rooms will accommodate that many. Just at the end of last term the boys' cook and assistant cook had a fight, a regular queue pulling affair. One took a big meat knife as his defense, and pokers and clubs came in for their share of the fray. Charlie tried to pull them apart and one of the schoolboys also took an active part as his father was one of the fighters. He would slip up behind when he found a chance and give the other fellow's queue a yank and it would have been ridiculous if it hadn't been so serious for the Chinese do get raving when they get angry and yell so at each other. They were finally separated and one put outside the big door into the street. When this term opened there had to be new men hired.

I must close for tonight—the mail leaves in the morning. We are not disturbed in the least in living here—you get all the scares in your newspapers.

....

May 8, 1894
We've been to two Chinese weddings in one week and maybe you would like to hear of them. Mrs. Atwood's cook, a big fine-looking fellow and a Christian who came to Shansi with them three years ago this fall when they came from Shan Tung, lately took a

notion to be married and married he must be! There was a beggar family (selling opium on the streets) with a sixteen-year-old daughter who rattled bones and sang for cash, and he seemed to take a shine to her and she to him. It must have been a "Romance in Missions" for her, for her life must have been a hard one and to leave it all for a quiet home in a room on Dr. Atwood's place with a Christian husband is a great contrast. We were all invited to the wedding and heard a great deal about it. First the cook got a friend called a middleman to arrange the affair for him, and the first important thing to settle was the price he was to give the parents for her. As she was a very useful member of the family they had to have a big sum (from a poor working man's point of view), so the price was put at 100 tiao, but finally came down to 62, which is about $33 of our money. Then he planned for a feast, the bridal chair (which is a gorgeous affair of red and tinsel), and the musicians. He also found out that they were not getting good shoes and stockings for her so he sent a clean white pair of his own to her (she has unbound feet), and a nice pair of shoes. He also bought wedding jewelry (earrings, chain, etc.); he seemed very anxious that his beggar-girl bride should have a fair wedding.

Early in the morning chosen, the musicians came to Dr. Atwood's and tooted, scraped, and drummed out their music all day at intervals, the noise being loudest with a fresh arrival of guests. There was a cart hired by the day which went back and forth for the invited ones, but as we live so near we simply walked around to their big gate and as soon as we were inside the band (?) struck up a welcome for us. The chair did not leave for the bride until after 12:00 with the musicians following the chair bearers and the crowd following the musicians. When the gate was opened for the procession, in crowded the outsiders until it was a jam. An awning had been arranged and a piece of carpeting spread on the ground and with some plants it made quite a pretty corner for the ceremony. The old women helped the bride out of the chair, led her to the place where they were to stand, and Dr. Atwood married them with a Christian ceremony. She had a long red veil over her face (the veil and an outer garment being hired with the chair), which was kept on until after the ceremony when she was led into the room which was to be her home. There she had to sit on the *k'ang* while the crowd pushed in and out to get a look at her, and she was not a bad-looking girl. There had been great feasting going on all day, but after the ceremony the big feast was eaten and it was all very good. The foreigners ate in Mrs. Atwood's dining room while the Chinese ate in the waiting room of the dispensary and other rooms, which ended the whole affair.

Today we went to the second wedding, which was at Mr. Davis's place. A young man who is on probation married a young girl who was baptized with her father and mother a few weeks ago. Dr. Atwood married this couple too and they seem to be very well suited for each other. We hope it will be a Christian home. This wedding was very similar to the other, except the musicians were only hired to follow the chair, and the crowd was kept out so it was a very quiet affair. One peculiarity of Chinese weddings is that the parents of the bride do not come to the ceremony, so when a young girl in China puts on the long red veil and gets into the shining red gilt bridal chair she bids good-bye to her old home for she has to live with her husband's family if he has any and wait on his mother. In the case of Mrs. Atwood's cook his folks live off so far that they will live together as foreigners do. But this young bride married today will go to his home, which is at Yu Tao Ho where we spend the summers.

Well, I must write a word about the "flying dragon" that came a week ago. I have been without a cook three months, and last week a young fellow came in with the courier, having heard in Tientsin that I wanted a "boy." His name is Fei-lung or "Flying Dragon," and when a dragon flies that far one most ought to take him in so I hired him for a month to see how he will suit. I hope he will do well by us. If he doesn't he will have to go as the two others did.

I must close as it is time to put Florence to bed.

....

June 4, 1894

The courier came in yesterday morning but no home letter— one from Jennie which will doubtless be the last for several months as they sail from San Francisco for Micronesia early this month.

Miss Gray visited here last week. She came out a year ago to marry Mr. McConnell, a young man in the China Inland Mission. The rules of their mission will not allow newcomers to marry until they have been here two years, so she is "living around" until the two years are up, which is not at all pleasant for her. He lives in the southwest corner of the province several days' travel from here so he cannot come to see her very often, and when he does come it is not very pleasant for some of the rules are so strict. He came over here the last time he was in this part of the province and we liked him so much—a Scotch-Irish gentleman of much good sense—and he said he enjoyed his visit here for it seemed homelike. Poor fellows! Some of them have to live pretty rough. Some of the friends call our home "Paradise Cottage," others "Rest Cottage," for they say it is such a restful change to come here.

My dear friend, Mrs. Russell, of whom I have written several times, broke down nervously last year and went to the coast. Her husband was afterward called there by telegram but she grew so much better that he came back a few weeks ago and came over to visit us. Their work you may remember is in Hsiao-I, fifteen miles from here. However, last week he sent a man over with a letter telling us that he had received a telegram that his wife had died the day before in Shanghai. She was such a lovely Christian. Her friend, Miss Whitchurch, who has lived and worked with her for nine years, is in England and it will be a great shock to her for they loved each other dearly. I only wish they could have thought it their duty to live in more comfort, but they lived just about as the poorer Chinese do. I feel sure if she had taken better care of herself and lived in a more homelike way with good nourishing food, she could have stood it much longer here. However much we may regret her living as she did we must admire the spirit of self-sacrifice and consecration. They were such a help and comfort to me when Donnie went away, and now in little more than two years she is gone too. I shall miss her for she was such a spiritual help to me.

It is not an easy thing to live here though it may seem so from your distance, but then we are glad and willing to if by living here we can help even a little. Many fall by the way and some are taken who cannot be spared, it seems to us who are left, and yet the work goes on—spreading here a little, there a little. Gradually the gospel is getting a foothold even in China. Year after year adds to the number of saved ones, and it will be joy unspeakable if we have something, even the least, to do with leading them to the Father. We need your prayers that we do not become disheartened.

I have made a few calls on my neighbors and have had a number come to see me, some of whom I like so much for they are so friendly and pleasant. But some of them just want to look around and see what we've got, and if they have visitors they must bring them in to see how the foreigner looks and what she wears. If they would only come and want to know something of the gospel how glad I would be to tell them as best I can.

I will close for this time. Florence and Stewart are well and happy.

....

August 14, 1894

Someone out here in China will soon be thirty-nine years old and I wonder who it is! There has been a mysterious hiding away of presents for several weeks and every day Stewart tells me not to look in a certain drawer in the bedroom, so I rather suspect there is "molasses in that jug." My last year in the thirties!

We go outside the city once in a while as much for Florence's sake as anything for it does her a great deal of good. But dear me! She will never know how to say "Git up" as we do in America when driving for they always say "Duh" here, and instead of saying "Whoa" they go "Dr-r-r-r" with a trill of the *r* that is quite an accomplishment. The last time we were out we saw several camels feeding along by the roadside. Stewart always enjoys them, but they are not such a rare thing here. We often see whole lines of them with coal or other produce tied on their backs.

We see the threshing floor, which is a large space of ground, cleared and pounded until it is even and solid, and then the grain is scattered over this while a donkey or so are made to go around and around tramping until the grain is trampled out. They don't waste anything so if it doesn't all come out this way they beat and pound it until it is all out. Then the grain is gathered up, dirt and all, and put through the fanning mill. They grind wheat too in this very primitive manner with two large stones, one above another, turned by a donkey.

The rest of the friends are all out to the valley this summer but Charlie has been having some more building done so we have had to stay in the city. Just now we have two guests—Miss Bird from Taiku, who has charge of the school now that Mrs. Clapp is away, and Miss Gray of the C.I.M., who is waiting to be married to Mr. McConnell, also of the C.I.M., this winter. It has been a real pleasure to me to entertain friends from different countries—Swedish, English, Scottish, Norwegian, Irish, Canadians, etc. They differ widely oftentimes in belief and methods of work, but somehow the Lord seems to bless them about equally.

I wrote to you of the death of my dear friend Mrs. Russell in Shanghai where she had gone to see friends off to England. She suffered greatly from head troubles and we have learned that she took an overdose of sleeping powder and after being unconscious over seventy hours she passed away. It has been very sad. Another one of our friends, Mr. Gulbrauson, who has been here often and who seemed so strong and bright and happy became insane and is now in Shanghai in very bad condition. This is a wearing climate and living as many of them do, exposing themselves to this terrible sun and out in all kinds of weather, causes many breakdowns. Just now one of our own mission, Mr. Williams, is very sick with some stomach trouble which Dr. Atwood fears is an abscess. It is anxious times when our friends are sick for we are like one family.

Don't I wish you could see Florence now! She is toddling all over the house and as she is such a tiny little body she looks very cute. Her mouth is the daintiest little affair you ever saw, eyes are blue with long black lashes, and her hair is a pretty brown and curls in back.

I must close now with very much love to you all.

....

September 11, 1894

We have had two couriers this week, one being delayed on account of bad roads and the other a little ahead of time, and each one brought a letter from Mother, but the rest of you seem to be keeping still as Quakers. You are having times at home aren't you? War right in your midst! If that isn't "brother rising up against brother," what can it be? It is enough to make men stop and ask, "What do these things mean?"

Maybe you think we on this side of the world have reason to ask questions too as Japan and China are quarreling over the "bone" Korea. Details of what is going on at the coast are slow to reach us and often unreliable. We hear a good many rumors of course, one to the effect that every hsien Magistrate* has been called on to furnish 500 taels (about $500) and that each province must furnish 2,000 soldiers. We have word sent to us to the effect that we need not be alarmed and may go on with our business as usual. We had felt no alarm for we seem so far away from the trouble that it is hard to realize there had been actual fighting going on. But maybe God has some plan for China—nations as well as people are often better for passing through deep affliction. However, there is nothing very definite to be learned from the Chinese, for every man will have a different story.

The other day Miss Gray, who has been here for three weeks, left us for the coast to be married to Mr. McConnell, and I went with her part way, being gone from home four days. We came to a village where we were told that the road was bad and we couldn't go the usual way. Another man said the road was good, another said it was bad. Each one we met, only a few rods apart, told just the opposite until even the carter and Ch'iao Ko Ling, my Chinese "boy," laughed. I told them if there were a hundred men there would be a hundred stories.

I had such a nice time on the trip. Miss Gray is the dearest woman friend I have in China, and of course I thoroughly enjoyed being with her. Then it was so beautiful out in the fields this time of year. Our road wound through fields of *kao liang,* a stalk with top something like sugar cane but the stalk is not very sweet and they use it largely for making wine. These fields and those of millet and a kind of small rice look very pretty now. The roadsides were pretty too with vines and grasses of which I

*County Magistrate.

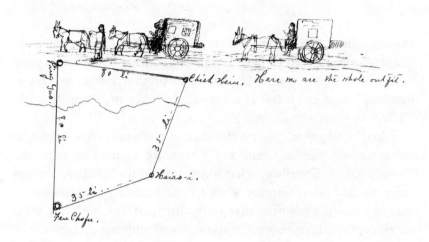

Ping Yao 80 li Chieh Hsiu. *Here we are the whole outfit.*

Hsiao-i.

35 li

Fen Chofu.

gathered quite a bunch and brought home to make the rooms pretty. The first day we went to Hsiao-I (about twelve miles), for some of Miss Gray's things, and the next day we went on to Chieh Hsiu for the rest of her worldly goods, having to cross a river by ferry, which was quite novel to me. We spent the afternoon and evening packing her things, some to take with her to the coast and the rest to be picked up on the return trip to the south of the province where they will live. The following morning we left for P'ing Yao, and as it was about thirty miles it took nearly all day. We reached there about 5:30 and met Mrs. Saunders and two Swedish friends. Mrs. Saunders is an English lady and has a sweet little daughter, Jessie, about the age of Florence.

After spending the night there I started home accompanied by Ch'iao Ko Ling and the carter. We had made a kind of circuit in the trip so I could get home in one day. The day was very cool and cloudy, which made it fine for traveling. I had to cross the same river, only in another place, and as I was the only foreigner I felt rather queer. The ferrymen waited until I got on the boat with my cart then said I must pay 300 cash for crossing. The usual price for one cart is 30 cash I think, but they take advantage of us foreigners when they can. I told them I wouldn't pay that much, so down I sat and there they stood chattering loudly. Finally, after keeping the whole crowd waiting, the "boy" came and said they wanted 120 cash so I told him to give 110, so we started for that was big pay.

But the horrid old ferrymen made fun of me all the way over. I only glared at them and as soon as the boat touched shore turned my back upon them and walked away with as great a dignity as I could muster. I gratified myself when the carter caught up with me by telling him those people had no manners.

We had to stop at an inn for dinner and I had a bowl of flour and water, scrambled eggs with onions, and some Chinese cakes. My stomach didn't take to this dinner so well, especially as the water was so bad, but I rested and was glad to leave for the fleas were bad too. Because of the good, bad, good road story, the carter went out of his way so far that we were till 1:00 A.M. getting home. They were glad to see me too when I arrived as it was the first time I had been away from Florence overnight, though Charlie took good care of her and they seemed to get along as well without me.

The building is all finished and we have been house cleaning this last week. The rooms are all good now for the schoolboys, servants, and Chinese teacher, and we have a pleasant home too.

Just now we are very excited for day after tomorrow if nothing happens Charlie and Stewart leave for the coast. We had word by the last mail that a Dr. Hall, his wife, and two children were to sail for China, coming to Shansi some time in August. We also heard that a cablegram had been sent to stop the party from sailing on account of the troubles here, but as we cannot know whether the cablegram reached them in time, there will be need for someone to go to the coast to meet them and escort them inland. They may not need to go farther than Paoting fu, which is a few days this side of the coast, and it may be they will go on to Tientsin. I am so glad it has been thought best for Charlie to go, for he has been about less than any other of the gentlemen, so the change will do him a lot of good. Stewart is just about wild because he will get to go too. They will take the cook along and he can cook for the friends coming back. They will be away from home over a month, I expect, and Florence and I will have to keep old maid's hall and do our own cooking, but that will be fun.

September 24, 1894

Charlie and Stewart have been gone nearly two weeks now and it will be several more before they can get back, especially if they go on to the coast. I hope they will go on to Tientsin for Stewart is so anxious to see the cars.

The house is pretty quiet without Stewart and things don't get mussed up as much, but we will be glad to have him back, noise, dirt, and all. When I ask Florence where Papa and Stewart are she says "Duh—duh," which is what the carters say to their mules when they want them to hurry up, so she remembers they started off in a cart. We went with them one day's journey and I intended to go on to Tai Yuen fu but the place where we stopped for the night was such a miserable hole that Florence and I slept in one cart and Stewart in the other, while Charlie, the cook, and the carters slept in the one empty room. It disheartened me so that I made up my mind to come back to my own clean home and bed and let them go on without us. The weather is very fine now and I hope they will have a good time.

Four years from this fall we will be going to the coast again,* I presume, if we live, and will go on and on across the mighty ocean. Oh, that big sea! I think of it often now, vast and awful, always in motion, never resting, all that water, deep and wide, always there, always the same. But there's no way of getting to America from here unless we cross one of the oceans.

I must close now and eat my lonely breakfast before Florence gets up. I am enclosing a fig leaf off my tree.

....

November 6, 1894

Well, Charles Wesley and Stewart are home again and you would be amused to hear Stewart rattle on about things he saw in Tientsin—cars and steamboats and jinrikishas and horses and buggies and a real church where folks went to meeting and a menagerie

---

*The usual missionary term was ten years, so it's unclear why Eva counted on only four more years instead of five.

where there were animals and birds, and so many things he could scarcely contain himself. They were in Tientsin a week so had plenty of time to look about. The Consul advised them to not stay any longer for there was a possibility any day that an order would be issued forbidding anyone to leave for the interior, and as they had no fancy to stay there all winter they left after being there a week. The foreigners were somewhat stirred up about the war as they feared that if the Japanese landed their troops the Chinese would fire their property about the first thing. There is a large foreign settlement in Tientsin, many businessmen, mostly English, and quite a large number of missionaries, English and American. It seems singular to have Japan and China at war while the big powers stand off and look on. China is so backward and unprepared and the soldiers are so untrustworthy that I don't believe China could make much real resistance. And if Japan does raid China it is hard to say what effect it will have on foreigners living here, but we have no need now to feel any alarm and do not borrow trouble.

Stewart and his papa were on board the U.S. warship *Monocacy* and were treated very cordially by our countrymen. Their sympathies were decidedly with the Japanese but they have to be neutral. It was such a treat to Stewart to take this trip and he will always remember it, I expect. Some of the friends wrote that he was a beautiful boy and quite won their hearts.

We had the pleasure of having Dr. Taylor, the father of the China Inland Mission, take breakfast with us this morning and visit an hour or so afterward. He has made a fast trip through this province twice now this fall. Mr. Russell was with him and of course we especially enjoyed him as he is an old friend. Dr. Taylor is not liked very well by the members of our mission and their methods of work are not very satisfactory in many instances, but like Paul we ought to feel that although "some indeed preach Christ even of envy and strife" . . . and "of contention, not sincerely" . . . What then? "Notwithstanding every way, whether in pretence or in truth Christ is preached, and I therein do rejoice yea, and will rejoice." The Chinese profess to be Christians and are baptized and often make fine stories for *China's Millions* or the *Herald,* but only a very small proportion of them are genuine. As to Mr. Taylor himself, many feel that he is a hypocrite but I believe he is a good Christian man, striving honestly for the salvation of China and not self-glory. Those of his mission that we have met we like very much and some of them are very dear friends. Some are unwise and too easily deceived by these crafty Chinese, but we all get taken in too often. His workers are genuine, I believe, but the Chinese Christians will bear a good deal of watching. Paul's experiences with those early churches are more real to many of us than they were before.

Because I am not able now to do very much active outside work does not mean that others are not doing everything in human power to lift these people up. We can only pray to the Lord of the harvest to send forth more laborers. I hope as the children grow to need less of my constant watching that I can have a larger share of the work. I feel that to have the goodwill of the people and to be liked by one's neighbors is a step toward preparing the way for more work afterwhile. Charlie thinks it is everything that he has a pleasant home here and surely can do more and better work than if the children and I were in America.

I must close now. We are all well and our sweet little girlie is doing better than ever.

....

Fen Cho fu, China
December 18, 1894

Dear Father and Mother,

Eva has several letters to write tonight and has asked me to write to you in her place. My failure to write has not been for lack of interest in you and what you are doing. I enjoy your letters fully as much as Eva, but she has relieved me of the labor that ought to fall to my share.

We are enjoying life in the same old way with not much to excite us, and with our encouragements and discouragements about equally divided. Eva and the children have just returned from a two weeks' visit to the friends in Taiku. I went after them and stayed one day. I did not care to have them come home alone as the country is rather unsettled. Not that there is any evidence of trouble in this part of the country. Everything seems to be very quiet, but on the road one is constantly meeting small bands of soldiers on their way to the seat of the war, and they are rather reckless and surly. Putting up for the night at the same inns with them is a little risky. Aside from this we feel very safe and have no fears from the people, who are friendly as usual, and our work thus goes on as before the war. The officials at Peking have issued a proclamation and sent it to the cities of the empire, warning the people against harming the foreigners who are here to preach the gospel. This of course is an additional assurance of safety, so you are not to think of us as being in danger because of the war, but as doing our work in the usual way.

Stewart and I took a pleasant trip to the coast in September and October. Traveling at the rate of twenty-five to thirty miles per day is a little tedious if one happens to be in a hurry, but once you make up your mind to take things as they come it is not so bad. The four days through the mountains are especially enjoyable and make up for many of the discomforts of the entire journey. Stewart enjoyed Tientsin best of all. We visited the U.S. gunboat and it was to him the best thing he ever saw. The Lieutenant Commander escorted him around to see the different sights and afterward said he told them all about how we lived and what we were doing at home and the men on the boat enjoyed him very much. Some of the friends at Tientsin spoke to me of what a gentlemanly fellow he is and praised him very highly in many ways. It almost made me proud. He is growing very fast and will soon be as large as his father. We had the pleasure of meeting our friends, Dr. and Mrs. Hall, and escorting them in to Shansi. We were gone from home just six weeks but as it was the first rest I had taken since coming to China I did not regret the time.

Florence is growing fast and is quite a bright girlie. She is our greatest comfort and I don't see how we could get along without her. Eva is a great big woman. Who would have thought the little woman on the farm in Franklin township would ever attain the stature she has reached. In some of the letters we receive from you you write as though you might be a little proud of her. I am sure if you could see her she would cause you no shame. She grows better every year, and the trials that we have passed through since we came here brought out the true womanly qualities that were always hers. The best people are her truest friends, and her love for you her parents grows stronger as she grows older.

We look forward to the time when we will be permitted to see you with great pleasure. Half of our ten years have already passed and the next five will pass still more quickly and it will be a pleasure to see civilized life once more. But we are not discouraged with our life here as we have many home comforts and all our necessities are supplied to us. Except for separation from friends and the depressing influences of heathen life, we would see no need of change, and if we can do something even though it be little to change these surroundings we shall not have lived here in vain.

I must close. We send love to you all. Though I do not often write you are in my mind and I am always anxious to hear from you.

Very truly your son,
C. W. Price

Dear Home Folks,

I can't let the letter go without a line from me for I am always so glad to get your letters. What will you think when I tell you that another wolf came into the city today in broad daylight having to pass through one of the big gates! With as many people as there are constantly moving about this sounds bold, doesn't it? Dr. Atwood shot the other one.

We are having some really cold weather now and I am thankful we are safe in our own home and not on the road. Our March shipment that ought to have been in two months ago has not appeared yet, so I guess the Japs have it in safekeeping. And the next shipment has only partly come in. We had a clock come in a box and it had been opened and rather roughly handled.

With much love to you all from Eva.

....

January 1, 1895

Here we are beginning a brand new year. It doesn't seem possible that 1894 is past. I can remember when it was 1865 for so long that I thought it would always be that and always had been. That was when George and I used to go to the post office to get war letters from Father.

We had two Christmas days this year, for Dr. Atwood's family took dinner with us on Christmas and the next day we had over fifty Chinese come to a feast. For our Christmas dinner I had pheasants made into a sort of pie and the "boy" made canned oyster soup. We also had potato balls, squash, bread and butter, spiced grapes, pickles, mince pie, dried raspberry pie, white cake, chocolate cake, and coffee with grapes and nuts. The boxed American Santa Claus didn't get here but there are a good many foreign toys here and the friends sent the children some. We had ordered an assortment of presents for the schoolboys too, and they are not in yet. It is difficult to get animals now to carry things on account of the war.

We expected the courier to get in today but he has not come. We are always a little anxious for fear they will be molested by the bands of soldiers who are straggling about over the country. It is hard for the people to believe that we have nothing to do with the war. They keep asking us if America is peaceful and they wonder why we don't go home. They ask us if we are afraid to go by Japan and if the Japs would let us pass. Poor old proud China! It opens the eyes of some of these people to know there are other countries big enough too to make war on this honorable country!

The school is not as large as last winter and I think it comes partly from the unsettled state of the country. People are afraid we will disappear suddenly. And some of the money shops don't like to lend us money if we run short because they are afraid we are not going to stay. When they see we do stay and their natural suspicions are quieted I think they will have more confidence in us than ever. The general uneasiness in the country makes it hard to know what to expect, but so far we have been treated very kindly.

....

January 29, 1895

This is the Chinese New Year time, a time of feasting, wearing new clothes, visiting, and having a good time generally. If they would keep their firecrackers still it would be pleasanter, but they do bang and crack night and day. The schoolboys have gone home for vacation except a few who have no homes and are glad to stay here.

Just now we have company, a nice little Swedish lady, Miss Nilson, who is soon to go to the coast to be married, and Mr. and Mrs. McConnell, who are just back from the coast where they were married. And such a disconsolate bridal tour! They are both sick— he had teeth drawn and has taken cold in his jaw and his face is all swollen, while she is sick with backache and other aches from riding in these miserable carts. I am glad they are here for there is no place on the road among their own mission where they could be so comfortable, and their home is over a week's journey south. Miss Nilson has been here nearly a month and it has been such a comfort to have her. She has done finely in the language and has been teaching me every day and we have made a good many calls. She plays with Stewart too and we will all miss her when she goes away. They leave for the coast about the first of March. I call her "daughter" and she calls me "Mamma" and says it is so like home here. I have enjoyed being able to have so many friends come to us and they all seem to enjoy it too. We look for Mrs. Davis, Mrs. Thompson, and Miss Partridge to arrive tonight.

Stewart has passed his tenth birthday and comes up to my shoulders and Florence is nearly two years old and a dear bonny girl she is.

We keep hearing reports about the war but nothing very definite or alarming. We are safer here than in some places I believe. Now I must close to make ginger cake for company.

....

February 25, 1895

We are quieted down now that all our winter guests have departed except that the measles is abroad in the land and Stewart is down with it. He has a bad cough but otherwise is not very sick. I presume Florence will have it too after a time. It is very fortunate it did not come while all the guests were here. Miss Nilson was here five weeks and Mr. Lundgren (to whom she is to be married) came over occasionally of course. Then Mr. Hoste, one of the famous "Cambridge Seven,"* was here for a day or so, and then Mr. and Mrs. McConnell were here more than a month. Mrs. Davis and Miss Partridge were here also. However, they are all gone their several ways and have their own work and interests which will make some time before we can expect to be together again. It is such a blessing to have so many foreign friends and visitors.

When Mrs. Davis was here we had a number of women stay on the place and she taught them nearly two weeks and I helped as much as I could. Now I go two afternoons a week to read with eight women, going to one place one afternoon and to another on another afternoon.

The school is just opening for the spring term but one boy is down with the measles and there probably will be more. There has just been a large arched door cut between the rooms in the recitation building so now the two rooms can be used to a decided advantage, especially on Sundays when so many crowd in to the service. We need a chapel very much, for in not having a room large enough to hold everyone there needs to be two services, one at Dr. Atwood's and one here. If we had a good chapel it would be great economy for one of the gentlemen could go out to villages.

We are always anxious these days for the mail to come in for we have no other way of learning definite news about the war. There are so many rumors that we never know what to believe. We heard that all the Chinese who had worked for foreigners were to be made to register, for what purpose was not known but the surmise was that all foreigners were to leave, then these Chinese will be tortured. The last word we had was that the Japs were within a few miles of Peking. We are very quiet in here and the people very friendly. They find it hard to believe that no other country is helping Japan, for they know it is a very small country compared to China. The different rulers and gov-

---

*Dickerson Hoste was one of seven young men recruited from Cambridge University by Dwight Moody to enhance the China Inland Mission—all seven of them were endowed with education, money, social standing, and athletic ability.

ernors seem to have a friendly feeling for America in spite of past experience so we hope and hope that nothing will drive us from the work here.

I must stop now and take Florence out in this fine sunshine.

....

March 12, 1895

I must send you a line by the courier who leaves in the morning for during these war times I presume you are more or less anxious. The last mail was to the effect that new troops had landed and they were nearing Tientsin. It is still very quiet in here and they are kind to us. They really seem to be as much or more afraid of their own soldiers as we can be, for when a lot of soldiers are passing through, the shops are shut and everything is as quiet as though there were no people about. They dread the time when the war is ended and all these soldiers are scattered over the land to pillage the country, for they have been so poorly paid and fed that they will be like a lot of robbers. That will be our most dangerous time I expect. We heard the other day that there is a prospect of the emperor coming with his household to Tai Yuen fu, about a hundred miles northeast of us in this province. There have been a lot of carts kept in readiness to move them if necessary. It will lower the dignity of the august person to be obliged to skedaddle like that.

Today is cold, snowing and blowing quite like winter. It is the middle of March though and we don't often have much cold after this time. Stewart is over his measles and Florence is having her time at it. She has been sicker than Stewart and has taken some cold so she coughs a good deal and is having a pretty hard time.

I have been reading a little book in Chinese that Frank prepared before he left China and am using it in teaching three classes. I go about a mile on Wednesday afternoons and read a chapter with two or three women; then the teacher's wife and girl are reading it and I go there twice a week plus the class of four out about six miles on Friday afternoons. Today there were seven baptized, among them our gatekeeper, the teacher in the school, and Ch'iao

Ko Ling, the boy who has lived with us so long, though now he is a real manly fellow. Two could not get in because of the storm. There are twenty-two members now besides the foreigners and I hope a church will soon be organized. It is a cause for rejoicing that every year brings some few of this people to confess Christ openly. Eternity alone can show how many are really in earnest, but if we do the sowing and tending, God will give the increase.

....

April 8, 1895

I was feeling pretty blue when Mother's good letter came as we had been having sickness for over a month with both children having measles and all, and if you could have seen me cry while reading it you would have known how glad I was to get it and to hear of the happy family gathering. Wouldn't it have been fine if we could have been four little mice behind the organ? We would have squeaked in on the chorus.

We are alone in the city now as Dr. Atwood's family has gone to Tientsin on a visit before the Annual Meeting, which begins next Sunday in Taiku. We will not be there as Charlie is ailing and is not well enough for such a journey. But the gatekeeper has brought in some plum or apricot blossoms and I have my flower seeds planted and the willow trees are in quite good leaf so spring must be here and that cheers me.

We had a letter from brother Frank from Ruk, Micronesia and he wrote of that beautiful country in the tropics—islands with palm trees, coral reefs, and the ocean. It surely is a place where every prospect pleases and only man is vile. The natives are still in a sad heathen condition but Frank is full of faith and zeal.

I am sending by this mail the Chinese book Frank wrote entitled *Christ's Life.* I am also sending some silk pieces which you can divide amongst you, the larger pieces being what the women buy to make their little shoes. The buttons are real "cat's eye" buttons from the south, and the beads are from a fragrant southern wood. The embroidered pieces I had on the sleeves of a garment for a while and the green and white stone I found in the valley is jade,

I understand. The cart and wheelbarrow will tell their own story, they are quite a perfect model of the real ones.

We are wondering what the outcome of the war will be. Many soldiers have passed through this region so there must be a lot of them around Tientsin and Peking.

....

June 4, 1895

Well, we are home again from our visit in Taiku and all are well and we enjoyed meeting the friends very much. We don't often go visiting but Charlie couldn't work in the school. We were gone four weeks. When we came back we had to dismiss the Chinese teacher in the boys' school. He was a good enough teacher but we found out he isn't a good man, which is very disappointing to us for he professed to be a Christian and was baptized in March. It is so hard to find reliable people among these poor heathen and now we will have to try another teacher, so you see it is rather discouraging. We surely make haste slowly in the growth of Christianity.

I am having the sitting room whitewashed again and it takes so long when we begin a thing of this kind. We have to take out every single thing, have three or four men come who build a scaffold, which takes a long time, then they each have a little brush something like a common paintbrush which covers only a small place at a time and they swipe and brush and brush and swipe, stop to drink tea, to go to breakfast, to go to dinner, to drink tea again, and so it goes for several days. We sit around patiently (or impatiently) as possible waiting for them to get one room done so we can settle it before they begin another. Each room takes the same amount of scaffold building, tea drinking, and puttering. It takes weeks if we whitewash the two kitchens as well as the two small bedrooms, a small bathroom, sitting room, and dining room.

Well, Florence is in bed and Stewart sits here making pictures. He says it is a picture of a restaurant and he has men stretched back in chairs looking very luxurious. It has been so long since he saw a restaurant and he was so young then that I think he has to draw on his imagination a good deal. As we were looking at the moon the other night he wondered if you saw it too. I told him you were probably working just then as it was daylight with you but at night you would see the same moon, three quarters full, and the very same stars. That is one thing we have in common at any rate.

We have a horse now, a sort of dappled cream and brown, and we have a big cow and a heifer and a smaller heifer calf that is as fine and large at four months old as an American calf! Then we have a dog, Kippy, a fat roly-poly dog—black and shaggy with white feet. And we have over fifty chickens that would remind you of home for their cluck and scratch and crow are just like Christian chickens.

Our garden is faring pretty well considering the dry weather and we have had onions, radishes, young cabbage, peas, and spinach and later will have new potatoes and green corn. We went into partnership with Dr. Atwood in the garden this year.

It is getting late so I will close with much love to everybody.

....

July 2, 1895

We are nearing the "Glorious Fourth" and I wonder what you will do to celebrate the occasion. The people here do not seem to have any patriotic love, for their firing of crackers and guns is usually to make it rain or not rain, or to scare away the devils. The other day it looked as though we might have a big storm and threatened hail. Our neighbors had a patch of opium about harvested and it never would do to have that spoiled, so they rushed around firing some great crackers with such a bang that it scared the hail devil away! (It only hailed just a little.) They doubtless fully believe it was their big noise that stopped it.

Sometimes about church time in the evening one of the temple bells not far from us is rung and sounds very like the old Presbyterian bell in Des Moines as it was ringing the last time for service— ding, ding, ding, ding—with a pause between each stroke. If only one could forget that these bells are heathen temple bells.

Our long delayed boxes are finally about all in except one. Some of the goods have been delayed almost a year. My carpet that ought to have been here last November is here at last and it looks very nice. It is about sixteen feet by twenty feet border and all and is just laid down as it doesn't pay to tack anything down in this dusty country.

Stewart is stiff and cross today as he and Charlie went out to the valley yesterday on horseback and went up in the mountains a ways. He has a playhouse in the back court made of poles and covered with mats—the coarse straw mats we buy here. It is about nine feet by twelve feet and seven feet high and he has all sorts of traps out there—wooden guns, an old valise, an organ made out of a raisin box, rubber bands and tacks, flags, and other things. I made him a big U.S. flag and it cheers us all. I had a woman make Charlie a silk flag for his birthday present last December and it is draped over the front door through which our visitors from many countries must pass. It never looked so pretty as it does out here.

Stewart plays soldier most of the time and enjoys anything about war. He only has two studies this summer, spelling and arithmetic, and he calls long division "long and hard diversion" as it keeps him at it a long, hard time.

School is out for July and August, though there are still several boys on the place. My flowers are looking fine. The oleanders, calla lilies, petunias, zinnias, geraniums, morning glories, portulaca, and snapdragons make the court look very pretty and are a comfort.

....

Fen Cho fu
China.

July 3, 1895.

Dear Grandma & Grandpa.
I have not written a letter to you in a
long time so I thought I would write.
I have been trying to practice
blacksmithing, but I put my stove too
near a tree and it looked as if it
was going to catch fire so I had to
put it out. I have a large playhouse
here is a picture of it
it is nice and large.
I think I will close now
your's Truly Stewart L. Rice.

Fen Cho fu, China
July 30, 1895

Dear Father,

With school dismissed for two months' vacation I thought there could be no reason for not writing to you. I usually give the letter writing into Eva's hands as she can do it so much better than I, but this time I will try it myself.

The children are very well. Stewart is growing very fast, weighs over a hundred pounds. He takes delight in working with tools, which he does not inherit from me. Perhaps it comes from the other side of the house. I am glad to see it but hope he will come to take more delight in study than he has shown up to the present time. I believe he will make a good man—he is improving every day, is not so impetuous or self-willed as he used to be, and is learning to have some respect for the rights of others. It is one of the hardest things in the missionaries' life to train our children without the help of the outside influences we would have at home. Boys will not be so strong and manly without coming in contact with boys of their own age. If he plays with the Chinese boys they submit to him in everything. He needs playmates who will make him understand that he is not the only one to take account of.

Florence is growing quite plump and we are very glad to see it, for a few months ago she was not looking strong. I do not know what we would do without her. She makes us love her more every day. Everyone speaks of her being beautiful, which is not surprising, but to us she is only sweet and good.

Eva is feeling very well. She and Miss Bird of Taiku, who is visiting us for a few weeks, are very busy drawing pictures of the different things in the neighborhood that would be likely to interest people at home. They have some very good sketches. Eva has quite a reputation in this province for her hospitable home and the way in which she entertains company. We have a goodly number of missionaries of many nationalities coming to see us at different times and are thus able to meet many cultivated and consecrated people, which is a great help to us socially and spiritually. I am glad for Eva's sake as it would be very hard for her to live here except for this break in her monotonous life. It is a very trying life to anyone, but to a woman necessarily kept at home a good part of the time it is almost unendurable unless they have in their own homes sufficient enjoyment and visitors to break the sameness. No one can understand what such a life as this is if they have not tried it. The wonder is that any woman can endure it.

We have been out to the mountains, eight miles from here, for a week's stay. There is a small stream of water running in front of the door and trees for shade and grass to lie on and take a nap or read the paper. It is a beautiful place and we enjoy it very much.

The war is over and we are happy at the result. I trust the whipping will do the Chinese good. They will begin to see there is some other place besides China and though they are the most numerous people they are not the strongest. If they get rid of some of their pride the gospel will find the way to their hearts.

With love to Mother and yourself with all the children, I must close.

Ever your son,
C. W. Price

....

Fen Cho fu, China
August 12, 1895

Charlie left us two weeks ago to visit the other stations. In vacation time there isn't much to do except the Sunday service. Well, last night a little after dark he came in and such a sight he was! The whole plain is soaked full of water, rivers full to overflowing and the whole country for miles knee to waist deep in water. He had waded water, had the horse fall and toss him head over heels into the water and mud, and all in all had a rather damp time of it. He came through in one day, however, and he says he had a good time while he was gone.

While Charlie was away I had some little trouble with the servants. On Sunday after the dinner work was done, I was in the sitting room and Miss Bird came from her room in the court and said she had seen three strange men go into the kitchen and she wondered if the servants were there. I went into the kitchen to see and sure enough there were three strangers who had evidently walked onto the place and into our house without leave or license. I told them to leave and then sent Stewart out to find where the servants were that they had allowed such a thing, and there wasn't a man on the place except these strangers. The gatekeeper had gone to his home to dinner and the others had gone out to the fair. It provoked me so to think they would do such a careless thing that when the gatekeeper came back I had him lock the gate and told him the boys couldn't come back until the next day. It made them angry to be locked out and have to sleep where they could, so they wouldn't come back the next morning but thought they would teach me a lesson by letting me do the work. I haven't kept house so many years to be scared by such a thing, so I went on as though nothing had happened. Pretty soon the servants from the other places began to come in and console with me about having to do the work. I told them that was a very small matter, that I was perfectly able to do my work. I also told them the servants couldn't come back until Mr. Price came home and said whether they could or not. This word was evidently carried to the sullen mutineers, for then the helper who had preached for us on Sunday came in to plead for them. I told him what a very serious thing it was for them all to go off and leave our property exposed to thieves and to leave us two women alone on the place with not a man to help us had we needed it. Finally, I relented and said they could come back but I should tell Mr. Price and he would be very displeased when he found out that they couldn't be trusted any better than that. So back they came and I acted as though nothing had happened and now Charlie is talking to them. I don't presume we were in any danger but it does give one an uncomfortable feeling to find mean-looking strangers in the house and no one else on the place.

Florence is a little mischief and keeps me jumping to keep track of her. I will find her paddling in the water with her clothes wet through to the skin, or in the cupboard or a hundred other things. She runs outdoors and that keeps me uneasy unless I can see or hear her every minute.

Miss Bird and I are going out to the fair after dinner to see if we can get anything curious or pretty. She expects to go home in '97. It is time to close now and I send love to you all.

....

September 10, 1895

Now Mother, I will tell you something if you will promise not to get too excited and not be too disappointed if the plan has to be changed in any way. We have asked permission to go home next year, and the mission has signed a resolution to that effect which goes to the Board for approval. Usually if the mission votes unanimously for anything it is as good as settled for the Board usually gives consent. But now, when the Board is so cramped for money, they may send us word that they can't afford it before our ten years are completed.

It will be a great disappointment to us if we cannot go but if the Board refuses permission we will just have to be patient and wait two more years. I was quite contented until we decided to ask permission and then I got so excited that for a few days I wanted to fly. It is mostly on Stewart's account that we feel the necessity of going earlier than the ten years. It is hard to live where the children are so shut away from everything helpful. If he were like many other boys, of a quiet disposition, it would be far easier for him and us as well. But a boy of his activity needs some outlet, and if it could be something useful it might make a great difference in his life. Here there is literally nothing for him to do after he gets his lessons. We don't want him with the Chinese, and there isn't any chance of his working at a trade, for the ways of working here are not worth much to a modern mind. While he was younger it was all right for him to play all the time, but now I feel that I must get him home, and it may be thought best for me to go with the children and leave Charlie here for a year longer. Anyway, I write you of the possibility. Our joy at seeing you all again will be mixed with sorrow at leaving the work and the people. I pray we are not being selfish.

We have been somewhat uneasy lately for there are such false reports being circulated about the war. Dr. Atwood's helper received a letter from a Chinaman near here and it is a good sample of what is going about. It is claimed that a secret order of soldiers, or some peculiar order rather, has entirely annihilated the Japanese. That Russia, England, and America, with other nations, came to help the Japs at Formosa, and that this band of "Black Flag" of China overcame them all and destroyed all their warships and put them all to shame. Of course, it is all a story to deceive the people and to incite them against us foreigners, and just how far it will go it is not possible now to know. The terrible murder of the English people near Foo Chow* may bring things to a crisis sooner than

---

*The massacre of ten missionaries at Ku-t'ien (near Foo Chow) on August 1, 1895, traumatized the mission effort in China. The attack was carried out by a vegetarian cult that may have viewed the Christians more as competition than as a pernicious foreign intrusion.

anything else. We wait now with some anxiety to know what England will do about it. If this dreadful deed is not followed up and the perpetrators beheaded, it will greatly lessen our chances to go on with our work here in safety. Our mission has sent a special request to Mr. Denby, the minister from the U.S., asking what we are to expect. It will be so long before we can hear that we will naturally be somewhat anxious. Chang Chi Tung, the governor of the southern part of the empire, is bitter against the foreigners and it is doubtless his fault that so many riots occur there. Li Hung Chang, the governor of the northern part of the empire, is friendly to the foreigners and it is due to this that we are as safe and quiet as we are. But with all the unsettled condition of things at present it is useless to say what will happen next. The Kingdom of God is to prevail over all this heathen idolatrous nation whether it come peacefully or by bloodshed. Christ came not to bring peace but the sword, for He could see that this was the only possible way to overcome the prince of this world. The devil is to make a mighty struggle against the work of the Holy Spirit in China, and we must be willing to go where duty calls even if it means suffering and danger if not death. Can we hope for the gospel to be established in the very stronghold of Satan and he leave anything undone to prevent it? The gospel has had to find its way into other places through the martyred bodies of many, why not in China? What does Revelations say about it? Rev. 6:8–11, also Ch. 7:13–17. God has not forgotten His children but He knows all they shall be called upon to suffer and all that must yet be suffered to accomplish the work to be done before every knee willingly bows and every voice willingly acknowledges Him Lord of all. We must trust Him to care for us and all the interests of the work. He that is for us is more than they who are against us.

But if I keep on this way you will think I am anxious to be a martyr. Well, I'm not. I wish the day of all such tribulations were over and the time had come for turning swords into plowshares.

School is begun again and we hope for a good winter's work. We hope we have a teacher now who will be a great help. He came in from the coast reaching here two days ago. He is a younger brother to my "Flying Dragon," the "boy" who came from the

va Jane Price, photographed in Oberlin,
hio, at about Christmas, 1885.

Charles Wesley Price, Oberlin, Ohio, 1887.

va Jane Price, Oberlin, Ohio, about 1889.

Stuart Leland Price, June 11, 1886, Oberlin, Ohio.

Donald Price, 1888.

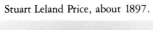

Stuart Leland Price, about 1897.

Florence Price, 1897.

Florence Price, 1897.

Eva Jane Price, Oberlin, Ohio, 1897.

Eva, Florence, and Charles in San Francisco before boarding the steamer to return to China, 1897.

George and Mary Alice Williams, China, about 1892. *(Oberlin College Archives)*

George and Mary Alice Williams, in their home in China, about 1892. *(Oberlin College Archives)*

The annual meeting of American missionaries, Tai 1893. *(Oberlin College Archiv*

Francis Davis (in Chinese dress) and Lydia Davis with baby William in Shansi, China, 1893. *(Oberlin College Archives)*

Francis, William, and Lydia Davis, Shansi, 1894. *(Oberlin College Archives)*

Rowena Bird in Chinese dress, about 1894. (*Oberlin College Archives*)

Mary L. Partridge and friend, about 1895. (*Oberlin College Archives*)

Mary L. Partridge and helper, dressed for travel, about 1898. (*Oberlin College Archives*)

A group of missionary children, 1893. *(Oberlin College Archives)*

Williams' house in the old
onary compound in Taiku,
1900. *(Oberlin College Ar-*

A meeting of American and English missionaries, 1898. *(Oberlin College Archives)*

The wedding of Ernest and Elizabeth Atwater, 1898. *(Oberlin College Archives)*

Dedication of the Memorial Arch, on which are listed the names of the Price family and other Oberlin missionaries who perished in the Boxer Rebellion. Dedication ceremony, 1903. *(Oberlin College Archives)*

coast over a year ago and has cooked for us since. We like his appearance very much. He has had about twelve years of training in the North China mission and some of the missionaries there are fine Chinese scholars, so we may hope he is well trained. Oh, it will mean a good deal to the work here if he is truly genuine and we somehow feel that he is, and that he can be just the one we need. His wife has not come in with him as he was not sure whether he would like it here or whether we would like him. She is a girl who spent some years in a Peking school and has unbound feet. I was quite disappointed that she did not come, for I want someone to help me work with the women and I don't like this fashion of the husbands leaving their homes for so long. It is quite the custom, however, in all business circles at least, for the man to go away and go into business, coming home every three or four years. I hope this teacher will prove good and reliable and that his wife will come soon.

Miss Bird left us for Taiku this morning having been here some ten weeks. She was looking much better when she went away than when she came and I trust the rest has fitted her for a successful winter's work. I knew her mother in Oberlin and I became sort of her Chinese mother. It has been a large share of my mission here to take in the workers for a little rest and it has done me more good than I have been able to give them. Just think what a flattering testimony came to me from Scotland by last mail. Mr. Russell, who has been with us several times and who is now at home for a much needed rest, writes in this kind way, "I am so glad you have been keeping open house and that some weary workers in the Master's vineyard have been refreshed through their stay with you. I think that it is a sphere which you fill exceedingly well. And while I should be sorry to see you out of Shansi, yet I cannot shut my eyes to this, that you would fill a more important and a larger sphere with equal love and sympathy." He doesn't know that I've received more than I gave and that we've entertained "angels unawares." It has been a blessed privilege to meet so many friends from so many countries and have them as guests in our home for a time. Most of them will likely never be able to come again. Many of the Scandinavian friends are gone into Shensi, a long journey from here, and some have died. Others have gone to their native land or moved elsewhere so far away that I can't hope to have them here again, especially if we go home next year.

We spent ten days in the valley during the past two weeks and had a fine time clambering over hills and eating meals in the open air. Florence enjoyed it and you may be sure Stewart improved the time with the water to play in. But we all enjoyed it and it did us good.

Now I must close with love to you all.

Yours lovingly,
Eva

....

Fen Cho fu, China
September 14, 1895

Dear Grandpa and Grandma,

I think my mother told you we were going home in a year. It will be hard to leave my horse Dandy and my dog Kippy but the going home will be enough joy. Florence is very cute and playful and is beginning to talk and sing. My father has a school. The other day he helped me build a playhouse for Florence and me to play in and we have lots of fun in it. I have a nice playmate in Edward, Dr. Atwood's boy. He is eight years old. I have a nice lot of little chicks, ten altogether, eleven counting the old hen. I just wish you could come and see us. Florence has a nice playmate in May, Dr. Atwood's little girl. She is three and a half years old. I look to the coming of going home as the coming of seeing Grandpa's workshop and learning to use tools. I have a copy book No. 3 I am almost through with, then I will send it to you, Grandma. I am in a fifth eclectic reader revised edition. Also in school geography No. 3 and a young folks physiology.

Yours truly,
Stewart L. Price

....

Jen Tsun, China
October 22, 1895

Dear Home Folks,

I have come several days' journey to Jen Tsun to visit Mr. and Mrs. Thompson before they leave next Tuesday for the homeland and am staying over to meet the Clapps, who are expected back here next week. I do wish she could have come to see you while they were in America. I left Charlie and Stewart to keep house while Florence and I ran away. I brought our gatekeeper along for an escort. He is over fifty years old and this is the first time he has ever been away from home, this far at least, and this is only about seventy miles. We came in a big *peng* cart with a carter, two mules, and a horse. You would smile to see the rig, but it is the most comfortable way I can travel. These carts are quite comfortable if one has plenty of pillows and mattresses though they do go slowly. It seems ridiculous to take a big cart, three animals, and two men and spend two days to go a journey of that distance, but that is the way things move in China.

We are all well or were when I left home last week. It will probably be two weeks more before I go back. I am going a day's journey tomorrow to Tai Yuen fu, the capital city of the province, to spend two days with Elsa Lundgren, the Swedish sister who was with us last winter. I have never been in that direction so will enjoy it.

This letter is rather short but with so much trouble in China I feel you would rather have a short letter than none at all. In answer to your questions, no, we have no protection at all here. We are at the mercy of the Chinese so far as any help from our country goes, excepting the protection of all treaties. As the treaties are often violated, we have grown to feel that to put our confidence in "princes" is of not much avail. The murder of those English subjects makes us feel how useless such things may be. If China were a truly civilized nation we could depend more fully on her stability. I will admit to being more uneasy over these recent outrages than most anything that has happened since we have been here. However, we have no special reason at this time in this province to be alarmed.

I look forward with much pleasure to the time when we can be home again. We hope to find all of you well and happy. Won't it be fine? It makes my heart beat to be here and see the friends getting ready to go away next week. It is quite exciting.

With much love to you all from your affectionate daughter,

Eva

....

Fen Cho fu, China
November 5, 1895

Dear Grandma and Grandpa,

I wrote a lettre to you saying I would send a copy book to you so here it is. I hope I have not made menney mistakes in it, it is old and smeared but I hope it will receive honor to its age. My chicks were killed by a rat all of them. I was sorrey but could not help it so they had to go without leave from me. Mamma has gone to Taiku we expect her back soon. My papa is writing a lettre to Aunt Jane his sister. A week ago we had a snowstorm. Edward came over today and we had a fine time. The boxes came the other day and in them were to nice dolls for Florence and a teaset for her. I have a nice big calf. I have named her Floss. She is a nice calf. It is a small family we have now—only papa and I to keep house and it is hard work for papa who has the school boys in the morning and me in the afternoon so it is hard work for him. We are sometimes asked over to dinner or supper at the Atwoods or Atwatters to eat so we are not lonesome as we would be if they did not ask us.

Yours truly,
Stewart L. Price

....

Fen Cho fu, China
November 19, 1895

Dear Home Folks,

It was such a treat to go off on a trip to see Mr. and Mrs. Thompson, who were about to start for the coast on their homeward journey. It is over two days' journey from here, but what of that? I had to jolt all the way in a big cart and my back had been aching dreadfully for nearly two months, but what of that? Charlie went on his horse a day's journey, stayed overnight with us at the inn, and then came back while we went on. Stewart stayed at home so Florence and I had the big cart all to ourselves with plenty of mattresses and pillows to make it comfortable, and I just enjoyed being out in the fields. The cart jogged along, the weather was fine, roads fairly good (leaving out the ruts), and I just rested with a hard pillow at the small of my back. I have grown to like traveling in China, strange as it may seem. What's the use of being in such a rush to get to a place that we can't take time to enjoy the journey? Rushing off at lightning speed as you folks do spoils the whole thing. You can't have a look at the trees, or the tangle by the roadside, or study cloud effects or outlines of hills; nor can you get off and walk a bit, and then have the comfort of being nearly alone with the big world outside. The friends in Tai Yuen are all English excepting little Elsa and her husband, who are naturalized Americans from Denmark and Sweden. I had as good a time as possible where friends were so many and my time limited. While I was away we had a regular "squaw winter" and one day I rode over the plains with every leaf, twig, branch, and bush weighted down with snow that had come suddenly upon us and found the trees still in full green leaf. The effect was beautiful. I had taken along blankets and warm wraps so did not suffer any from cold. I have never seen so much snow before in October.

My cook had been away several weeks, as he had gone back to Shan Tung after his brother's wife, and he came into Taiku while I was there so we came home together. Mr. and Mrs. Clapp came at the same time so I saw them before coming away and they looked so natural that it was hard to realize they had been away to America since I saw them last. Mrs. Clapp regretted not seeing you but I can realize how much she had to do and how many friends of her own to visit. She said in many ways it was harder to come back to China than it was the first time. It was harder for one thing to leave the beauty of the homeland and come back to dreary China. Nothing but love for the work would induce us to come back. However, I have grown to love the outdoors here but maybe when we get home we will wonder how we could have thought this plain beautiful. It is beautiful though with the mountains on either side and trees scattered all over, with the many fields fresh and green in spring and summer. But just now it looks barren and brown excepting the green fields of winter wheat. There was quite a procession of us coming home as the cook had not only brought his brother's wife with him that long journey but his own wife and four children as well, because when he reached his home he found the whole family sick with ague and the house surrounded by water. So he bundled up the whole lot and we hope it will be good for the work to have them here. We like the new teacher and his wife very much. She is twenty-four years old, has unbound feet, reads very well, sings sweetly, and being somewhat educated and a Christian I trust she will be of much use to the work.

We are invited out to Thanksgiving dinner, so you see we are not quite out of this world. With very much love to you all.

Your affectionate daughter,

Eva

....

December 17, 1895

There must be a little letter, at least, sent from us at this Christmas time which is so near at hand. We are planning to give a feast for the schoolboys, servants, and a few outsiders. We have some toys to give the schoolboys as we sent to Boston for $5 worth and they sent marbles, horns, Jack-in-the-Box, animals that squeak, and other things. I hope they will enjoy them. They always enjoy the feast and the big bag of candy, nuts, popcorn, and fruits we give each of them.

Christmas always comes before I am ready for it and I still have sewing to do, and mittens to crochet for the teacher and his wife. The days just seem to fly and night comes and finds very little done. I am to have the tailor come in a few days to fix some Chinese garments and do other sewing. The teacher's wife does nice work and has made Charlie some Chinese socks but her eyes are not good so I am afraid to give her much work. I like her very much and she takes hold of the gospel work very well. Last Sunday the room was packed full for Chinese service and I was the only white body there. The teacher preached from Luke 19:10 and I believe it is "The Son of Man is come to seek and to save them that are lost." He has been well trained and preaches very earnestly, and is teaching the boys to sing so they can sing independently. Several of them started and carried through "Watchman Tell Us of the Night" last Sunday and did it well (in Chinese of course).

Stewart can scarcely wait for Christmas to come. I have a drum and sticks, a stone paperweight, a microscope, and candy for him. There was a big doll for Florence, but I didn't know she could open the bureau drawer so easily and one day she came walking out in the sitting room carrying her baby, tickled most to pieces. I found another place for it the other day and I expect she wonders what has become of it. I have a tea set for her also which she has not seen.

I gave Stewart a little tea party the other day and invited the other foreign children, Ernestine and Mary Atwater, Mabel and Edward Atwood, Florence and Stewart. They looked very cute at the table eating their ice cream, cake, and candy.

The prospect of our coming home this year is not very bright now, though we may hear more about it soon. But at the most the Secretary only expects us to stay two or three years longer and they will soon pass, won't they? We'll get there some day if all goes well and will make up for lost time.

I will close with much love and a "Merry Christmas" to you all.

....

Fen Cho fu, China
December 17, 1895

Dear Grandpa and Grandma,

I wrote to you last in November but this is Dec. and near Christmas too only 8 more days. My papa's birthday comes 3 days after, then New Years, 5 days after my Birthday, and in March Florence Birthday too. By the way how do you like the copy book

I sent you. My mother remarked that it was heavy. So it was but that dont matter, it is all the better. I will tell you why, because I want to send you lots of love so the larger the package the more love I can get into it. I hope that next year I will spend my Birthday and Christmas with you in the home place. Now last but not least I would have you send my love to the friends at home and hoping you are well I close with love.

Stewart L. Price

....

Fen Cho fu, China
March 11, 1896

Dear Father and Mother,

Stewart is very sick—has Bright's disease* in its worst form. The doctors say we must get him home as the only hope of prolonging his life. He is very weak and may not be able to stand the trip to the coast. But as it is our only hope of keeping him with us for a few years longer we must take the risk. If all goes well, we will be well on our way to America when this reaches you. But we shall travel slowly and be obliged to make numerous stops. We will write you again at Tientsin.

Eva is so busy and is feeling so badly she has asked me to write you a few words about the matter. Perhaps we can both write more fully next time. You will understand why I do not write more at this time. One year ago Stewart looked so rugged we had no thought of such a thing coming to him. Now he seems to have lost all his life and activity and is so very poor one would scarcely recognize him. It is very hard to think of his never being well again but we must all bow to the will of our Heavenly Father. "He doeth all things well."

With much love to you both and all the friends.

Sincerely your son,
C. W. Price

*Chronic kidney disease.

....

Tientsin, China
April 13, 1896

Dear Loved Ones,

I will send you a line from here hoping it will reach you before we do. Stewart is very much better than when Charlie wrote and we are all far happier and more encouraged. We hope the journey home will help him and that being able to diet him will cure him. We begin to hope now that he will be well again some day, but for weeks we had no such hope. He has been growing stronger since we left home so that the friends along the way are surprised at his looking so well.

It has been a very sad getting ready to go home for us and sad to leave the work and friends, not knowing when we can come back.* But it has been taken out of our hands. We are to go to Shanghai starting day after tomorrow and will be off for the States as soon after as we can arrange about tickets, etc. The past week has been busy as we are getting into new clothes, which is no small matter after living inland for so long. We will likely go to San Francisco first and consult some physician there as to what to do and where to go, and if they think we should stay in California it may be that we will not go farther for some time. If the doctors advise us to go to any special place it may be some time before we see you after all, but you know how glad we will be to see you all again. We will get our "best foot foremost" by the time we see you so you will not know how blue we have been.

Your affectionate daughter,
Eva

....

*Eva had wanted to leave China, but she must have felt that their work was cut off too abruptly. The Prices left for the United States, expecting to return to China if Stewart's health permitted.

S.S. *Belgic*
May 19, 1896

Dear Home Folks,

Here we are nearing our own land and loved ones once more. If nothing happens we will reach San Francisco tomorrow so I will have these few lines ready to send on by the first mail. It will reach you maybe a few days before we do. I can scarcely wait now that we are so near—compared with being in China. We are getting tired of traveling and living in trunks, having been on the way since the sixteenth of March. We have no definite plan as yet but think we will leave San Francisco on Thursday. Charlie thinks he will take Stewart to Clifton Springs in New York as soon as possible where he can have special care and diet.

We haven't had a very pleasant trip over as it has been so cold. Not a single bright warm day since we left Japan, and we've all but frozen besides being dreadfully seasick. It will be so good to get on land again and get to Mother's where we can get something good to eat! Deliver me from steamer and hotel cooking. A piece of good corn bread and a glass of buttermilk would taste better than all these flip-flaps.

Florence has been so good and everybody makes a great fuss over her, so it will be no wonder if she is spoiled. She says she is going to Gramma's and get a cookie to put in her pocket. We'll soon be there if all goes well and will talk instead of trying to write on board the steamboat. Just think! Almost seven years since we left! Kiss Pa on the tip of his nose for me.

With much love to you all.

Affectionately,
Eva

....

San Francisco, California
May 21, 1896

Dear Family,

We were so tired when we reached the hotel here and had a washing to have done, so decided to rest over Sunday before starting on the R. R. journey. If nothing happens we plan to leave Monday at 6:00 P.M. It is such a rest to be off of the heaving water though we are still dizzy from the voyage. It was a tedious job getting our things through the customs and nearly all of yesterday afternoon was spent in having our trunks ransacked and tumbled up, and it is provoking business to have your nicely folded and packed clothes tumbled topsy-turvy. But we are through now with all that kind of business if it did cost us $7.50 to get our things through. We have great reason to be very, very thankful that no accident or harm has come to us in any way all these weeks of travel by land and sea and in all sorts of vehicles.

We are all feeling very well now that we are on land again. Stewart has stood the journey very well. He was very low and weak when Charlie first wrote about him and we did not think he would live until we got to the coast, but we feel far more hopeful about him now.

We are all enjoying the fruit here, the cherries and strawberries especially, as we have not tasted any all these years. Yesterday was a beautiful day for us to come ashore and we stood around in the sunshine like ducks after a rain, but today again it has been dark and rainy until we begin to think we left all the sunshine behind us in sunny Shansi.

I will try and send a line sometime later but it will not be many days before you will have us all down on you, so brace up!

With much love,
Eva

....

Distraught over Stewart's illness, Charles and Eva retraced their steps all the long weary way back to America, a return trip they had hoped to make in the not too distant future with such joy.

Back home, their hopes were alternately raised and dashed as Stewart was treated in Lincoln, Nebraska, and Des Moines, Iowa, and although Eva had heretofore mocked the notions of faith healing espoused by some of her China colleagues, Stewart's condition led the Prices to seek the services of a Chicago faith healing institute. After that, they returned to Oberlin,

Ohio, where Professor Churchill urged them to use "tissue remedies." They even pondered a return to China the following year so Stewart could be treated at a health resort for foreigners at the seashore at Chee-fu.

....

While Charles states that Stewart has "Bright's disease," a rather vague catchall for kidney disease, at least one physician diagnosed the disease as diabetes. This latter diagnosis seems the more likely.—R.F.

....

Stewart Leland Price
November 5, 1884–February 7, 1897

Rev. 21:4 And He will wipe away all tears
from their eyes; and there shall be no more
death, neither sorrow, nor crying, neither shall
there be any more pain: for the former things
are passed away.

Oberlin, Ohio
February 10, 1897

Dear Loved Ones,

God is comforting our hearts as no other power could, but the burden of sorrow is heavy. If you could have been here and could have seen the sweet face as it was, free from his great affliction, you would have felt with us "it is far better—he is eternally well, safe, and happy now." The mystery of God's will in thus taking our children from us will not be revealed to us here but we shall know hereafter. Oh! Those words Dr. Brand chose for our comfort: "He shall never hunger, nor thirst. David perceived that the child was dead, therefore David said unto his servants, Is the child dead? And they said, He is dead.

"Then David arose from the earth and washed, and anointed himself, and changed his apparel, and came into the house of the Lord, and worshipped, then he came to his house; when he required, they set bread before him and he did eat.

"Then said his servants unto him, What thing is this that thou hast done? Thou didst fast and weep for the child while it was alive; but when the child was dead thou didst rise and eat bread.

"And he said, while the child was alive I fasted and wept; for I said, Who can tell whether God will be gracious to me, that the child may live? But now he is dead, wherefore should I fast? Can I bring him back again? I shall go to him but he shall not return to me."

Mark 10:13–16. "And they brought young children to him, that he should touch them: and his disciples rebuked those that brought them.

"But when Jesus saw it, he was much displeased and said unto them, Suffer the little children to come unto me, and forbid them not; for of such is the kingdom of God."

Rev. 7:16–17. "They shall hunger no more, neither thirst nay more; neither shall the sun light on them, nor any heat. For the Lamb which is in the midst of the throne shall feed them and shall lead them unto living fountains of waters; and God shall wipe away all tears from their eyes and there shall be no more death, neither sorrow, nor crying, neither shall there be any more pain; for the former things are passed away."

Our hearts go back to you all, knowing your love and comfort that you share with us. We must be brave and strong in His strength. Stewart loved you all, and I am glad we were with you for even the short time we were. Now, as our loved ones gather over on the other shore, one by one, it makes us look forward with joy to when this warfare and pain, mystery and disappointment will all be over.

Your loving daughter,
Eva

PART FOUR
Return to China
MAY 1897–DECEMBER 1899

Oberlin, Ohio
May 7, 1897

Dear Home Folks,

The days are flying by and we will soon be on our way back to China. We must all be brave and put our best foot foremost. We are enjoying the springtime and trying to get all ten years we are to be away in these few weeks. We went to the woods yesterday, the first time in eight years that we have been in the woods, and Florence enjoyed picking the flowers and getting moss. We came back by the cemetery where Stewart's body is—the first time I have been there since the service. It is a beautiful spot.

Mr. Thompson of our mission, who is now with Mrs. Thompson and baby in Wisconsin, has resigned from the mission, but we hope our letters and the one from Secretary Smith will cause him to reconsider his decision.

It begins to seem more real that we are actually leaving our dear ones and our land with all its privileges.

Love to everyone,
Eva

....

Why the Prices decided to leave their beloved family, friends, and country and return to China can only be understood by others so wholly dedicated to commitment and sacrifice. Had Stewart not become ill, the family probably would have returned home in 1897 and remained in the States for his schooling. Now that he was gone, there was no compelling family reason to stay. To remain close to loved ones at home would have seemed to the Prices to be selfish. Their work in China was unfinished. They had no choice but to return.

Eva found it hard to be reconciled to the thought of two homes, one in America and one in China, with an ocean rolling between, but like moths drawn to a flame, their destiny was inextricably interwoven with the plight of the people of Shansi.

So they again turned their faces to the West and the long arduous journey ahead. Like a fly entombed in amber, they thereby sealed their fate.
—R.F.

....

San Francisco, California
September 1, 1897
Dear Home Folks,

Well, there is but one more day of happiness before us. To-morrow we go aboard our sea home and will be miserable I expect for the next month. We have three remedies which sympathizing friends have given—chew gum, wear a fish skin next to the stomach, and lastly, Antipyrine. We went on board the *Coptic* yesterday just to take a look at our place of misery.

We have to go to a missionary meeting this afternoon so I must not write more now. I shall think of you all every day. My mind will often go back to "Cro' nest" where we left the home of Pa and Ma.

With much love from Eva

....

San Francisco, California
September 2, 1897
Dear Father and Mother,

I want to send you a few lines to say good-bye before going aboard ship. We have had a very pleasant stay here and are feeling quite well and ready to face the torture of a sea voyage. Already I can feel it coming on.

I wish we had more time so as to write a long letter but we have been very busy since coming here and have only a few more minutes. I shall write at the first opportunity and of course Eva will keep you posted about our movements and general condition. When our ten years are up we will have another jolly go-round. I must close with very much love to you all.

Sincerely, your son,
C. W. Price

....

San Francisco, California
September 2, 1897

Dear Home Folks,

The day has come and almost the hour for us to go on board the *Coptic* and be carried off and away from you all. Our trunks have been taken and just a little breathing spell remains in which to send a last message of love to you all. There is a kind of aching somewhere—I can't just locate it—and the waterworks begin to squeak as if they had a mind to set to work.

My heart aches at leaving you all and the homeland more than it did eight years ago. My capacity for loving has enlarged in all the discipline of sorrow we have had and I love you all more perfectly than ever before. May we all live more fully for the "other home" where we will not have to say good-bye.

With much love to you all,
Eva

....

On Board the *Coptic*
September 3, 1897

Dear Home Folks,

Well here I am, just as I expected—sick, sick, sick. The horrible grinding, screwing motion as I came down to the cabin last night to wash Florence upset me and took away all my brave resolve not to be sick this time. So all day today I have been here in my

OCCIDENTAL & ORIENTAL STEAMSHIP CO.

List of Passengers sailing from San Francisco, September 2, 1897, per S. S. "COPTIC," Voyage 22.

COMMANDER . . . . INMAN SEALBY, LIEUT. R. N. R.

CHIEF OFFICER . . . FRANK HART   CHIEF ENGINEER . . . . R. GORE

PURSER . . . . . . C. L. GOODRICH   SURGEON . . . . . .J. MOLONY, M. D.

For HONOLULU.

Mr. O. St. John Gilbert	Mrs. Chas. Hoadley
Mrs. F. C. Smith	Miss A. P. Appleton
Miss L. S. Watson	Mr. B. F. Vickers
Judge A. W. Carter	

For YOKOHAMA.

Miss Randall	Mr. Paul Jordan
Mrs. Chas. McCreary	Miss M. C. Clark
Miss Martha Aldritch	Mr. Uboldi
Mr. Parravicini	Miss Etta Birdsall
Miss Mabel Cluness	O. D. Richardson

For KOBE.

Rev. C. A. Clark	Rev. S. L. Gulick
Mrs. C. A. Clark	Mrs. S. L. Gulick
Mr. Admont Clark	Miss Sue Gulick
Mr. Edward Clark	Mr Luther Gulick
Mr. Grover Clark	Mr. Leeds Gulick
Miss Louisa Clark	Miss E. Wainwright
Mr. Wm. H. Gill	

For NAGASAKI.

Dr. R. I. Bowie	Miss Anna K. Stryker

For SHANGHAI.

Mr. A. C. Hunter	Mr. D. Nesbit
Mrs. A. C. Hunter	Dr. O. T. Logan
Rev. C. W. Price	Mrs. O. T. Logan
Mrs. C. W. Price and Child	Rev. J. B. Thompson

For HONGKONG.

Mr. Chas. N. Niblett	Miss Irene Fuller
Mr. Theophil Wyss	Mr. Hugh Taylor, Sr.
Mrs. J. H. Ransom	Rev. Hugh Taylor
Mr. William B. Jones	Mrs. Hugh Taylor
Mrs. J. H. Thorndike	Miss Ella Taylor
Miss S. F. Richardson	Miss Martha Taylor
Mr. Thomas Halstead	Miss Isabella Taylor
Mrs. M. L. Halstead	Miss Isabel Griffin
Mr. Robert Clark	Miss Grace H. Webb
Mr. Bruno Mencke	Miss Harriet Miller
Miss Willma Ross	Miss Jane Hall

From HONOLULU to YOKOHAMA.

Mr. A. Emanuel	Mr. W. H. Hamilton
Rev. J. G. Jackson	Miss Margaret Scott
Mrs. J. G. Jackson	Miss Georgiana Bancus
Dr. T. J. Edwards	Miss Emma E. Dickinson
Mr. H. T. Edwards	

berth. Charlie has been here too, much of the time, and Florence joined in on the chorus of upheaval once. Since then she has played about very comfortably. The report says we have made 311 miles in 22 hours.

Saturday, September 4

Here we are about 700 miles from land, 355 miles since yesterday noon. I am sitting up on deck in my chair wrapped in my new steamer rug and can look away off on the bluest of all blue waters. When you get a tub of rinsing water too blue then you can imagine something of how the ocean is now. Nearly everyone is better now and able to be on deck. I haven't been brave enough to go down into the dining room for meals but if it stays as calm as it is now I shall try it. The stewardess has brought me something on a tray for breakfast and dinner. Charlie is more comfortable and Florence quite like herself.

The first day out was really cold but today is much warmer. There is quite a number of missionaries on board and if we all get to feeling well we can have a pleasant time. We saw whales a few hours out from San Francisco blowing the spray till it looked like fountains.

The last three days have been somewhat monotonous with one exception. Yesterday afternoon we had the pleasure of passing the *Gaelie,* a steamboat bound for San Francisco. She passed very near to us—it seemed almost as though we could have thrown a stone on her deck but then there was no stone and she was farther off than she appeared, no doubt. If only they could have stopped so we could have sent a letter back by her! We are expecting to land at Honolulu tomorrow and will leave this letter to go back on the first boat but that will be over a week. So far we have had a very smooth trip; this old *Coptic* runs as level as a boat-car it seems to me.

It was five o'clock when I came up on deck this morning. There have been squalls the past two days and this morning the showers were chasing each other on the water and we got a drenching too. The awnings kept the actual rain off, but the deck was soon sopping wet with the mist. I sat curled up in our chair, well wrapped in my

rug and big cape, and enjoyed it so much. I had the rainy side of
the ship to myself as the others chose the dry side. This was very
early and since then the weather has cleared. There were rainbows
this morning and you know the old saying! It is delicious now on
deck and yesterday I imagined I smelled new mown hay—think of
it, away out here how many hundreds of miles from land? I will
copy my report of the miles as they are posted up each day. We left
on Thursday, 2:00 P.M. At noon Friday the report was 311 miles,
Saturday 353, Sunday 354, Monday 347, Tuesday 354, Wednesday
(today) 367; to Honolulu from S.F. 2,086.

Wednesday morning

By looking very closely now we can see the island of Malachi*
or Leper Island way off at our left. It gives one a queer sensation
to know that after rushing and swishing through miles and miles of
water we are again nearing land. Yesterday and today so far have
been fine. The sea is truly beautifully blue and if one isn't seasick
we can get up quite a lot of sentiment just seeing the white-capped
waves sparkling in the sunshine. The so-different blue of the sky
with fleecy clouds and the pure air make one understand how poets
and painters can rave over marine life. However, I have never seen
a painting yet which comes anywhere near this color of the deep
blue sea! Perhaps it remains for me to become famous in an attempt
in that direction. There are some sixty-seven first-class passengers
on board, some of whom leave us at Honolulu today. One sees all
sorts on such a trip as this. There are two "painted beauties" on
board bound for Shanghai, I hear. Poor girls!

Well, this must be the last page of my letter. One is too excited
as we near port to write coherently. The faces of the passengers are
taking on a shorter, wider appearance as they come about "viewing
the landscape o'er" though there is still a deal of "water scape"
lying between. We expect to go ashore and spend the night with
the Leadinghams. It will be good to walk on dry land again. Say
what you may, when there are but a few planks between you and

---

*Molokai. Eva apparently did not know that the island was spelled differently than
the biblical name, as they are pronounced the same (Book of Malachi—last book
of the Old Testament).

the briny deep for weeks, it gets monotonous. But it is fine to get into a big tub of salt water the first thing every morning. We have been more comfortable on this six-day trip than ever before.

With very much love to you all, everyone.

Affectionately,

Eva

....

Steamship *Coptic*

September 14, 1897

Yesterday was Sunday, September twelfth, today is Tuesday the fourteenth. Where has Monday the thirteenth gone? Dropped off our calendar and we have really lost a whole day unless we come back this way and pick it up. When we come to this longitude on the Pacific, off goes a day—going west. Adding a day going east brings us all straight with the outside world.

We went ashore at Honolulu and the ship came into the wharf. Last time we had to be taken ashore in a little boat to say nothing of the skill it required to go down the stairs by the side of the ship and step off into the dancing unsteady craft, and it was expensive—a whole dollar I believe. And there was Mr. Leadingham to greet us and we felt very important too when we went ashore to have a carriage there waiting to carry us up on the lower slope of "Punch Bowl" to their hospitable home. What a beautiful, beautiful view they have from their piazza of the wonderful coloring that comes of the different depths of water, shading from the intense blue off to paler, paler, until green seems to be made prominent, with pale sea-foam green breakers capped with white over the coral reefs, and backgrounded by mountain and valley, sky and clouds! I told Mrs. Leadingham she ought to be a better Christian from having this always to look out upon. It is an expensive place to live though, so there is no rose without its thorn.

We called on the Bowens, saw Percy Pond, called on the Binghams (children of the first missionaries to these islands), and I sat in the rocking chair of historic fame—the first one ever seen on the Hawaiian Islands! It was handmade but what of that? Had not Mrs. Bingham rocked all her babies in it? And did she not die in it? And is it not now a sacred thing to these her children?

We had a pleasant drive along some of the pretty streets and saw the part of the palace in which the late queen was imprisoned. Then it was time to go to the boat again and to say a good-bye to our friends. We thought our "good-byes" were pretty well over when we left Des Moines, but they keep stringing along all the way across the Pacific! Even when we get to Tientsin we will have to leave old Oberlin friends, and what is more, will be turning our faces away from you all and placing weeks of time between us as we go on over the mountains away from steamboats and railways. But then, "where duty calls or danger" and then who knows—there may be railroads into Shansi within a short time.

And now here we are ploughing our way through the vast Pacific at the rate of 366 miles the past twenty-four hours, which is the best run we have made yet. If nothing prevents we shall be in Yokohama by Sunday night. It has been rougher the past few days and in consequence Charlie has not felt well while I have dumped about and put in most of the time reading (there is a good library on board) and sleeping. I took a fine bunch of grapes to Charlie yesterday and today some good tart apples helped us out. I wish I could remember just what the chief engineer, who sits at our table, has told us of the capacity of this old *Coptic*—eighty tons of coal a day to keep up steam and hurry us along! We will take on coal again in Nagasaka [sic], Japan, for the run to Hong Kong and back to Nagasaka where they will recoal again for the run back to San Francisco. Most of the freight are barrels of nails for the ports in Japan.

....

Sunday

Well, we are less than 200 miles from Yokohama now. We had a good helpful service this morning led by the Episcopal clergyman, Mr. Jackson, who came on from Honolulu. The sea is unstable today and some of us do not feel remarkably bright, but we have come all the way from San Francisco across this wide heaving sea and have not had the guards on the tables once to keep things from skidding off. Yesterday we saw a large school of porpoises (there must have been hundreds) leaping their way along through and over the waves. It was quite a break in the monotony. A few flying fish, one or two gulls, and a passing ship make up the "outside world." Florence is very little trouble as she has some little playmates on board. We shall likely reach Cape King in the night but shall hardly get in port before early morning. We have to get washing done and I shall try and buy a few little things for some of the home friends. Our letters will be sent on and by the time you get them we shall be across the water.

....

Tientsin, China
October 9, 1897

Dear Father and Mother,

Eva probably will not be able to write this time as she has been quite sick, but she is improving very fast and we hope she will soon be as well as ever. While in Yokohama she was taken very sick with what the ship surgeon said was fish poisoning caused by eating fish that had not kept as well as it might. They buy fish for the entire voyage at San Francisco and keep it on ice and the result is the passengers are in constant danger from eating it.

We were one week from Yokohama to Shanghai and she was very sick all the way and was scarcely able to ride to our stopping place in the ricksha. The house was so poorly kept and being on a public street the noise was so continuous we left for Tientsin sooner than we otherwise would and before Eva was really able to travel. The four days to this place were very rough and the forty-mile car ride over a very rough road taken with it was almost too much for her and she has not been out of her bed much since our arrival. We have a very good physician, Dr. Smith of England, and he says she will be all right in a few days. I write thus fully because I am sure you will wish to know all about it. You will not feel uneasy about the matter for there is now no danger at all. On our next voyage we will fight shy of fish!

We expect to be able to take up our journey for Fen Cho fu

in about one week. We are a little anxious to start for it is growing late and we will probably meet with cold weather in the mountains, but we shall not think of starting till Eva is entirely well. We have a comfortable place to stay and except for what is keeping us here would enjoy it very much. In Yokohama we bought a few of those picture rolls you admired so much and about a week ago sent some home to you and several other relatives and friends. I trust they will reach you in good condition but am a little fearful as the Chinese postal system is not very reliable and the road is long.

Florence is feeling very well and is having a good time. The one desire of her heart now seems to be that we should buy her a "baby puppy." We have sent out to see if we can get one. I expect we will spoil her giving her so many things, but she will have very little to amuse herself with when we get to Fen Cho fu.

Mr. Thompson, who has been with us since we left San Francisco, will not wait longer for us as it is uncertain when we will be able to start, but will be on his way next Monday. We are sorry we are not to be with him and he seems to be reluctant to start out alone. It is a tiresome trip at best and for one to take it alone would be much more so.

It may be that Eva will be able to write so her letter will go on the same steamer with this, but I will urge her not to attempt it until she is entirely well. We are very glad to be able to write so favorably of her condition. Surely the Lord has been very good to us. It seems a long time since we saw or heard from you but we are fairly started on our ten years of waiting. We pray the good kind Father to bless and keep you.

Ever your son,
C. W. Price

....

Tientsin, China
October 13, 1897

Dear Mother, Father, and every chick and child of you all,

To cheer myself I've been rereading all the kind words we received from you while at the hotel in San Francisco, and it makes me homesick and I want to see you all so much. I love that little "cottage on the hill" and the folks who belong there. I will promise you now, if you will all live till I get back, I will stay somewhere in the region of Father and Mother as long as they live. I'm just a little homesick thinking of the woods, which must be looking beautiful now, and of the old cat and kittens and those who go in and out of the little brown cottage.

The doctor says if I keep on improving that we may start for the interior next Monday, so Charlie is rushing around making arrangements for the journey. The weather is delightful now, clear, bright, and bracing, and we begin to want to move on.

We will long remember the pleasant drive "Old Billy" took us, and a thousand and one pleasant things—the goldenrod on the road to Granger and all those good days and times we had together. I hope there will not be too much difference between heaven and earth for we do love some of these things so much.

I was keeping track of the distance we were coming up to the time we reached Yokohama and I planned to write up the Inland Sea and our going ashore at the different ports. But as I was doubled up in my berth all that time with fish poison, you will just have to imagine it for not a glimpse of the Inland Sea did I have. It was a great disappointment to say the least. I might enlarge too on getting ashore at Shanghai, the journey up the China coast just after a typhoon had stirred up the waters, the getting ashore at Taiku, and the fearful jolting the thirty miles of rough railroad gave me, but it is all over now and I am about well and all things begin to brighten and say "Cheer up."

The enclosed letter (with translation) we received from our Chinese teacher who is glad to welcome us back.

Affectionately,
Eva

....

Mr. and Mrs. Price,

Peace to both. I am at Li Man Chuang* in the hospital, and everyone is at peace. Every day I preach to the men and tell them

*Li Man and Li Man Chuang are the same place. Chuang simply means "village."

they ought to repent and believe Jesus, leave darkness and turn to the light—leave the false and turn to the truth—be upright, true men, and trust the Savior for all things and be what will please the Heavenly Father. Ch'iao Ko Ling is in the hospital where he gives the men medicine and also gives the needle to the opium patients. He teaches the men that Jesus is the Son of God and who came to the earth to save men and gave His own life for our souls.

We truly want to meet you if you are willing and can tell us what place we can see you by writing very early if you please. No matter what place we will be there to meet you. We will be very, very glad to see our good friends—more glad than to receive gold or silver. May the Lord constantly be with you. Amen.

Mr. Liu

....

In an inn 25 miles from
Huai-Lu (why-loo)
Chihli province, China
October 31, 1897

My dear Home Folks,

We are likely to meet the coast-going courier any day and I want to have at least a short letter to send on by him. We may miss him entirely here in the mountains but I would not like to meet him and have no word ready to send back. We are anxiously hoping the incoming courier will overtake us for it will be such joy if he has letters from home for us.

We are creeping along on our journey and will soon be dating our letters from the old place. We left Paoting fu last Tuesday, October 26, and had level plains for the first three and one half days, and yesterday morning began the climb over the mountains which lie between our province and the coast provinces. It is bad enough to cross mountains by rail, but to climb, crawl, slip, tumble, and jerk over them hung between two mules is an experience I assure you. I never get over being nervous in a litter. Four times a day do I sit in terror (and on an inclined seat) while the men, four of them, puff, pull, and tug to get me up and the thing teeters and totters, quivers, quavers, jostles, and jerks the whole day through. Do you wonder we get seasick? I think of you so many times and wonder what you would think if you could see us. Then, when one of the mules falls flat, which lets the whole affair come tumbling as Charlie's front mule did last evening, you will not blame me for having my heart in my mouth when climbing up and up over the dreadfully slippery rocks worn smooth by constant travel. Strangely enough the mules seem to fall even on level roads. Some of these mountain places are very dangerous. What are called the four "Heavenly Gates" are dreaded, as the ascents over the passes and the descents on the other side are paved with huge flat stones worn smooth as glass in places and the way is very steep. It would mean a roll if our vehicle were to tumble here. Even more than these do I dread the places where the litter swings out over chasms—there are several—though accidents are rare as far as we have heard.

Feng-Lin, Jennie's old cook, appeared on the scene in Paoting fu, wanting to escort us inland. We already had a "boy" we had picked up in Tientsin who was quite efficient, but knowing the amount of packing up twice a day there would be in the litter journey and how much work it requires preparing meals we decided to have his help also. We took four and one half days across the level plain from Paoting fu to Huai-Lu and as we did not aim to get off before 7:30 A.M. and have been in for the night before eight o'clock, it has not been as trying as when we came out eight years ago with a little baby and were routed out between 3:00 and 4:00 A.M. in the cold, dark mornings with no chance for a proper breakfast. We traveled sometimes as late as ten o'clock at night. But we decided we would rather have daylight and breakfast before starting, even if it means being on the road days longer.

Yesterday morning we were in Huai-Lu and for some reason the servants and litter men wanted to stay there for the weekend while we wanted to push on by traveling Saturday. But when you have to insist on anything with these Chinese you might as well let it go unless it is principle, for they will make it cost you dearly. The litter men dallied, fussed, and jangled with each other until it was nine o'clock before we left the inn. Then when we stopped for dinner at 1:30 they dallied until 4:00 before getting off, fussing all

the time. When, about 4:30, it began raining slightly, the whole
force became fairly frantic for a Chinaman abominates being out in
the rain, and although it was scarcely five o'clock and we were still
twenty li from the place we had chosen as our Sabbath resting place
we were glad to "turn in" the first fairly decent inn we found. We
would not have given in, but when it is raining and growing dark,
mules falling, rocky roads, and growling servants, with your own
discretion urging a surrender the better part of valor, one does not
need much persuading. So we turned in in time to get all the traps
carried to shelter before dark. Is it any wonder we were so reluctant
to part from our houseboat in Paoting fu and the kind boatmen?

In Paoting fu we took tea twice with the Ewings, met Miss
Gould and Mr. and Mrs. Pitkin. If I could have sent you a picture
of Mr. and Mrs. Pitkin's parlor you would think they must be well
fortified against the disagreeable outside surroundings in having
such wealth of beauty and talent as offsets. The luxurious couch,
beautifully rich "Art Square" on the floor, Egyptian screen bought
in Cairo, easy chairs and grand sweet-toned piano (made to order),
and, what made me green with envy, the ability of Mr. Pitkin in
playing and that of his wife in singing. She sings beautifully while
he is nearly perfect in accompanying. What resources! When one
is nearly frantic with the poverty in music, refinement, cleanliness,
and uprightness of this benighted land!

And what surprise do you think we had when we reached
Paoting fu? Louise Partridge was there to meet us! She had ridden
that long distance over mountains and fording rivers, on horseback,
accompanied only by a "boy." But when we stopped at this "emer-
gency inn" she was so disgusted with the idea of "giving in" to the
Chinese that she rode on (being on her horse) and her "boy" after
her. This would not have been so dreadful in itself, though we must
wish she were not so heady, but going off into the dark, rain, and
loneliness as she did, she went away from their bedding, which was
on one of the pack animals, from our food, company (!), and with
but little money. One of our "boys" claims he has been out fifteen
li ahead this morning trying to get track of them but could hear
nothing of their whereabouts. Not knowing where she is it is impossible to send on her bedding and we can but wonder where she is
and what she has done to make herself comfortable or even safely

protected in the cold, cheerless inn for over the Sabbath. She ought to have realized how we would worry.

Florence was quite feverish last night, has poor appetite, and says it makes her sick to be in the inns. No doubt it will take her some time to become acclimated to the dirt and unattractive places. She seems quite sensitive about the disagreeable things such as sores, blind people, beggars, and such repulsive sights as we are seeing every day, heartaching for us, to say nothing of one so young.

It is pitiful to see these people carrying home their bundles of leaves, grass, twigs, stalks, and in fact everything which will help keep them warm here where coal is so expensive. And it is pitiful to see that the fields and even roadsides are actually raked and look as clean as though swept with a broom. It looks tidy, but oh the poverty that makes it necessary. There is a regular traffic in following up the animals passing along this great highway and gathering in baskets the droppings from the animals. When we first start out from an inn, the animals having just been fed, these men and boys follow after us very closely so as to get the first chance. Yesterday one small youth followed my mules shouting "Hsia lu—hsia lu" which, being interpreted literally though at the risk of shocking you, means "Drop your manure, mule, drop your manure." I think they burn that which comes from camels though most is used for fertilizer for their fields.

So far we have had quite an uneventful journey over land, though Charlie's front mule fell flat last night just as we were about to stop for the night. We are spending Sunday here and have found it very quiet and good to rest from our labors on the seventh day. This morning Charlie was singing a verse from that classical gem, "There was an old man and his name was Uncle Ned." Florence evidently thought it quite unbecoming to the day or his dignity and came to me with "Mamma, why does Papa sing that?" Charlie asked her, "What do you sing?" "Why I sing 'Jesus Loves Me.'"

I must stop and fix the bed for the night and we will be off again tomorrow.

Very lovingly to everybody,
Eva

......

Jen Tsun, China
November 11, 1897

Here we are at one of the stations of our own mission at last. We had a wretched journey over the mountains as I anticipated. What with rain, slippery roads, sick mules, and sick folks, we had a time of it. The mules fell many times, some of the tumbles quite serious, and all of them startling enough. I was very nervous the last day in the mountains and walked the greater part of the way. We were nearly fourteen days coming 300 miles.

When we were about four days on the way Charlie began to complain with his stomach and was not at all well. After reaching here we went for Dr. Hall who lives about ten miles away and he has helped him so we hope to go into Taiku day after tomorrow to stay over Sunday and will be going on to Fen Cho fu next week, I presume.

There is an engineer in the province now in the interests of a railroad from the coast into this province, and if that is ever built the really tedious part of the journey will be done away with and I will not dread the journey so much. We missed the courier, who passed us some place on the way, and our letters have been sent on into Taiku and we will have to wait to get them.

We had expressions from the friends in the mission signifying their pleasure at our return, but the long journey, sickness, and the prospect of having to settle our household goods again have taken the enthusiasm out of me and I feel pretty well discouraged, especially when there is such a poor outlook of money from the home churches to carry on any work.

We are having beautiful weather now, clean, bright, and warm as May. If this were only a Christian country and you were all here it would not be bad after all. Everything seems dirtier and more repulsive than when we went home, but we will get used to it again. Think of seeing men, right out in daylight ten feet from our litter, taking their pants down to obey the call of nature, and also to hunt lice! Land sakes! And then the sores and deformities we have seen all along the way are enough to sicken and dishearten one. It surely does require a good deal of heavenly grace to enable one to stand it, and my supply has dwindled very low and I feel much like a heathen myself. All the way along I have been thinking of all the home friends, comforts, and opportunities and privileges for our little one in the homeland and the dearth of such things here. I don't mind it so much for our two old selves, but for these sensitive young hearts it is so different.

When I write next we will be in our own home again and it will be a relief after this long siege of traveling. The past year with all it has held for us has not been a restful one. Please write "Cheer up, cheer up."

....

Fen Cho fu, China
November 21, 1897

At last I am able to date a letter from our old home, two months and twenty-nine days after leaving San Francisco. The way has seemed long and tedious and the task of settling looms up like a mountain, but we are here and can take our time. This morning the ground is white with snow and more falling so we are thankful indeed that we are here and not out on the road. Florence took cold the last day out, is quite stuffed up, but is playing happily.

We stayed with Mr. Thompson in Jen Tsun five days, then went into Taiku, and from there out to Li Man to see the friends there. As to Miss Partridge (Louise) and her madcap career,* the friends said she arrived in Li Man looking as though she had been through flood and flame. We left Taiku for home with two of those big lumbering, dragging freight carts, one for the boxes and one for ourselves. Imagine the very heaviest two-wheeled dray with a rough straw mat fastened over a frame like a mover's wagon, a white horse in the shafts with a poor little bay horse in front, tandem, and moving oh so slowly. We were nine hours going seventeen miles and had to travel until eleven o'clock at night in order to get through to Fen Cho fu in two days. When we were

*See letter of October 31, 1897.

about five miles from this city we were met by two of the "boys" from Dr. Atwood's who had come out on horses to see if we were on the way, and after paying their respects hurried back to let the friends know of our whereabouts.

The plain looked very pretty as the sun was setting with the tall pagoda in the distance, the mountains misty purple, and the quiet of the fields. When out about two miles, we saw a "boy" coming along a path toward us smiling a welcome as far as we could see him and it proved to be Kung Hau Chi, the cook we had for three years, and before long we saw quite a procession—Dr. Atwood, Mr. Atwater, our old gatekeeper, one or two more servants, and several schoolboys. They all greeted us very warmly and walked back with us. We came in the city gate once more and were soon at our own big gate. The rooms were lighted and warm, for Mrs. Atwood had come over and made them look as homelike as possible. We spent yesterday opening boxes, putting up the "Boon Range," and getting out dishes (to find only two broken), and are now resting the "Seventh Day" preparatory to a big week's work to come.

There is a Chinese service out in the school court and they are all out there excepting Florence and I and Mrs. Atwood and her babies. Two of the Atwater girls and Edward are in Li Man in Miss Graham's little school. She and Mr. Atwater are to be married next year, then there will need be someone else to teach school.

Think of us now in the old home looking forward with eagerness to the coming of the mail, hoping each one will bring letters from you all.

....

December 7, 1897

The last courier was a full week late as he had a big carbuncle on the back of his neck and was not able to travel. When he did come what a feast we had! As is often the case he came just before dinner when there was no possible chance to read letters so I gathered them all up and carried them to the table with me. There is a lot of comfort in just looking at the outside of letters but I know it was precious little dinner I ate. And as soon as possible we drew up our chairs alongside the sitting room fire and I began to read them aloud. There was a baker's dozen from friends and one from Father and Mother which I saved till the very last on the principle that the best better come last.

The past weeks have been full of getting settled and the boxes opened and things put away. Our goods from San Francisco could not come on the *Coptic* with us as she was full, so came straggling along after us. There are still three boxes on the way somewhere. The goods shipped from Oberlin, including the range, were here some time before us. We heard reports while on the road that our stove was likely to be pretty well smashed and we held our breath and ourselves in readiness to find nothing but pieces. But when we finally had the box opened we found two quite unimportant breaks and succeeded in setting it up with very little trouble. The "boy" thinks it fine. Our barrels of dishes too came in for their share of anxiety but when all unpacked found but two pieces broken—one oval vegetable dish which I mourned over most, but then, was not the mate to it safe and whole? (This morning the "boy" came in to show me that he had broken this so now I am disconsolate unless the dish mender can fix it.) But this is the way it goes. We have to see our household treasures get smashed if we go around the whole of creation with them. We have been so thankful Stewart's picture was all right. The friends here think it very good and some said it looked as if the face ought to speak. Our rooms look very pleasant and tidy now that we are at last settled.

I went into the kitchen the other day after the cook had gone out on the street, and didn't I put in two good faithful hours of hard scrubbing! The breadboard, tables, floor, and all were just dreadful. Didn't I get lye, soap, and hot water with plenty of elbow grease to work, though? My how I scrubbed and scoured. When the chap came back he found the floor clean enough to eat from, but it hasn't been swept even since.

Charlie is settling back into the harness again and has enough to keep him pretty busy.

Now dear ones all—it is not necessary to tell you what a blessing your letters are to us here so I shall expect letters from you all very often.

....

January 31, 1898

Here it is the last day of January of a new year. Just now there is a station class of over thirty here for two weeks' instruction, but best of all Mrs. Clapp is here to visit us and she has done me so much good. She is more like a sister than an ordinary friend. With only one other lady in the station, Mrs. Atwood, it is rather lonely. I haven't been off the place since we came back excepting over to Hsiao-I once to see Miss Whitchurch and over to Dr. Atwood's a few times. Don't ever imagine me a model missionary for I find that home ties and the blues affect me much as they do "ordinary" people and it is harder to live here now than it was before. If ever you have thought of us as always going about with a Bible under our arm and dressed in black broadcloth à la typical missionary, you will not again after this confession. I speak for myself, not Charles Wesley. He's typical enough. He and Dr. Atwood and Mr. Atwater are busy, with the help of native Christians, teaching the station class. They have morning and evening services every day and teach separate classes forenoons and afternoons, so it keeps them very busy.

The Davises, who are in America, may not be sent back next year. His health is not very good and we are afraid that the committee will not send them back. It will be such a trial to Mrs. Davis especially, whose whole heart seems in this work, and I dread to think how she will suffer if they are not allowed to return. It will be a strange providence that will keep such a capable, enthusiastic, faithful worker as she is at home. We learn the Davises and Mrs. Thompson (whose husband came with us) are to be in Oberlin this winter.

The weather still keeps very mild—no rain, no snow—and the fields are dry. No soil in the world, however, is better fitted to withstand drought than this loess formation.

A rose geranium which I got from Mrs. Stanley while in Tientsin and a pink geranium from Mrs. Atwood are blooming, and Mrs. Bagnall in Paoting fu gave me an English violet. I also have two pots of hyacinths and a rose bush budded, and I brought a petunia and two pots of pansies from Mr. William's garden in Jen Tsun. The gatekeeper brought in a dwarf cherry and they are a great comfort.

....

March 1, 1898

Charlie and Dr. Atwood are back home after a two-week trip to Tai Yuen fu, the capital of the province, to attend a convention of foreign and native Christians. The day they started home it began snowing and snowed much of the three days they were on the road and for as many days after reaching home. Consequently, we have had as deep a snow as we ever have seen in China, but I have enjoyed it so much, perhaps because I could sit in my warm comfortable home and look out without having to be out in it. How pure and clean the compound looked for several days, but then the inevitable dirt began to show and spoiled the beauty.

Charlie came pretty near being mobbed the other day. There is a literary examination being held here and a large number of people are in town because of it. Some came to take the examination, others to sell things, but it has brought a class of people here who know nothing about us excepting their dislike for us and their desire to see us driven out. Charlie thought he would take a walk one day outside the city and as he went around by the west wall he encountered several hundred of these strangers. Whether it was because of his foreign clothes (he has not put on Chinese dress this time) or whether Stewart used to be a protection as the Chinese all like our children and Charlie always had Stewart with him before, or what the reason may be, this crowd hustled him, jostled, crowded, and hooted at him and threw clods of dirt at him, one hitting him in the eye, and were altogether impudent and daring. One of our neighbor's boys, a lad of about fifteen years, was in the crowd and went to Charlie and walked along by him as a protector! Why the crowd let him alone is a wonder for a man who attempted to shame the crowd for the way they were acting was hustled out of the way in a hurry. Charlie did not run, though he felt like it, as that would have made the matter worse. The lad led him in a roundabout way through the city avoiding the main street, which was packed with people, but Charlie said about 200 followed them home (although he didn't stop to count).

As there is no school on our place this spring the doctor is using the rooms for his women patients, there being over thirty (with some children). Mrs. Liu is teaching them and we hope it will be more useful than a school.

Florence sits at the baby organ playing and it sounds quite harmonious. She sways her body and bends her head quite professional-like. At the table the other day when she had finished drinking her milk she said, "I've drinkened it all up. Oh, I 'most said drankened—I make so many 'stakes, don't I, Mamma?" And she chuckled and giggled as if she was ahead for once!

Our "boy" Kung, who has had a time getting his wife, is to be married in a week. He wants a Christian wedding, but I find myself questioning the motives. He says for one thing he doesn't want any false worship connected with it, which sounds encouraging, but he also says it will cost less than a heathen wedding. Our friends here all think he is a sincere Christian so we better call it prudent thrift! One of their customs is that about a week before the wedding the groom sends a man to carry presents to the bride, so last week Kung went to his mother's twenty miles away and got the silver ornaments belonging to the family to send to her. He brought them in to show to us after he came back and he handled the precious things as tenderly as he would a baby. While he was showing them to us he said, "Women are such a bother here in this country—you have to send them so many things and make such a fuss when you want to get married—now in your country they don't have to bother, do they?" I told him sometimes they gave fine clothes and rings and such things—it was just as they pleased, there was no fixed custom. "Well," said he, "if a man has a lot of money here he sends fine clothes, but everyone has to send ornaments and money." So yesterday the basket of things was sent. He couldn't trust the "middleman" who had managed the affair, as he said he was afraid he would steal some of the things! So one of our men went along as a responsible man!

I put in a little box—a cake of Ivory soap, a towel (red and white with red embroidery at the ends), two spools of thread (one white, one black), a paper of needles, a handkerchief, a fan I bought in Oberlin and hadn't used, and some pretty cards. Kung seemed delighted and came in with his polite bow and "Thank you." It will cost him less to have the wedding here as it would make it pretty expensive to send four men to carry the bride in her red chair all that long distance to his mother's home, so they are to come here and live for the first few weeks, after which he can send his little bride home in a cart—a much commoner and less expensive thing! His mother is to be here this week, and I have given him permission to use a room in this court for himself and family. So next week there will be a grand pow-wow here—music (Chinese music without which they could not possibly be married) and feasting. Don't I wish you could all be here to enjoy (?) the fuss. Well, he is a good "boy" and has been with us most of the time since we have been here, and deserves a good send-off.

Now I've finished the gossip and will have to say good-bye. I wish I could see you all!

....

March 14, 1898

Dear Home Folks,

We are "Marching" along though it seems queer yet to write 1898. March has fulfilled her reputation so far, for we have had regular blustering snowy weather. Last Tuesday the sun shone for the first time for several days and Tuesday was our "boy's" wedding day. The day before was lowering and chill, but they had some sort of preliminary feast for the men on the place and those from the doctor's, and Kung's mother and sister who had jolted a day's journey in a cart over wretched roads in order to be here for the wedding. We prepared a large room in this court for the family and wedding party, and Kung bustled around for days much as a foreigner might have done hanging curtains and making everything cozy for his bride. When Dr. Atwood, in arranging for the ceremony, asked him what the girl's name was, he had to admit he didn't know the given name but he thought the surname was "Fan—yes it was Fan." My cook brought in a nice-looking cake, which he had baked in a long dripping pan, which was frosted with white and decorated beautifully with pink characters and curves. "Well," thinks I to myself, "we're going to have a nice cake anyway," and I poked my finger in the edge and saw it seemed very light and nice and promised to taste as well as it looked—but lo and behold! what did he do but carry it off for the Chinese and we never got a smell of it. The day for the wedding as I have said was sunshiny and I was glad, for maybe the superstitious Chinese would think our Providence specially favored a Christian wedding. The musicians came on the place along toward noon and made the day hideous with their clashing of cymbals and squeaking and tooting. Three of our men mounted our dashing chargers and rode out until they met the bridal chair coming, whereupon they wheeled and gallantly galloped back to tell the glad news. Then our cook took a long string of firecrackers and just as the procession came in sight toward the entrance gate set them off, and as he whirled and whirled, bang, fizz, pop, they went one after the other until the whole string was popped about the time the chair was inside the compound. They claimed the firecrackers were just a happy addition, much as the small boy in America thinks when the Fourth of July comes, but I have my suspicions that they were scaring away the devils. The chapel compound was about full of curious lookers-on and it must have been a rather trying time for the little bride as she stepped out there with not a single acquaintance except the woman who had come with her (it isn't the custom for the bride or her relatives to come to the wedding feast), and I wondered if she wasn't frightened to be set down amongst so many strangers and to be led into the chapel by one of our young women and be stood up there before foreigners and her husband-to-be, who was a perfect stranger to her, while some queer rigmarole was gone through with. She, who had never before heard a hymn, or a prayer, or wedding ceremony, to have to stand there and listen to it all—why even the "boy" sweat, and he has been with us years! After the ceremony the "boy" took hold of his bride's hand, which again is contrary to all Chinese custom, and assisted her over the steps to our compound and led her to the room in this court. She had a long red veil over her face all the time so no one had seen her face, but after she was seated on the *k'ang* it was taken off and everybody had the right to crowd in and stare at her—it is a sign and requisite of modesty that she sit through it all without lifting her eyelids or quivering an eyelash. I think she is modest for she did neither all the time I was in the room. Think of it and think too of not getting a taste of the wedding feast which had been eaten before the ceremony, and think of having to sit in one uncomfortable position for hours and be stared at! There was a little low table in front of her on the *k'ang* on which was a Chinese "wedding cake" made of their bread-dough, and dates stuck in thickly. It felt hard and dry as though it might be very stale—the "boy" again may have studied economy and bought a leftover one, though I don't know whether he furnished it or whether it was sent in by her folks (maybe 'twas)—and by the side of this "cake," which was about fourteen inches in diameter and six inches high, was a neat little bundle of onions.

Maybe you will not be satisfied with this letter all about the wedding but it is over now and next time there will be a chance for something else. We are all usually well. Today, Monday, the sun is shining brightly. With much love to everybody.

....

Fen Cho fu, China
April 24, 1898

Dear Father,

Eva has several letters to write yet so I offered to write to you this time in her place. I have no doubt you will be disappointed to get my scrawl in place of Eva's racey, newsy letter but perhaps you can make it do for this time.

I have been out for a ride and to preach in a village about six miles from here. I call it going out to preach though the pleasure of the ride is usually taken into account. I have a very good little horse; I say "I" because Eva will not have anything to do with him. Perhaps she will get up courage to take a ride after a while. This is the kind of work I expect to do for the next two months in addition to preaching to the hospital patients. I take some tracts and go to the village and sit down on a block or stone in the shade and rest till the people gather around. It does not take long to get a crowd. It is much harder on me than preaching in the chapel. On the street the people feel free to talk and ask questions and I get very tired by the time I am ready to leave the village, but the ride home alone is a rest. One can have time to think without fear of interruption.

Today on my way home I thought of the great difference between the people of the village I visited and we of America. They are as a rule bright and quick, but what is there in their life that we would desire. It is a fight for the necessities of life, and death without hope. If we are in close quarters now we can hope for something better in our conditions, but with them there is no hope for anything better ever in this life. What wonderful things God has done for the people of America! And how little we appreciate His blessings! Yesterday a man told me he could not understand why his village was not prosperous. They have rich lands and are industrious but their houses are falling down and everything seems to be decaying. I asked him how many people in the village (500 or more) did not use opium. He said about ten. This explains the matter and the man saw the point. The only hope for them is in the gospel which so many people who enjoy its advantages treat so lightly.

We are getting on very well. Florence is growing very fast and her health is good. She has a playmate in Dr. Atwood's girl who is one year older than herself and they are together most of the time. I wish you could see her again. We have two cows and a calf which with our horse make the stable look quite like a home barnyard. I bought a bull the other day as I am thinking of starting a dairy. I do not suppose I can sell any of the milk but no matter about that. I believe in helping to improve the country and livestock does not cost much here. The horse cost but $15 and paces very well. I could not stand to ride a trotting horse.

I have been out to the valley eight miles from the city trying to rent a place where we could stay for a few weeks but the prospect is not good. It is very pleasant out there and quite a change from the dusty city, and I will be disappointed if we cannot get a place. However, if we cannot get what we want we must be content with what we have. "And be content with such things as you have, for He has said, I will never leave nor forsake you" is a text we would do well to take into our hearts and lives.

I wish we could get some strawberries started. I brought some strawberry plants in with us from Tientsin but they failed to show up this spring. It was too late to replant them when we arrived so by the advice of a friend I put them in the cellar for the winter. I suppose we will try seeds next time.

Is it possible there can be any danger of the United States going to war with Spain? It scarcely seems possible but it may come to that. I suppose when you get this everything will be settled or war will be in progress. I sincerely hope the Senate will not fail to ratify the treaty annexing Hawaii—it would be too bad to let those islands go to some other country.

Ever your son,
C. W. Price

....

Fen Cho fu, China
May 6, 1898

Well, here we are again in the midst of one of the biggest musses you nearly ever saw, what with tearing down walls, putting in waterproof bricks around the foundation of our rooms, and building new bedrooms, with an upstairs. With half a dozen other irons in the fire we may expect to be in a muss for the next three months. Somehow ever since we came into this place it has been tear down and build up. Just now they are soaking bricks in hot rosin and oil and putting them under the dining room walls. They do this very cleverly and neatly by taking out a small portion of the old foundation at a time. Then they will fix the sitting room in the same way and lay a hollow tile floor which we will have painted instead of the rough floor full of cracks. When this is all done and two windows lowered and the new bedrooms all finished, we can go upstairs and look out over these walls toward America. The new addition will have a hall for the stairway and a bathroom and bedroom downstairs with two bedrooms upstairs. I can hardly wait until it is all done and we are settled again. We will have to carry a debt of $500 until we get a grant from the Board, but the mission voted to have it done so we are in it. If the Board refuses to make the grant we will run off and climb a tree.

When Mr. Thompson was here he took some pictures of the children and of the Chinese and if they prove to be good we will send you a sample. He tried to get one of the "family corner" in the sitting room and we had to sit still five minutes, it being an interior and not a very good light. After about three minutes Florence said, "Oh, my nose itches" but she stood it a few seconds longer and then up with her arm and gave the nose a vigorous rubbing, so I feel pretty sure that that picture will not be a success. He tried to get another by flash light and there we all sat in the dark, silent and expectant, while he fumbled around in the dark and tried to light his flash light powder. He would strike a match, apply it to the powder, then jump back, but the thing fizzled as bad as some Fourth of July firecrackers, so that was a failure too. He tried two plates on our second "boy" with his mother, sister, and bride. I hope these will be good.

My flower seeds are planted but not many are up as yet. We have four pie plant [rhubarb] roots that Dr. Atwood gave us and some day we will have a pie plant pie maybe.

We have the mat shade up over the house court to keep out this hot sun for a few weeks. We could hardly live here without it. Yesterday we had a high wind and how nervous it made me. Dust, dust, dust, in and over everything, even our teeth. I had a time tidying up our habitable rooms this morning.

Oh, it is such a rest when the gang of workmen go home for their meals! It is the only quiet time we have through the whole week. They come in at six o'clock mornings, work till eight o'clock, go to breakfast, back at ten, stop fifteen minutes for drinking tea about noon, go to dinner about one, and back to work at half past three. Then they work till six, drink tea again for fifteen minutes, and then work till dark. They do so much chattering—worse than a lot of magpies—that it seems like water to a thirsty soul when they go off the place. The school court now has a lot of women patients in the rooms, and the bedroom where we have to sleep while the others are being built opens into this court. At night when we want to sleep is just the time they all want to be clacking away with their tongues. Finally their tongues give out and all is quiet till 6:00 A.M. when it begins again.

Day before yesterday Mrs. Liu and I went to the south suburb and made calls, having been invited by some women who had been here visiting relatives in the hospital. There must have been about fifty families living in one enclosure. We went through a big door from the street into a perfect network of narrow passageways between high walls and through an occasional tunnel from one court to another. Our escort, a young boy, took us from room to room, where we stayed for a few moments with each family. In one place there seemed to be no one but an old serving woman and three or four men, one of whom seemed disturbed by our coming and in his opium smoke looked very sour and glum. The elder man of the party, however, was very gracious, gave us seats, and chatted very pleasantly. He had been to Peking, Tung Cho, Tientsin, and even to Shanghai. All the while the opium lamp was burning away on the *k'ang* and the smoker glared at us. I finally asked who of their number used opium (the room was full of fumes), and they pointed to this man. We had a little talk about opium and its evils and the man halfway smiled, agreed that it was wholly bad, but no doubt was at it as soon as we left, which was very soon, and we were both glad to be outside again. I am so pleased with Mrs. Liu on all occasions that bring her in contact with strangers as she is very modest, but intelligent and earnest, and it is such a help to have a woman of her intelligence and Christian training to help in the work.

We have a word in Chinese pronounced le high (spelled *li hai*), for which I have never yet heard a good synonym in English, that is until Florence gave it to us the other morning. She said, "If it hurts badder nor you are bigger dat means lihigh." Her grammar is an awful reflection on my teaching but her definition expresses it exactly. She says nearly every day, "Mamma, I love you more than the sky is big."

....

May 27, 1898
Yesterday brought us nine good letters and the ones from Father, Mother, and Wallie* among them. It was the very best

*Wallie was Eva's youngest brother, Samuel Wallace Keasey.

letter from Father I ever received. It did me so much good to have him write such a funny letter. The letters were every one of them full of love and good cheer. I had been out to a village yesterday and had felt depressed and "heartachy" about some of these people who are so poor and want to find comfort, but when I came back and had all these good letters to read it was a great uplift I tell you.

Oh, if you could just live here a little while you would not wonder that we appreciate our home and friends more every day. There is so much dirt, so many horrible sights, and so much to depress one, you would be patient with us even if we do want an "upstairs," lace curtains, and English violets. We often see men whose faces have been terribly torn at some time in their lives by these big ugly wolves that come even into the city sometimes. Yesterday I saw the worst looking one I have ever seen. There really did not seem to be a bit of flesh left on the bones of the man's face—just the scarred skin drawn over the bones, the eyes set back in the sockets, the teeth all exposed, the nose gone, the flesh of the cheeks gone, no lips. It was simply dreadful to look at him. So many have sores or are blind or crippled and so many are dirty and in different stages of heathenism. Some few, we believe, of this mighty number are sincere believers in the One True and Living God, and it is that belief and in the hope that others will be saved that we can live on here. One learns to sympathize more perfectly with the feeling of our Savior when He said, "How often would I have gathered thy children together, even as a hen gathereth her chickens under her wings, and ye would not!" And there are so many times when we do not know what to do with such texts as we find in James II verses 15 and 16. We surely need be "wise as serpents and harmless as doves."

Florence and I rode out to the valley yesterday and spent a few pleasant hours with Mrs. Atwood and the children. Mr. Atwater is to be married in a month's time if nothing happens. Mrs. Atwood will not be sorry, for it has become quite a burden having care of his children so long. She has had the two babies for nearly two years. The two older ones have been going to school to their future mamma who is a fine young woman and will make a good mother for them.

We are all usually well and the building goes on very smoothly. Charlie bought a grate when we came through Tientsin last fall and it is in the lower bedroom. He superintended building the chimney and setting the grate and the other day the head mason called me to see and hear the fire he had made in it to see if it would draw. It made noise enough to draw us up the chimney so we feel pretty certain it will be a success. It is the first one these people ever saw and the workmen are so delighted, as we are.

The men are at work now putting on the poles for the roof. These will be covered with thin roof boards and then they will put on about seven inches of mud (made of clay and straw) and finish up with the tiles. It all makes a very heavy roof. Father would be greatly interested to see how these men work. The ceilings will be covered with paper as is usual here, but I am having cheesecloth put on first, then covered with the paper and afterward white-washed. It will be very much stronger than paper alone. It takes Charlie and me both to boss these men, but our ways of doing things are very different. They have no level such as the "spirit level" and use a sort of plumb line which is a cord with a brick tied to the end. The cord broke at one of the corners of the new rooms and I noticed the edge was not real straight in consequence.

We have heard that it was no accident which blew up the *Maine* and we hear you are at war with Spain. Telegrams from our land reach China by way of England and it takes two weeks for news to come in here from the coast. We cannot help feeling a deep interest in what our country may be doing even if we are way off here.

I must close now with much love to you all. Florence is taking her afternoon nap—she is wearing the pretty little ring Father and Mother went down in the rain to buy, she remembers that. Charlie is reading the latest "War Telegrams" until his old soldier blood is getting hot.

....

June 20, 1898
Are you at war with Spain? The rumors we have had are to the effect that the States are giving Spain some hard hits. War is a cruel

thing at best, and it is to be hoped this one will soon be over. We seem to be quiet here in China or at least there is no disturbance near us. What may be going on at the coast is not known by us but we suppose Russia, England, Germany, and Japan are wondering what the next move is to be.

As to ourselves we are still listening to the sound of the hammer and saw, cries for "more mort" by the masons (only they call it something else), and superintending the painters. The stairs are up and floor laid in one room upstairs, roof all on and plastering done so you see we are beginning to see through to the end. It will take these thick walls some time to dry out enough to sleep in the rooms (one of the outside walls is two and a half feet thick), but in the meantime the woodwork and painting can be finished. I actually got the painter to mix colors until I found a tint that is very satisfactory. They use such strong colors and combine them in a very loud fashion sometimes. When we decided to repaint all the woodwork I took my oil paints and mixed a sample which the painter matched. By taking white, Naples yellow, vermilion, and brown in the right proportions we made a very pleasing tint which is warm and cheery. When my wallpaper comes in this fall, which I ordered from San Francisco, our sitting room and dining room will be very pretty and I can hardly wait.

For a change we have the school court full of patients and it is heart-wearing work to see what distress and pain some of these poor people suffer. I would not want to be a doctor in China. I go in to see one little six-year-old fellow who had a large stone fall on him in such a way as to tear nearly all of the flesh off the thick part of his left leg next to the body. I held his hand the other day while the dreadful-looking wound was being dressed. He is brave too and I give him Mellen's food and milk as he can scarcely eat enough to keep alive. Then there is a young woman with gathered breasts and we give milk for her little two-month-old baby. But worse cases come at intervals. One of my friends has a large growth under her tongue until it has almost filled her mouth. I hope Dr. Atwood will be able to cut it out. Last week there were two bad cases, one man (a bridegroom) attempted suicide because his father-in-law and he had a fight over some money which he did not give as he promised.

The sum was about $2.50 and he cut his throat and lived seven days before being brought here for help, but it was too late and he only lived a few hours afterward. Another man was angry at the Lord of Heaven for letting it hail and he grabbed a gun and was going to shoot the hailstorm away. The gun burst and blew his hand all to pieces and he had to have his arm amputated. That is what he got for trying to fight against the Lord.

But oh dear, it seems as if there is nothing here but misery and dirt and distress. It knocks all one's theories all to pieces to live in this land. If the germ theory is true one wonders what keeps these people from dying by the thousands. For instance, I took my little boy some milk this noon, and his mother used the nastiest old rag to wipe out a bowl to pour it into and then gave the milk to the little fellow to drink. If they have any left they let it sit in the room with not a thing over it and it makes one shudder to think of drinking it after a few hours. No use talking to them about covering it carefully. They never heard of a germ and wouldn't care if they had!

We are usually well. Florence is playing the music box and the Chinese children are listening.

....

July 6, 1898

We are alone in the city now as the rest of the station are off for the summer in the valley. Mr. Atwater left on Monday for the capital of the province where he will be married. They will come back to the valley where his children are and there will be a mother again in the family. The only disagreeable thought that creeps in my mind is that in less than four months after his first wife died he was "booked" for another one. They have waited a year and more to be married, but he didn't wait very long before he had a wife in view.

The carpenters still keep pounding away on a door or two, then their work is finished. The painters are putting in the last ceilings, then have the stair steps to paint when they too will be done until the wallpaper comes. The sitting room and dining new addition

Hull

Bed room

Bathroom

Sitting room

Coal; only this place doesn't stand square

Dining room

Kitchen

cellar

washroom

coal house

stable

well

2

room floors look so pretty. They are painted and will be so easily kept clean, and as they are hollow tile floors they will dry too. We have a lot of brick pavement laid around the house as brick and labor are cheap. Florence has a fine run now for her tricycle. Such hot days as this though she keeps in under these thick roofs until the sun is down. It has been so hot for a few days and nights that I have put in most of the time wiping the sweat out of my eyes and fanning myself at the rate of twenty knots an hour. I will be so glad when the heated season is over. Dr. Atwood was in today and he says they have felt the heat greatly at the valley so we are not the only ones.

Charlie went on a visit to the other end of the mission last week and we are glad he got back before this dreadful heat came on. While he was gone I had every dragon's head on the place taken down, had a big gateway torn down (I've sent you a drawing of it), and those who want dragon's heads for ornament can buy some of ours very cheap.

Just now we are anxious for war news so it seems like a long time between mails. We take the *Independent* and *Advance* so get some good editorials. Charlie almost swears by the *Independent.*

How often I think of you all and have a deep longing to see you. We're doing no missionary work these days—it's all we can do to be good ourselves.

....

> Fen Cho fu, China
> August 3, 1898

Dear Father,

Eva is away and has asked me to take her place writing to you. She will follow her usual custom by next courier. We have been in a rather serious job this summer and both feel rather tired. I suppose Eva has told you of our new rooms. It may not seem so hard work to oversee workmen as to do the work yourself, yet when the workmen are Chinese and the weather very hot, the job is not at all desirable. We have found it so at least and are very glad the summer is nearly past and our building almost finished. The Chinese are a little hard to manage at times and we must be on the lookout or they will get ahead of us. However, we are going to have some very pleasant rooms and will get them built for considerable less than any of our friends thought it would cost.

The mail has just come in, no foreign letters but the paper printed at Tientsin brings us the news that Santiago [Cuba] has been taken. That was about the first of July and we have been waiting all this time. We are very glad the war is going so favorably to our side and also that Hawaii is now a part of our own country. That is one wise thing our Congress has done.

You will excuse a short letter this time as the courier is waiting and I did not know I was to be detailed to write till it was really too late. Florence is very well and has grown so you would scarcely know her. She still remembers you all very well. We often speak of you and pray for you every day to be kept by the Father we all love.

Your son,
C. W. Price

....

Fen Cho fu, China
August 17, 1898

Can you hear the drip, drip, splash, splash of the delightful rain we are having? Oh, it is so refreshing after the oppressive heat and drought to have it rain and rain and rain. It is by far the heaviest rain we have seen since we came back and seems to be making up for all the "water pot" showers we have been tantalized with all year. It is testing the new roof too and we find a leaky place. I had some fine castor bean plants in this court which had grown to be some nine feet high with leaves nearly two feet across. Some of them are lying flat this morning, but maybe they will stand up again when the rain is over.

The last mail had no foreign letters and the coast telegrams were about three weeks old, so no knowing what has happened with the war since then. Poor Spain! Her glory and power dwindle and dwindle. How true all history has proven God's word to be.

The nation that forgets God has never prospered, though for a time it may seem to spread itself like a green bay tree.

Florence is perched up here beside me on a chair with a book pretending to read. She will be a perfect bookworm I fear when she can really read. She talks of the time when she will go to "Merika" to study while we stay here without her "and teach the Chinese about Jesus."

It is predicted that in less than three years there will be a railroad through here and then we shall expect to see some of you coming to visit. Maybe I will have some of my fine plum jelly to give you. The "boy" made some last Sunday evening before I knew what he was up to and I told him he must never do so any more at all, at all.

With very much love to every one of you. Day after tomorrow I'm forty-three years old. Oh, my!

....

November 21, 1898

The last mail brought us dreadful news of the death of Miss Brown of Shou Yang mission. She, in company with Miss Shekleton, started in a big cart to visit a village about four miles from there. When in sight of the village, as they were going around a bend of the river in the mountains, the cart fell over the edge and plunged down some fifteen feet. There were two native women in the cart as well and they were all thrown out, and Miss Brown fell in such a way that the cart was on top of her. Aside from the terrible shock none of the others were injured, but Miss Brown's body was pressed down in the mud and water and it was an hour before she was dug out. The doctor said she probably died instantly and her features were very peaceful and composed. From this we trust she was spared suffering the agony we feared from the nature of her death. She was a beautiful Christian woman and was ready for the summons which came to her so suddenly but while she was about her "Master's business." The saddest part is that it was so long before her body was taken out. The Chinese are a peculiar people and are very reluctant to render any assistance at such times. People passed by but would not help and when finally some men did come they stopped to haggle over the price they would be paid. Such things make us feel that some Chinese are scarcely worth being saved, but if Christ had stayed away from this world because of the cruel treatment he was to receive at the hands of his own people we would not have the assurance we do have now.

Dr. Hall of our mission developed symptoms of the same disease Stewart had and has been ordered to the coast hoping the change will help him. We went to help them get ready for the journey and were away from home three weeks in all. We could sympathize with the Halls perhaps better than others in our mission because we ourselves so recently were called to go through a similar trial. It is harder for them in many ways for it is the father of the family who is afflicted and they have four children, two of them but babies. They had to leave their home and work just as we did, not knowing when if ever they could return. This meant for them, as with us, disposing of their household goods in such a way that if they could not come back some things would be sold, others to be sent after them. These things are so hard. It means too that long, long, tiresome journey to the coast with aching hearts because the plan and hope of our lives seem overturned. We helped sew and pack, for a lot of sewing is needed for a family of six at the beginning of such a long journey with winter coming on. The doctors at the coast may order them on to Japan or even to America and that means a long time living in trunks. Mrs. Hall was quite worn with so much anxiety and work.

We are to have our station with us for Thanksgiving dinner. There will be fourteen or fifteen of us, children and all. We hope to have goose as there are lots of wild geese a few miles from here while it is nearly thousands of miles to a turkey! If the man fails to bring the geese we will try ducks and if they fail we have chickens of our own.

We are usually well now. Florence looks better than she did all summer. The three weeks' visit did us all good. We were at that end of the mission to welcome the friends, Mrs. Thompson and babies and Miss Bird, when they came back from the homeland. I am so glad Miss Bird could go to see you.

Since the Chinese government has taken charge of the post office work in Tientsin there are a lot of letters lost. Hope this will reach you.

....

December 7, 1898

I'll scratch off a few lines as the courier leaves tomorrow. What do I find to be so busy about that I have so little time for letters these days? We have breakfast at 7:30, then English prayers and study the lesson for Chinese prayers, then some eighteen or nineteen of us gather in the sitting room for Chinese prayers, which last a half hour. From nine o'clock to ten o'clock I read Chinese with the teacher and then the rest of the day flies as though on wings—sew, visit Chinese, write, or something until supper time. After supper, with Florence in bed, I have two hours with the teacher and his wife teaching them English. We have lots of fun and I laugh much more over their mistakes in English than they do over mine in Chinese. He is so anxious to learn that I hope we can keep at it all winter.

Oh, if you could only see the Christmas present that came into the court today! We wanted a rocking horse for Florence so showed the carpenter a picture of one which he thought he could copy. He brought it today and of all the queer-looking animals in the whole wide world this looks the queerest! One could worship this for it is like nothing else under the heavens or on the earth. And then Florence had to be out in the court and see it, so what kind of a surprise will it be anyway? She thinks it's fine! I sent for a book for Charlie's Christmas present and it came out in the boxes and he has read it through already. So that's the way our Christmas presents go. Mine is even worse. Charlie ordered a writing desk for my birthday present. It was so long in being finished and so long in getting home afterward that now it has to do for a Christmas present as well. And my birthday 'way back in August!

Mrs. Liu and I went out to a village some six miles from here a week or so ago. It took us most of the day but we had a good time. Mrs. Tung (doong) got dinner for us and the whole village turned out to see us so we felt quite like a circus. We went to Shih T'a last week and go again tomorrow, and hope to go once a week this winter. There are only nine boys as yet in school so Charlie has time to look after Florence when I go away.

I cried when the mail came in last time. Why? Well, there was a picture of my father and mother and I just cried, yes I did. I am so glad to have them and they are behind the glass door of my bookcase where I see you every time I look up. They are worth more than their weight in gold.

....

December 20, 1898

Well, the carpenters actually have made two very respectable-looking rocking horses after the fearful-looking beast they first attempted. It was a great heavy thing, a load for two men, with stiff legs and doleful hang to the head. The rocker too was almost straight. But by staying here on the place where we could oversee them, they cut the thing down about half, made a new head and neck and new rocker, and finally got one to look something like a real horse. By buying a horsetail to use for tails, forelocks, and manes I hope to have a pretty present for Florence and for the Atwater girlies.

Mrs. Liu and I have been in fourteen homes within a week. My chief errand has been to invite women here for Christmas dinner. There will likely be fifty or more besides an indefinite number of children. It will help us get better acquainted and I hope and pray that by some means we may get hold of more of the women. The men are to have their feast over in the chapel and there will likely be as many as the women. I hope the weather will be good for some of the women with little children are to come from outside the city. It has done me good to see the friendliness with which the people have met us. We already have two more invitations to teach women in their homes. I feel so helpless and inadequate in attempting to teach the important truths of Scripture, but fortunately for our encouragement the Bible says, "Thou has kept these things from the wise and prudent and revealed them unto babes." But how like a mountain the work in a heathen land is with this difficult language and the dark superstitions and dense ignorance of the people who never heard of there being a true God much less a loving heavenly Father. The attempts seem failures so often, but who knows at what time some truth will spring up in some heart and bear even a hundredfold?

....

Fen Cho fu, China
January 4, 1899

Dear Father and Mother,

And so the war is over at last! It wasn't much of a war but it has made us here in China feel quite proud of our country. From the last account we are led to infer that we retain the Philippines and we are glad of that.

We are all very well. Having plenty to do we have no time to think of being lonesome or dissatisfied with our surroundings. Work is the only thing that can make one content to live in China. We are in the condition of the sailor climbing the mast who so long as he does not look down has nothing to fear. We try to keep our minds on what is ahead knowing full well if we stop to think of the pleasant surroundings and loved friends we have left behind our life will be full of regrets. That is not saying there are no pleasant things in China, but taken as a whole our life here, aside from the knowledge that we are doing the will of our Heavenly Father, must be one of endurance.

The longer I live in China the more I learn about the people. What I mean is, we are constantly learning something that gives us an insight into the character of the people. A man was brought into the hospital a few days ago who had his leg broken and Dr. Atwood asked, "Who will take care of you while you are here?" "I have no one." "Have you no relatives?" "None." "Have you no wife?" "Had one but sold her to get money to buy opium." "That is a very bad thing." "The wife was very bad also." The stoical indifference of this man could not be equaled among our American Indians.

There was quite a pitiful case came in to the hospital a few days ago. A man had fallen from a ledge about forty feet high and he lay at the bottom more than twenty-four hours before his friends found him. Wolves and leopards are quite thick in the mountains and of course he was in considerable danger, but he and his friends did not seem to think much about it. He is very badly hurt but will probably get well.

Florence is growing very fast. You would not think she is the same little girl that had such good times at Grandpa's a few months ago. We send lots of love. May our Heavenly Father bless and keep you all.

Ever your son,
C. W. Price

....

Fen Cho fu, China
January 15, 1899

We didn't get a single foreign letter by last mail. The courier just missed the steamer I presume, and only brought me a card from the *Independent* saying they were too crowded for my story. So that precious story had to go under! Never mind, when I become famous they'll be sorry!

Did Charlie tell you about our happy Christmas day? You may wonder how I managed to entertain seventy-six women and children, but I had open house all day. The guests first looked about at their ease, then twelve at a time sat down to eat at the dining table, dessert of grapes, nuts, Chinese cakes and candy and tea being the first course. Then we went into the recitation room in the school court where tables were prepared for the feast. The old women, mothers with little babies, and expectant mothers sat on the big *k'ang* while others sat on the less comfortable benches around other tables. I went about among them urging them to eat and you would have enjoyed seeing the gusto with which they attacked the bowls of food.

After the feast the women struggled upstairs on their little tied up feet, and one appreciative sister cuddled up on our bed on the soft eiderdown quilt, while one of her neighbors explained to me that Mrs. Chang's bones wouldn't ache so if she had such a soft bed to lie on. They were delighted with everything until it came to going downstairs. Some of them sat down and shuffled from one step to the other. It gave me a good chance to point out the disadvantage of their poor little maimed hooves. The foot-binding just makes little stumps of their feet.

The men feasted in the chapel, which Mr. Atwater had decorated with evergreens, Chinese lanterns, and mottoes. This feast was only for church members and probationers, while mine, I fear, was for more sinners than saints.

Will you promise to not worry and fret if I tell you that Florence came very near a dreadful accident the other day? This is the second time she has narrowly escaped a dreadful death. I have not thought anything of leaving her to play about the house alone if I wanted to go out to the room where there are some women staying. And I have left her here while I went to service Sunday mornings, for she has always been so careful and not inclined to get into mischief. I feel that the Lord allowed the accident to happen while I was here to help her. If I had been out she probably would have died. I sat here reading and all at once heard her scream. I ran upstairs where she had been playing and met her starting down and her clothes were on fire! Half of her apron, a new gingham, was burnt badly and her thick dress was burned through to her skirt. I put the fire out by throwing my arms around her and gathering her clothes up in a tight wad. She had been trying to build a fire in the toy stove Eltha gave her and in some way her clothes caught fire and it looked as if they might have been burning some time before she noticed it. I think she learned a lesson by her fright that she will never forget! She has had the stove over a year and this is the first time she ever got matches to light anything. If I had not been right here and she had run downstairs, the draft of air would very likely have made the fire blaze so she could not have been saved. We feel that nothing but God's good providence spared us an awful tragedy.

....

January 28, 1899

Have you had such a mild, bright, dry winter as we are having? Last fall the rain fell incessantly all through September. The people complained "too much rain," and for the first time since we lived here the Mayor of the city ordered the north gate closed and it remained so several days. The rain continued all the same until the Lord saw fit to drive away the clouds. Since then there has been no rain and only a dozen or so flakes of snow. The people now complain because of the drought and the winter wheat will be spoiled and flour is expensive. Consequently, the Mayor ordered the south gate closed and for several days the whole line of traffic and travel toward the south submitted to the inconvenience of going a mile or so out of the way hoping by this act of self-sacrifice to influence the gods to send snow. But no snow came and so the gate was opened. The theory is that rain or snow comes from the gods and by submitting to discomfort the gods will send rain. In drought the closing of the south gate is in order, but if too much rain, then shut the north gate. The south gate is called the fire gate, the north the water gate. By closing the fire gate the clouds will have a chance to form and rain or snow will come. The water gate keeps the rain back and drives away the clouds.

Last week I had an experience. I took a native woman, Mrs. Chang (Jang) and we went off some thirty-five li from the city to stay at a Chinese sister's house. Mrs. Hou (Ho) is a baptized Christian (or at least she professes to be a Christian), a widow of some means, and is above the average Chinese woman in intelligence as she can read some. She was here Christmas and then stayed on two or three weeks to be with a friend who came with her to break off opium. She went out to villages with me four times while here so we had a chance to get somewhat acquainted. However, I did not exactly enjoy my overnight visit as the women nearly all use tobacco and the room was filled with smoke, and this, with eating Chinese food, gave me a headache. Mrs. Hou's stepchildren are grown and the men are off in another province doing business so Mrs. Hou and the wives live together. The family stayed in to see us get ready for bed. It doubtless was interesting to them to watch a foreigner undress. However, I left on my underwaist and drawers and put on my big long nightdress and they thus didn't get to see much after all. Mrs. Hou, Mrs. Chang, and I slept on the not very big k'ang and I slept in the middle with a "dear" dirty sister on either side!

The other women and children left soon after I was robed for the night, and Mrs. Hou and Mrs. Chang got ready for bed. They both unbound their feet to let me see how a bound foot looks. Oh, what a horrid-looking thing a bound foot is! It is awful to think of slowly crushing and changing the shape of a human foot until there is no more resemblance to a foot than to a block of wood. The great toe is left unbound but the other toes are all made to reach toward the middle of the foot underneath. The heel is brought forward somewhat to meet the ends of the toes, making the instep bulge up and often breaks the bone. Oh, what a shapeless thing it is! The process of binding is so slow but yet persistent that the agony must be awful. I don't see how they ever can straighten out the toes and change the shape back to anything like a real foot. Some of the Christian women try to and the agony of unbinding and trying to straighten the feet is worse if possible than the binding. Their bound feet feel cold and lifeless, like touching a bone. The skin and bone are all that is left for the flesh seems all absorbed. No wonder some of the women think I have cotton stuffed inside my stockings!

How can these women suffer so, then make their little girls suffer the same, and all for fashion! I said to them, "You laughed when you saw me undressing because our ways are not the same, but I want to cry when you undress because of your deformed feet." I let them look at my white fat feet and they frankly said it was very bad to bind their feet. The sentiment of the country is changing and now many of the better-educated men, regardless of Christianity, are trying to change the fashion. They begin to see the stupidity of it and that if they ever want their women to rank with the women of other lands they will have to take away this hindrance. How it cripples them. They totter about and could never cope with free-footed women, but it will take a long time to change as the women themselves will be the last to give it up as they have been taught for so long that it is a mark of beauty and that no man would marry them if their feet were large. It has been a sign of refinement and culture and good morals, as a large foot is supposed to belong only to bad women. The bound foot is one of the shackles that Christianity is taking off from this land.

I went from Mrs. Hou's to Hsiao-I and spent a night with our

English friends. One notices the responsiveness and congeniality of Christian fellowship more after being with the Chinese and more than ever appreciates the blessings that come from Christianity.

....

March 15, 1899

I get pretty lonesome here, in fact I'm really blue. Did you think missionaries always were bright and happy and hopeful? Well, there may be some of that kind but they are not out here. It is only by taking a wide look out over the whole general missionary field and seeing what has been done and what seems to be God's purpose that we can stand to live here at all. Mrs. Atwater and I went to call on a friend in the south suburb last Friday. The streets were fearful because of mud and stench and the places and people seemed dirtier than ever and a flea jumped into Mrs. Atwater's cup of tea.

We had a terrible dust storm several weeks ago and when the gale came it just whirled and swirled around the house and into every crack and crevice of our poorly made doors and windows. I even felt the grit on my teeth. There had not been any snow yet this winter and no rain since last September so you may know there was plenty of dust. Then when the wind fell it began snowing and when we got up on a Sunday morning everything was white and clean.

Come over and play on our new organ, the first one we have ever owned! It is a Mason and Hamlin five octave, thirteen stops organ with a very sweet tone. Mrs. Goldsbury brought it from Massachusetts when she came out in 1889, the same year we came the first time. Dr. Goldsbury died from typhus fever and she had to return home leaving all their furniture here. Then Dr. Hall came out to take Dr. Goldsbury's place and he bought the organ. Last year he developed symptoms of the same disease Stewart had and had to leave his work here, so the organ was for sale again. It cost us $60, freight and all, and I believe the first price paid for it was $120. Now when guests come who can play, there will be a good organ for them. I can't play much but it is a great comfort to have it and it is an entertainment for Florence too. Like Stewart, she seems to have a natural ear for music.

Dr. Atwood's family left two weeks ago today for the coast so now we are left five days from a doctor. But I try not to think about what may happen for the Lord knew we were to be left here just this way, and if it hadn't been His purpose for us He would have arranged it differently. I am sending that story of mine by them as it isn't worth paying postage on clear from here. If they mail it to you after they get to Wisconsin it will not cost very much. I sent it to the *Independent,* paid forty-five cents postage, and what did they do but mail it back again with "special regrets," but at my expense! I thought maybe you might mail it to the *Advance,* 215 Madison Street, Chicago, Ill., and see if they will have it. If not, keep it until I become famous—then it will sell for a big price!

I will enclose with this letter one of the "gods" the Chinese paste up in their kitchens the night before their New Year, where they stay until about a week before the close of the year at which time they have their mouths smeared with taffy to keep them from telling tales out of school. Then they are burned, taffy and all, but the "god" is supposed to go off into some sort of heaven where they stay for a week at which time a new "god" is pasted up.

We have had the pleasure this week of a few days' visit from an English friend, Mr. Brewer, who lives a day's journey away. It is such a joy to have guests come. Florence is as delighted as any of us.

....

April 12, 1899

Mary and Celia Atwater (seven and three years old) are staying with Florence and me while all the others are away to Taiku attending Annual Meeting. We did not go because the Williams children had been having whooping cough. Florence gets pretty lonely now that Edward and Mabel Atwood are gone. The Atwaters live a mile away so we don't see much of them. So we four are alone here, miles away from any other foreigner.

There are over twenty boys in the school now so I guess the

doubt about its getting a good start is done away with. Charlie has been pretty nearly discouraged at times and then again would be full of hope. I am glad the school is filling up for it is work Charlie likes better than some kinds, although he takes his turn leading the evening meetings for the opium patients and preaching on Sunday. Not many ministers in the homeland have as little leisure as these missionaries around us. Charlie has a helper in the school and when he is not here the work goes on. He will be home Friday or Saturday if nothing happens. Mr. and Mrs. Atwater and their other two girls, Ernestine and Bertha, will be gone a week longer. Florence is delighted to have two "sisters" for so long and they all play happily together.

Just now I am more farmer than missionary as I have five hens sitting, and as we have two cows now I tend to the milk and the butter-making myself. My churn is a small stone jar holding not over a gallon and I had the carpenter make me a lid and dasher. What if the handle is part of an old broom handle? I enjoy doing it anyway.

A good many women have been coming in lately and that always takes a good deal of time for they want to hear me play the organ, look at my plants, hear the music box, and invariably want to go upstairs. An upstairs is something new to them and they make great work getting up and a bigger fuss still getting down. The sewing machine is upstairs and that being of great practical use is of more interest to them than the organ and other things. One day one woman asked me what I gave the "iron tailor" to eat. I laughed and got out the oil can and told her he lived on oil!

They seem to appreciate the photographs I have on exhibition and are always very pleased to see pictures of my "mu-ch'in" and "fu-ch'in." One old woman said one day just after I had told her how far it was to where you live, "Can you see over there and see them?" These people have such strange notions about us. They think our eyes are different so that we have the power to see long distances and even into the very earth itself. I was very glad of the opportunity to tell her that our eyes are just like the eyes of the people here. We found out the other day that the gatekeeper had been refusing to let some come in and he was plainly told that the next time it happened and we heard of it he would be dismissed. One missionary who lived not a hundred miles from us bragged about their gatekeeper, saying, "He's as good as a watchdog and keeps the people away." But I don't fancy that myself.

Day before yesterday was "King of Animals" day and everyone who owns a horse or cow or donkey or mule had to pay tribute to the god who has such animals in charge. I don't know how many cents per head, but if they wanted to be sure of keeping them through the year they must pay the tax or it would not be at all certain that their animals would live.

If you knew how we prize all home letters and how many we have to write to different friends scattered throughout the world you would send us a line very often whether you got one from us or not. Florence often speaks of you. She is up in her room now, I hear her humming.

....

May 23, 1899

The last mail brought the pictures you sent and I was so glad to get them, and especially the soldier one. I show the picture to everyone. Just now Mr. Ogren is here and when I showed it to him he said, "Your father has such a kind face." Thank you so much for them. Did I cry? Well, when the package was opened and there were three little girls with their bright little eyes looking at me I let the tears come to the edge of my eyes then choked them back.

We took a day off last week and went out to the valley. It was so dusty though that I didn't enjoy it very well. A fair was in progress at the mouth of the valley and our carts had to plod their way through a great crowd of people and hundreds of wares spread out by the roadside. Not once did we hear "foreign devil" and they were pleasant and friendly looking. These fairs are strange places. A man has a few wares, maybe nothing more valuable than a lot of old mended shoes, Chinese shoes at that, but he will walk miles and carry his traps and spread them out on the ground for sale. Another will have pipes, tobacco pouches, or cheap little looking glasses or some such trinkets. There they sit in the hot sun, day after day, while the fair lasts, perhaps four days. Then they pack up their poor little things and trudge on to another fair some place carrying their goods on their backs or hung to a pole across their shoulders. We saw some going away having bought a pig or one of the big bushy things used as brooms, or a wooden pitchfork or some such goods. Those who have better things to sell usually have a large square awning fastened to a pole which they can shift to keep out of the sun. Others have regular tents, but there are hundreds of articles hung across ropes stretched from pole to pole. Women, two at a time on a single donkey sometimes, will go to these fairs and oftentimes they walk miles on their little feet just to be in the hot dusty crowd and blazing sun for a day.

We did not tarry at the fair but went on up the valley some four miles to our summer place where we ate our lunch, lay on cots and rested, or sat under the trees by the side of the stream. Mrs. Ogren, a Swedish friend, was with us and Ernestine and Mary Atwater were also along. I made ice cream before we started, packed it well with ice, and by lunchtime it was very nice. The road is so stony up the valley and these horrid carts so jerky that I haven't been worth anything since and am tempted to not try it again this summer. Our home is so pleasant now that I'd rather stay here than bother about going away.

Spring has been quite backward for Shansi, and for a while I feared my flower seeds were all dead under the ground but now the sweet peas, mignonette, portulaca, and some others are up and should be bright enough after a time. We went out from the city twenty li and got rose bushes, lilacs, flowering almond, wisteria, and peonies and sowed grass seed all over our back court. Our strawberry plants are in blossom, peas also, and lettuce and beets are coming up. We have had some pie plant, which came from some seed from Dr. Atwood's plants, which gets better each year. Little by little we will get these things around us. The peach trees (I brought two pits with me you remember, from a basket of nice ones you had while we were there) are growing nicely.

I have over ninety chickens and they are doing well in spite of cats, snakes, weasels, and hawks. I have to keep them in a small yard with a wall around it and twine netting over the top, and at night they are put in a smaller place with wire screen over the top. In spite of all this precaution a snake found its way into the coop one night and had killed one when Charlie heard the fracas and went to the rescue. I stepped inside the coop to make the little things settle down and put my hand right on the snake not knowing what it was that was making them so frightened. As I was in my nightdress with just Chinese shoes on I scrambled out in a hurry, and Charlie pounded the snake. It got away but was found the next morning and had some more pounding, which killed it. Snakes are not common here but this one got in through a hole in the wall and though only about three feet long it was after my chickens and had to die. A hen with seventeen eggs hatched out sixteen chicks, which I think is doing pretty well for a Chino-American hen!

It is time for the mail to be put up so I must close. We think of you often.

Lovingly,
Eva

....

June 20, 1899

Are you longing for rain as we are? It is 'specially aggravating to sit here listening to the rumble of thunder off to the southwest of us with little hope of any rain coming here. Somehow so many showers pass around Fen Cho fu. So often there is rain in the mountains and at places farther out on the plain, but we don't get any. The south city gate has been closed again and the shopkeepers have built little altars outside their shops hoping the gods will honor their worship by sending rain. Everything is so dry and the dust is dreadful.

We have had guests the past month. Mr. and Mrs. McConnell are here for the summer to escape the dreadful heat at their station 200 miles south. Their home is in a sandy region near a bend in the Yellow River and it is very hot there. They have a baby, born in Scotland, and this is his first summer in China, which makes them anxious for him. Children as a rule do not stand the heat well in this province.

About two weeks ago we were favored by a call from a Mr. Shockley, agent of the Peking Syndicate, who is traveling through the provinces on the hunt of petroleum. He came walking into the court one morning and it seemed good to meet someone in foreign clothes and who wasn't a missionary. He has a large retinue with him but the rest stayed at the inn while he came here for dinner. We sang "America" (he is an American too) and wished he might stay longer. What with our "thirteen stops" organ, the large Brussels mat on the floor and my beautiful (?) oil paintings, he will be able to tell of the luxury of missionaries. He had been traveling for weeks far in the interior and had been even away from any cart roads, following bridle paths over mountains, so it was probably a treat to get to a civilized place. He had an English-speaking Chinaman as interpreter and had a cook and plenty of foreign stores, so doubtless fared well so far as food was concerned, but he was glad to meet white folks and have a look at our latest papers. (And they were weeks old!) He came across the ocean with the renowned Hobson* who declared to him that the papers greatly exaggerated that kissing business!

Mr. and Mrs. Ogren left yesterday for their station 200 li from us. We will be their nearest neighbors. They have very few of this world's goods but have a *Jeh hsin* (warm heart) for the work among the people.

Mrs. Chang, the Chinese friend who went to a village with me and stayed overnight, attempted suicide last week. She and her daughter-in-law had some trouble and it resulted in that. She was saved, however, and I trust it may be a warning to her. Oh, these poor women! They are not very strong.

After killing two snakes, guarding with wire screen against cats, weasels, hawks, and other prowling varmints, my chickens are

---

*Richmond Pearson Hobson (1870–1937) won the Congressional Medal of Honor for his heroism in Cuba during the Spanish-American War. A popular hero, Hobson purportedly kissed 417 young women at a reception held in Kansas City during January 1899. A naval officer, Hobson was assigned to salvage Spanish ships in Hong Kong.

dying with pip, gapes, lice, and various other diseases. So I fear my boasting will all go for naught and out of more than a hundred there will scarcely be a healthy chicken live to tell its own tail from that of another.

....

July 19, 1899

When the thermometer is nearing the nineties you will surely not expect much of a letter and yet I don't like to let the mail leave this evening without carrying a letter to let you know we are well.

Today there is an occasional cool breeze at this north window of mine. This is the first time I ever had a room of my very own. Mr. McConnell has promised to take a picture of the view from this window some time and then you will see for yourselves that there is something else than walls, walls, walls for me to look at. If only the picture may show the distant mountains and the big, fleecy clouds!

If you could have heard the uproar in a neighboring court last night you would have thought pandemonium was let loose. Two men seemed to be quarreling and I could hear, "Ta-pa, ta-pa, (dä-bä, dä-bä) strike, strike" and then a blow and a regular fight was on. Such yelling! It was about nine o'clock and for an hour there was a regular fracas. It set all the dogs in the neighborhood to barking, and such a time! One man who seemed to be the maddest and yelled the loudest finally got to boo-hooing, the first time I ever heard a man cry when he was quarreling.

Mr. McConnell has been ill but he is about now so that is over. I wonder what the doctors would have called it if there had been any within sixty miles of us—doubtless diphtheria, or congestion of the brain, or apoplexy! He was very bad for a few days with his throat and head, which was fairly purple with the blood that seemed to center there. The helper Dr. Atwood left in charge of the opium refuge came and injected antitoxin into his arm twice a day for three days and the sore throat was better very soon. His head was greatly congested for several days and it is a relief to have him about again. I think he caused the trouble whatever it was, for during the hottest days two weeks ago he had his "boy" draw a tubful of cold water twice a day direct from the well, and sat with his feet in it a good deal of the time. It seems reasonable to think it drove the blood to his head. However, we can't say surely it was that but I hardly think he will try it again.

With much love to everybody and thank you for your letters. Yes, I know I ought not to get discouraged!

....

September 13, 1899

Charlie's school is begun and there are some encouraging features. There are twenty boys already in and if we had the money we could take more. Some of these boys are paying 1,000 cash per month instead of 500 as formerly, but even with that it does not pay for the food they eat, which costs about 2,100 cash per month. The other expenses such as the cook, fuel, the native teacher, books, and other things the Board makes certain grant for, but it is not enough so we have to bear a part of the expense ourselves. Charlie is keeping close account but the expenses run up. We pay the native teacher 8,000 a month (about $5) and he boards himself, wife, and baby, so he is not likely to get rich very quick. The boys live chiefly on millet, vegetables, and some white flour. I think Charlie allows the whole lot of them about two pounds of meat a week, not much for twenty boys but that is more than they would get at home.

Some of the boys are very bright. The advanced class in arithmetic is in compound numbers now and some others are just able to write the foreign figures up to one hundred. They know nothing of the foreign method of numbers when they come and are glad to be taught. This, with geography, is all the secular studies they have, their chief work being learning the gospels so as to recite verse by verse, a catechism, *Evidences of Christianity,* and *Old Testament History.* The native teacher teaches them to write Chinese and read the Chinese classics. All the work is in Chinese of course except writing our figures in arithmetic. They are anxious to be taught English but the mission will have to decide about that I presume.

I had a letter from friends in the Richfield, Ohio, church where

Charlie was the year before we came out here and they are sending a Christmas box to help make it a good day for the boys and women who may be with us. One friend is to support a boy in school. In these little ways we feel they are interested in us and our work, if we are thousands of miles apart.

We have had guests this summer and they keep coming occasionally all along. Mr. and Mrs. McConnell spent the whole summer here and since they left other guests have come to spend a few days with us, one from Sweden, one from America, one from New Zealand, and one was born in Africa of English parents but has lived mostly in France and Switzerland.

Mr. Thompson, who came out with us two years ago, will soon be on his way back to America as his wife died a few weeks ago and has left him with two little girls, one a baby two months old. He thinks it best, and it doubtless is, that he take them home. Mrs. Williams with her three girls is leaving too. So many calamities have overtaken this mission that one wonders who or what the "Jonah" on board can be.

It is cool and cloudy now but I fear there is not to be much rain. There has been so little rain this year and no snow all through last winter to anything like wet the ground, so the fields are very dry and fall wheat will scarcely sprout. Food is becoming dearer as a consequence and the people will likely suffer.

I will put in a little slip on which Florence drew what she called "Mother and Law." She had watched Mr. McConnell take photographs and she drew a lot of different ones, and when she was showing them to me explaining who they were, she came to one saying, "Dis is de mother" (pointing to the tall one), "and dis is de law" (pointing to the short one)! She had heard us talking about mothers-in-law!

I must close now with very much love to you all.

....

September 26, 1899

This is a blustery day more like November than September. We have had a little drizzle of rain but not enough to do any good when the earth is so very dry except lay the dust. People begin to talk as if there may be another famine here. There was one eighteen or twenty years ago and hundreds* of people died from starvation. Millet now is double in price to what it was a few weeks ago. A Magistrate a few miles from here had forbidden the price of food to go any higher and forbids a bit of food to be taken out of the district to be sold, no matter what the price is in other places. It shows they are becoming anxious. The fall wheat has been sown but does not grow because of drought. A year ago this month it was raining incessantly, which was the last real good rain we've had.

Next week Mr. Thompson and his little motherless babies and Mrs. Williams with her three girls are leaving for America. Our number of children grows smaller and smaller. The two older Atwater girls have gone away to school. An English family living at Shou Yang (four days' journey from here) have brought out a tutor and a governess for their only child, a boy of eleven, and they are glad to have other children come to live with them so as to make enough for a regular little school. We shall send Florence I expect in a few years if they still keep it up. It will be so much better for her to study with other children than to be alone. She was letting "Dickey," one of the chickens, play with her finger the other day and he jerked her ring off and that is the last we have seen of it. I was very sorry about it.

You might find it interesting to hear about one of the queer things the people here submit to. Those who make the carts have been making the axles a little longer and then a little longer still for some reason, until the axles would rub against the walls as they went through the city gates and made a big bother about passing other carts in these narrow streets. To overcome the difficulty and to make everyone owning a cart shorten the axle, the authorities ordered tall heavy stones set up endwise on either side of the track through all gateways, and it has caused a lot of trouble. After a time the axles will all be shortened, but in the meantime the crowd waits behind a cart stuck in the middle of a gateway with the patience of Job!

*It was estimated that one-third of the population died in the famine-stricken areas.

October 11, 1899

We have actually been off on a little vacation since I wrote before. As the time drew nearer and nearer for the friends to leave for America we felt that we would like to see them again, so at the eleventh hour we made up our minds to go to Taiku. They were to leave on Monday and we reached there on the Saturday before, so there was not much time to spare.

When they left the city Monday afternoon there were seventeen carts and some six horseback riders in the procession. Their party had six carts and the rest were for those who wanted to escort them a little way out of the city. Before they left they held a service in the chapel in Chinese, and sang "God Be with You Till We Meet Again," and some tears were shed. It is one of the hard things in our lives here that there is someone nearly every year going home, not knowing whether they can come back again or not. Homes are broken up and household things disposed of, and we are made to feel forcibly that here we have no continuing city. Our numbers grow less and less instead of being recruited. Mr. and Mrs. Clapp, Miss Bird, and Miss Partridge are in Taiku station (Mr. Williams too when he comes back from the coast), and the Atwaters and ourselves are here. Maybe we will dwindle away a few at a time until we are all gone. Mr. Williams has just finished building a fine large house, two stories high, but unless the Davises come back it will not be occupied I fear unless Mr. and Mrs. Clapp and the young ladies move into it. It is a well-built house and stands on a large plot of ground in the south suburb of Taiku and they have a fine view of the mountains.

Since I began this we have been outside the city for a cart ride. Charlie says we're to go twice a week now for we've been staying at home so closely I get the blues dreadfully. Tomorrow Mrs. Liu and I, with her fat little three-month-old baby girl, expect to go to Mrs. Hou's, thirty-five li away. We hope to get back before night by starting early. It is where I went last winter and stayed all night and was most choked by their tobacco smoke. Florence will go over to Mrs. Atwater's and play with the little girls so she will not keep Charlie out of school. He is to have four of the most advanced boys in an English class. It is a new departure and will have to be tried to see what success it will be.

We hope to get a whole handful of letters from everybody. Good-bye with much love to you all.

....

Fen Cho fu, China
October 25, 1899

Dear Father and Mother,

I am going to write you a letter as Eva is busy getting our winter clothing ready for use. We have had a tailor on the place nearly two weeks and a woman has been sewing for us about the same length of time, so you see we are not to be without clothing. The woman who is sewing for us has a hard life. Her husband is an opium sot and abuses her shamefully. He has sold her oldest girl to get money to buy opium and threatens to sell the others if she does not keep him supplied. The family is almost in a starving condition and the worst of it is we do not know how to help her. Money given her would go into her husband's opium pipe and we fear it would be the same with anything else we could give her. Cases like this, which are very numerous, are very depressing to one who is at all sensitive.

There was a beautiful stream of water by the roadside for part of our ride into the countryside last week, which made Florence very happy and I am not sure but two old gray-headed people enjoyed it about as much. It is good for Eva to get out and is something for Florence to look forward to. I can remember when I thought a man at fifty years ought to be considered a sage, and I have passed that nearly two years. Yet I do not think I ever passed a more peaceful happy year than the last. There have come sorrows into our lives within the last few years and they have left their mark, but our Heavenly Father has full compensation for all He calls us to suffer. There are yet things that may come to us that we can scarcely dare to think of as a possibility. We often speak of what a trial it would be for us to be obliged to part with our girlie. At times it seems to us that our lives are all centered in her. What could we do without her? I believe we are learning the lesson of trust that God wants us all to know.

Florence is enjoying herself very well these times. Today she has become the possessor of a kitten and is very much pleased. Yesterday she called me to see Madge, her little dog, sitting up in a corner holding her doll in her arms and it was too funny. She has a litter after the plan of the mule litters which she has them carry around, and though it often comes to grief she manages to get someone to repair it for her and starts on a new journey. She has not been at her studies for nearly a year till about two weeks ago, and hence had forgotten about all she knew. She seems to be getting along very well now and within the last week has commenced the never-ending struggle with numbers.

Eva's work, aside from taking care of me, consists for the most part in receiving the women callers who come to see what we look like. More than 200 have called since last June. She occasionally visits the villages. I fear it is too much for her to ride so far in the carts. I wish we had a better way for her to get around.

The people are having a hard time of it now. Grains of all kinds are nearly double the usual price. The scarcity is caused by lack of rain and there will be a great deal of suffering this winter. This is a rich country and produces abundant crops if the rains come in the season. If not, there is a shortage. At the best there is little more than enough to support the dense population and with a shortage there is always suffering. The work we are doing will also be hindered to a certain extent. But we will go forward, doing the best we can and God will take care of the rest.

We send our united love to you both and to all the rest.

Very truly your son,
C. W. Price

Fen Cho fu, China
Nov. 13 1899
Dear Grandma:—
I love you and
Grandpa very much.
I wish I could see you.
I have lessons every day
With love,
From Florence

Fen Cho fu, China
December 6, 1899

Charlie is very busy these days for he is the only foreign man in the station, Mr. Atwater being away for two weeks. Besides the school, there are some forty men breaking off opium and there are two services a day with them. With the help of Mr. Liu and the medical helper, Mr. Li (Lee), they manage to get the work done, however, and seem to be happy. Charlie was called over to a neighbor's last week to shoot a mad dog, and he bravely shouldered his musket and after four rounds really killed the beast! Brave old soldier!

There are five women here now breaking off opium and there are four babies besides, which doesn't make it easy if they all fuss at once. Teaching women is very uphill and discouraging work and opium sots are among the worst. But if Christ gave His very life-blood for them and suffered death itself, I ought to be glad to do something, especially because He suffered it all for me as well as them.

We had three guests come to spend Thanksgiving day with us, and Mr. and Mrs. Lundgren were here nearly a week. The Thanksgiving dinner was not much of a success for there was no turkey, no cranberry sauce, and the chicken dumplings would have sunk the Spanish fleet quicker even than Dewey did, but we were happy and enjoyed ourselves.

Still there is no rain or snow and the winter wheat has about all dried up. The dust is deep, deep, and I do not know what these poor people will do. There is suffering now and what there will be by spring is hard to say. They are poor, poor as Job's turkey. It makes me begrudge the food I eat when I know so many around us have so little to eat. It is one of the hardest things in our life here to see these people suffering for the necessities of life and yet find no way to help them, only to tell them to be Christians. Heaven grows more and more attractive to me. To be in a place where sin and sickness, sorrow or death cannot enter is a wonderful thing if we can only realize it. Our Heavenly Father has wonderful things in store for those who love Him and trust Him as their Savior.

Florence is well and seems happy, if she is the only foreign child within thirty miles. Her tricycle has been a great comfort to her, and the Chinese think it very wonderful that she can manage it so skillfully.

My friend, Mrs. McConnell, has been very sick since they went back to their station and expects now to go home to Scotland in the spring. Mr. Davis has returned from America but Mrs. Davis will not come until the spring. There is some hope of a doctor coming out then.

May joy and all sweet peace be with you all.

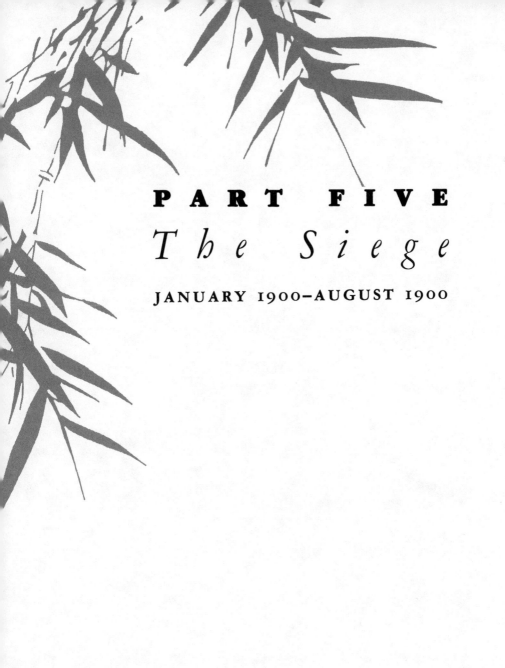

PART FIVE
The Siege
JANUARY 1900–AUGUST 1900

The China mission was dangerous. The danger was not that associated with being shipped into a war zone, although in view of China's weakness even this was possible. Rather, the dangers of spreading the gospel in China were more mundane. However we might fault the missionaries for their self-imposed isolation from the hustle and bustle of Chinese life, we must recognize that the risk of disease was a genuine worry. The experience of the Fen Cho fu mission is justification enough for a missionary's preoccupation with the lack of cleanliness in Chinese society. Perhaps even more frightening than physical illness was the mental and emotional cost exacted by work in China. The stress of an alien environment coupled with the frustration of attempting to convert a race that was confoundingly blasé about the state of their individual souls was more than some could stand. Thus, it is far from surprising that one of Eva's friends had gone mad, and another—a close friend—had ended her life with an overdose of sleeping powder. Nervous breakdowns and severe depression dogged the Shansi mission almost as much as physical ailments. Clearly, missionary work in China required an extraordinary level of commitment and courage, for only commitment and courage could have sustained mission workers through such deep personal tragedies as those suffered by Eva and Charles Price.

Yet the strength of conviction that allowed missionaries to withstand the severest testing was simultaneously a grave weakness. Mission workers were psychologically closed to the possibility that neither they nor their religion was needed or welcome in China. In truth, the presence of missionaries in China during the waning years of the nineteenth century was evidence of the deteriorating Chinese state rather than evidence of a thirst for Christian salvation. More than God stood with the missionary, for behind the man with the Bible was the Western gunboat. Dubbed "muscu-

lar Christianity," the gospel preached in China was a threat to local stability since the shield of Western military might extended beyond missionaries to include native Christians. Unfortunately, Chinese converts were notorious for using the leverage of their foreign religion to resolve disputes with their neighbors or with local government officials. Even the missionaries of Fen Cho fu, who had vowed not to interfere in the business of local Chinese government, did, in fact, intercede on behalf of their flock.

Reaction to missionary activities was inevitable, and it appeared, perhaps, most visibly and violently in China's inner provinces, where distance diluted the effectiveness of Western military might. The 1890s saw serious anti-Christian unrest in central China, including a major revolt in Szechwan, a province to the southwest of Shansi. This uprising, led by a coolie nicknamed Yü "the Wild," engulfed large areas of Szechwan in 1898–1899, and it was peculiar. Although initially directed against Chinese Christians rather than the government, the revolt inevitably came into conflict with the Chinese state, which belatedly moved against the rebels. Yü "the Wild" was captured and given what by Chinese standards was a remarkably light sentence, life imprisonment. The rebel slogan, "Obey the Ch'ing, exterminate the foreigners," was a notion that many in government could hardly fault. Indeed, the rebels acted out what many Chinese officials felt.

Shansi, however, remained relatively calm during the 1890s. Despite their poverty, the citizens of Shansi were noted for their docility, and as the Price family entered the first months of a new century, the ferment of the rest of China seemed as remote as American domestic politics from the isolated Christian outpost at Fen Cho fu.—R.F.

....

Fen Cho fu, China
January 2, 1900

My dear Home Folks,

We'll soon get used to never again writing 1800, but as yet it seems strange to write 1900. Christmas has come and gone and so has Charles Wesley's fifty-second birthday. Usually we have had a lot of women and children here Christmas but we decided to let it go this year. We expected to have presents for some of the people, as our Richfield church wrote of sending a box of things besides a box of Ivory soap for my women, but it has not come yet.

In two more weeks Charles's school will be out for a month and he and Mr. Williams plan to go off on a tour to find a place that would be good for a new station. The winter has been very busy and the opium refuge has been full of men and there are over twenty boys in the school. I have had ten women here breaking off opium and have tried to teach them something of the True Doctrine. Mrs. Liu is a great help to me with the women. There is one poor old body here now—she is not over fifty but she has been using opium over twenty years and she is having a tough time. Poor miserable women!

Last Sunday before service time I read to Florence in English about Christ before Pilate and Peter's denial. Mr. Liu had charge of the Chinese service and he chanced to read the same lesson in Chinese. When he had finished she turned to me and said, "That's just what you read, Mamma," which surprised me as I didn't know that she knew enough of Chinese, especially Bible Chinese, to understand what was read. March 18 will be her seventh birthday.

They are having an anxious time in the provinces east of here and some of our friends have their homes guarded by soldiers, but everything has been very peaceful here.

With much love from us all,
Eva

....

February 14, 1900

Just now we have been having a somewhat anxious time, for Florence is having what we suppose is whooping cough. She seems pretty well in spite of it in the daytime but at night after she has been asleep for some time she wakes up almost strangled with the phlegm in her throat. I have been keeping a candle burning all night for it must be dreadful to wake up choking and in the dark. I hope she is over the worst of it as I am so worried when she is sick and every cough makes one more gray hair on my head! How do folks stand it when they have a big family and they all whoop at once?

Do you hear of the trouble the Christians are having in two provinces just east of us? There is a native secret society called the "Boxers" who say they are going to overthrow the Protestant religion in China. They are persecuting the Catholics too. Just how far they will be allowed to persecute missionaries and their converts is not easy to say. They have ruined the homes of some forty church members where our friends, Arthur Smith and his wife, live, and they have killed one missionary belonging to an English society. But the last report was that they were to be taken in hand and a stop put to that kind of business, but one can't trust the reports that come from the Chinese themselves. So far in Shansi we have had no reason to fear any trouble. The people who come about us are friendly and this province is considered the quietest and its people the gentlest of any province in the empire.

The winter has been cold and dry with very little prospect of rain or snow. Food takes another rise today because of the continued drought. One wonders what these people will do if it continues.

Today is the thirteenth of the Chinese new year, and tonight is the parade of lanterns. The streets are all decorated with tissue paper banners and hangings of different colors and look very gay. We don't often go out at such times. There is always such a crowd that we feel safer at home.

....

The unrest mentioned in passing by Eva in her letter of February 14 undoubtedly concerned her more than she was about to reveal to the home folks. The disturbances occurring to the east of Shansi in the provinces of Shan Tung and Chihli were not simply peasant riots of the sort so familiar to Chinese history, but rather actions aimed explicitly at foreigners and Chinese Christians. That was worrisome, for virtually all the missionaries in Shansi had, at one time or another, personally experienced the hostility of those they had come to save. The "Boxers," as the adherents of the antiforeign movement in Shan Tung and Chihli were called, seemed, to many Western eyes, to be as bizarre as they were dangerous. In a quite accurate description of the "boxing" ritual, Charles Wesley Price could barely suppress his scorn:

> *. . . they began with boys, ten to eighteen years of age. The so-called mysteries connected with the organization appeal very strongly to a people so full of superstition as these, and after a few days it grew very rapidly. The drill, if it may be called so, consists in the boy repeating four short lines of some mystic words, bowing to the south and falling backward, going into a trance, remaining lying on his back for an indefinite time, rising endowed with wonderful strength, boys of twelve being as strong as men. They brandish swords and spears, not seeming to be skillful in handling them but merely to show strength, and place themselves under the power of their symbols. They claim to be invulnerable. . . .*

Boxer claims of invulnerability to swords and bullets were always disproven in the first volley of gunfire. Yet even some well-educated Chinese Christians conceded that Boxer leaders possessed some sort of supernatural power.

If Boxer beliefs confirmed missionary beliefs about the gullibility of the heathen, the foreigners could ill afford to be smug about the Boxer slogan, "Support the Ch'ing, exterminate the foreigners." The revolt of Yü "the Wild" had already broken the veneer of local law and order to reveal a widespread patriotic xenophobia, more patriotic than the Ch'ing government itself. What made the Boxers a threat more serious than Yü "the Wild" was the official blessing given the movement by government officials such as Yü Hsien, the governor of Shan Tung province. Reports that the Boxers of Shan Tung province carried banners inscribed with the name of Yü Hsien were truly alarming, and the foreign community, upset with the apparently blatant connivance of Yü Hsien with the Boxers, successfully pressured for Yü's dismissal from the governorship of Shan Tung. While the new governor of Shan Tung set about brutally suppressing the Boxers, the old governor, Yü Hsien, was reassigned, on March 15, 1900, to the governorship of Shansi province.—R.F.

....

Fen Cho fu, China
May 9, 1900

Could you look in today you'd find Charles W. with a holiday as the native teacher took the school out to the valley to a fair, and so he is taking time to write a few letters in interest of his "Academy." Work cannot be carried on here without money any easier than at home.

We have had so much wind and very little rain this year so far and I am becoming almost frantic for the dirt is dreadful. There came a high wind in the night a few nights ago and I could feel the dust over my face and teeth. It makes me so nervous to see everything covered with dust, but there's no use in fretting for we've a lot to be thankful for. So long as we have a good comfortable home and plenty to eat and wear with hope for the future and so many friends and blessings we ought not to complain. The lack of rain and the many high winds that dry up the crops so badly (as well as send dust over my house) mean far more to the Chinese than simply discomfort. What will they have to live on another year?

There is a lot of typhus and smallpox about but we have to become indifferent to all such things if we live here. We see so much of the misery and sad things of the world here. Mrs. Chia had another baby girl and when it was a few days old her husband pawned the covering she had and urged her to get up and go out as a wet nurse. She took a violent cold and is now very low. The baby died and when I asked about its body the oldest little sister said, "It died." "Yes," I said, "but where is its body?" "Oh, it was thrown outside the gate." A neighbor said quite unconcernedly, "It's our custom here to throw away dead bodies of little babies to the wolves." I question very much whether the little thing died a natural death, but the mother would have died too if I hadn't had her brought into a room here now and I shall keep her until she gets strong again or dies. They have nothing to live on except what she can earn so it means we will have to help them to food until she gets well again. She has been a patient little woman and is a probationer, but what a dreadful prospect she seems to have even if she gets well so long as her husband lives. She has been delirious and talks of going to heaven. I believe God will make up to her in joy and light all the misery and darkness she has had here, and I can scarcely hope she may get well. Oh, if I could give you a true picture of her miserable little room which she has to call home, and which is all she has in the world—a room black with dirt and smoke, the larger part taken up by the *k'ang* on which the whole family sleeps and where the baby was born, no food in the house, nothing but rags and the bedding which we have given her. You would wonder as I do that anyone can care to live on, and wonder too that there seems such an unequal division of things in the world. Some have all and more than they know what to do with, while others starve. I feel so ashamed to complain at certain trials when I contrast my life with hers for what am I that I should have better than she? This is only one little bit of the misery there is all around us.

Our Annual Meeting began April 15 and the friends from the other end of the plain came down here. We had meetings in our sitting room, and all took dinners with me so we had a merry time. There are only thirteen of us here so it was not a very big "all." Mr. Davis, Mr. Williams, Miss Bird, and Miss Partridge were with us over a week, and Mr. and Mrs. Clapp visited with us after the meeting closed. Miss Searell, of Hsiao-I, was here over a week since the other friends left so we have been let down very gently. I am thankful every day for this big comfortable home and that so many friends come to see us.

You ought to have seen my monthly rosebush a week or so ago. There were twelve deep crimson double blossoms on it. It smells like a tea rose. I have a geranium, an oleander, and another plant that has blossoms, besides two dishes of the beautiful Chinese water lily.

....

Despite its reputation for calm and order, Shansi province began, during the month of June, to show signs that it was not immune to the infectious antiforeignism of provinces to the east. The grave problem of drought in Shansi, a problem that so worried Eva, became a convenient peg upon which to hang antiforeignism. The missionaries were blamed for the lack of rain, and rumor had it that the missionaries were able to drive away rain clouds by fanning with all their might. As if this story weren't sufficiently fantastic, the rumor was embellished with the claim that the missionaries at Tai Yuen fu did their despicable fanning in the nude. Such rumors would have been even more frightening had there been a Boxer movement in Shansi, but neither the provincial authorities nor the mission-

ary grapevine had detected any Boxer presence during the early days of June. The suppression of the Boxer movement in Shan Tung had, however, succeeded in forcing the Boxers into neighboring areas. The region from Paoting fu to Tientsin was in Boxer hands, and the connecting railroad had been destroyed. The option that the Shansi missionaries had of fleeing to Peking or to the safety of the coast in the event of unrest in their province was fast disappearing.—R.F.

....

Fen Cho fu, China
June 6, 1900

Dear Loved Ones,

You will probably be uneasy in these very troublous times if you don't get a letter every mail. It is hard to say just how much personal danger we are in. It has not seemed to be the policy of the "Boxers" to harm the foreigners beyond the injury to their work through the native church members, but that is hard enough to bear. As if "Boxers" and the bitter persecution were not enough, there must be, on top of all, this famine.

I have written a long letter to the Des Moines *Leader* which I am hoping they will publish, and if they do you will maybe see that and know what the situation here is. I have also written to the *Advance* hoping by this means to get help from some source so as to be able to help this distressed, starving people. One's own food all but chokes one when you think people around are starving. We live plainly, cutting out all extras, but even then we will have very little with which to help. There is a great deal of sickness and death all about us because of the drought and high winds. Mrs. Chia is still here with her two little girls who have also been down with something. I was uneasy for a few days as the Chinese said they had the typhus fever and as I had been in and out I knew if there was danger of contagion that I was pretty well exposed and had exposed the others. But it could not have been typhus for they are about well again and no one else is sick, for which I am thankful. With the school here it would mean a serious business if such a disease broke out.

The people want us to keep the school through the summer so the boys will be sure of plenty of food. It will mean a pretty big expense to us if we do for I presume they will not be able to pay as they have been doing if this famine keeps on. Oh, how we long for rain. Clouds have gathered often lately and it has thundered encouragingly, but no rain comes. If it does rain soon they could plant millet. It keeps one strung up to a tight tension all the time, what with famine, and "Boxers," and all the various rumors we hear.

It is likely we shall have to give the couriers a layoff for they risk their lives every time they make the trip to Paoting fu. That city seems to be in the very midst of the trouble and all along the road there is a great deal of danger. So if you do miss some letters you must not think it strange for we may have to wait till this blows over. Don't urge us to go to the coast or to go home, for we're safer here than we would be on the road now. If we wanted to get away ever so much, which we do not want, it would look like deserting the native Christians and leaving it all for them to bear and they have enough without that. If money comes so we can help feed these people it will make a lot of friends for us and must do the work good.

Mr. Williams in Taiku had a narrow escape the other day. A crazy man had been to their place and was not let in. He afterward met Mr. Williams on the street on his way to the bank to draw money, and flourishing his sword the crazy man demanded $300. And on Mr. Williams telling him he hadn't money to give him, he thrust at him with his sword after first seizing Mr. Williams by the arm, but fortunately the sword was dull and only made a black and blue spot on the breast. Mr. Williams said, "I didn't stop to ask questions or for explanations, but took to my heels successfully." The Magistrate sent a guard and had the crazy man escorted out of the district where he was turned loose to bother someone else.

These are surely troublous times whether they are the troublous times the Bible refers to as coming in the last days or not. What with wars and rumors of wars, pestilence and famine, false teachers and "itching ears," there are signs enough. But as Charlie says, the best thing to do is to go quietly on attending to our business and do the best we can.

We are all well and as happy as circumstances will allow, putting our trust in Him who is our leader and for whose sake we are here. We probably are less worried than you are, and I hope you won't worry much. Florence has quite a curiosity to see the "Boxers" but I hope she'll not get the chance.

With love to you all,
Eva

....

If Eva Price seemed, on June 6, 1900, expectant of Boxer trouble, her fears were soon realized. Two Boxer organizers entered Fen Cho fu around the fifteenth of June and, according to a journal account kept by Charles Price, began seeking recruits through public displays of "boxing." In all probability, however, the Boxers had been in Fen Cho fu for some time. The sudden appearance of Boxers in many areas of Shansi during the middle of June strongly suggests that the preceding months had been spent in covert organizing. Boxer activity in Shansi had actually begun in mid-March, not coincidentally with the arrival of the new provincial governor, Yü Hsien. By the middle of May, Boxer attacks on Chinese Christians had begun, and within two months the antiforeign movement was active in half of Shansi's local districts.

The Boxers capitalized on the perceived strangeness of the missionaries by weaving horrifying tales of the supernatural abilities of the foreigners and the evil of their intent. Foreigners, it was claimed, could cut from paper human forms that would come to life and roam about doing harm. The story that foreigners were hiring vagrants to poison village wells was circulated even to the throne. Another was that by drawing the Chinese character for "ten" (which resembles a cross) on house doors, agents of the foreigners were able to afflict household members with illness. But the most terrifying tale of all was the one which asserted that foreign ships seized off the China coast were found to be carrying grisly cargoes of human eyes, blood, and female nipples. As fantastic as these stories were, they found a receptive audience.

By the twenty-fourth of June, the situation had grown quite ugly in Shansi's capital of Tai Yuen fu, where insults and death threats were openly directed at Chinese Christians and foreign missionaries. In blessed contrast, Fen Cho fu remained relatively calm, thanks largely to the local Magistrate, who did what he could to protect the missionaries. Nevertheless, on June 24, Charles Price and Ernest Atwater felt obliged to go to the Magistrate and ask for a proclamation forbidding the harassment of Christians. The Magistrate dismissed the growing anti-Christian sentiment as talk and nothing more but agreed to issue a public proclamation. The document was never issued, for in the meantime the Magistrate had learned that Boxers and Chinese government troops had put the foreign legations in Peking under siege. Times were becoming very difficult for the Magistrate of Fen Cho fu, but they were to become even more difficult for the missionaries.

During the last week in June, both Eva and Charles began to keep a journal of events; both chronicles eventually made their way to the American Board of Commissioners for Foreign Missions rather than to Des Moines, Iowa.

That the Prices began journals is a reflection of the conditions at Fen Cho fu during the summer of 1900. Mail was simply not getting out; Boxers were stopping travelers, and any Chinese caught carrying foreign correspondence was extremely fortunate if he were not killed. The Price journals, moreover, were implicit recognition of the possibility that neither Eva nor Charles would survive the storm gathering in Shansi.

Charles rather than Eva was the more prolific journalist, which again reflects the unusual turn life had taken for the Price family. Eva was the better writer, but the crisis had increased her wifely duties and domestic chores. During the miserably hot days of July, Eva was cooking three Western-style meals a day for a contingent of ten, and under these circumstances her thoughts remained her own.

The incessant barrage of rumors, false alarms, and intermittent antimissionary incidents kept the Fen Cho fu mission in a state of unbearable tension. The pressure was unquestionably a true test of faith for the Chinese Christians, for they could save themselves by simply recanting their belief in the foreign religion. No such option, of course, was possible for the Western missionaries. Although Charles was proud of the loyalty of Fen Cho fu's small Chinese Christian community, defections were soon enough to appear. Gradually, with the exception of one or two, the Chinese Christians rejected Christianity. The impact of a conscious campaign of psychological terror against the Christians could hardly have been greater than the uncontrolled pendulum swings between imminent Boxer attack and promises of protection that kept the Fen Cho fu missionaries on edge during the late summer of 1900.

The frayed nerves were not the fruit of some wicked plan, but rather the effect of deep contradictions within the Shansi official bureaucracy. There seems little doubt that the Magistrate of Fen Cho fu was doing all that he could to protect the foreigners under his jurisdiction, but at the same time he was duty-bound to at least give lip service to the governor's antiforeign pronouncements. The local Magistrate was truly a man caught in the middle. Yet it was he and he alone who kept the missionaries from harm.
—R.F.

From Eva Price's Journal
Fen Cho fu, China
June 28, 1900

It may be well to keep notes of these troublous times in which we are now living. It is hard to realize we are the same persons who, for more than ten years, have lived here in peace and quiet, with no greater obstacles in our work than the natural hindrances found in a heathen land. To be reviled whenever we go on the street or among strangers is not a serious trial. In fact, we look back over the years now and wonder that we ever called any of our experiences "trials." Maybe the day will come when even these days will not seem so dreadful. But now and then are so far apart as to make it seem impossible to ever forget the present anxiety.

For months we have been anxious because of drought and feared the suffering that would probably come upon the people, not thinking it would be of any special meaning or menace to us. The past two months have marked such changes that we feel the pressure from lack of rain nearly as keenly as though starving.

After the Annual Meeting, which began the fifteenth of April, we heard first of the new element that has entered our lives. For months our sympathies had gone out toward the friends in Shan Tung and Chihli provinces because of their trials with the "Boxers," but we never expected to know by experience what it has been to them to suffer daily, and hourly even, the constant wearing anxiety of such conditions. We know better now.

After our meeting, Miss Partridge was the first to go back to her station and sent word from Taiku: " 'Boxers' within five li of Li Man. I am warned to not go on." That was our first introduction to these present dangers. About the middle of May, the "little fire" had kindled simultaneously in different districts throughout the province. The first serious reports were brought by the C.I.M. friends who had attended the Ping Yang fu conference. Near Hung T'ung several Christians were attacked and robbed of all their household goods. The leading elder of the church there was nearly murdered as well as plundered, and others received bodily hurt in connection with the robberies. Still it seemed "far away" from us. Within a few weeks we heard they were in our own city in several places drilling and drawing large crowds of restless adventurers. Daily within the past two weeks we have had fresh causes for uneasiness. We have learned what . . .

....

June 29

Just what we have learned that I was going to write I shall never remember, I fear, for since the words were written we have learned what it is to meet danger, to have the feeling that we were facing death itself, and to realize as never before the power and majesty of our great Heavenly Father. Two weeks ago friends came to us for a visit partly, and partly to be in a safer place. Miss Eldred came from the district where the greatest outbreak has been, Hung T'ung, and Mr. and Mrs. Lundgren from Chieh Hsiu, sixty li away. Since they have been here we have thought and been able to talk of little besides the dangers around us. We tried to even pass a rule that we would not talk about it, but our hearts have been too full. Often just at nightfall disturbing letters or rumors have come in until for several nights we have not slept as usual. Last Sunday the most distressing rumors came that all the foreigners in Peking had been killed. Our mail has been shut off, so we have not been able to learn anything authentic. Later in the day the Kuan* posted a notice in favor of the "Boxers." Again, later, he put up another saying foreigners must be respected. Every day since there have been such conflicting rumors that one has been all but dissected. Our hearts have grown faint one hour to be lifted again the next.

On Wednesday evening we took the precaution to pack two trunks with most necessary things, and the next day they were secretly buried in the chicken house with a box containing most of our money. We seemed to be momentarily expecting an attack in which we would at least be robbed if nothing worse. To put out of sight the most necessary things seemed wise. This was done without the knowledge of the servants so far as we know.

Last eve we sat out in the court as usual trying to be brave and forget the situation. I went in about eight to help Florence get ready for bed. Just as we had finished, Miss Eldred passed hastily along the hall and called out in a quiet voice, "Mrs. Price." I answered as quietly and followed her into her room. "They have come. They are over at Mr. Atwater's now." I went back and had Florence dress again, but she only thought it a funny freak. We packed another box of clothes that would be needed if we were not harmed and went about as quietly as possible, fearing to hear from Mr. Atwater's. A man came shortly with the word that the Atwaters had fled to the *yamen*,† and their house was being looted. "They will be here before very long then," was our only thought, and no one can imagine the terrible suspense of the next hour as we went about dreading we knew not what. For days we had lived not knowing what an hour would bring forth. We heard Dr. Atwood's house and the chapel were to be destroyed. The "nightshirt brigade" formed and sallied out one night on a false alarm, but now that the tension was broken we expected the worst. The servants bound up their heads with dark cloth to prevent being seen and to get their queues where they would not be easily taken hold of. They sharpened case knives as weapons of defense. The "nightshirt brigade" put on revolvers, gun, rifle, but in none of these things could we trust. We

*Local Magistrate.
†A *yamen* is a government office. In this instance, it refers to the Magistrate's office.

kept crying to God to deliver us. Definite word came soon that the Kuan had furnished an escort for the Atwaters, and they were back in their home. A note came from them telling briefly of their experience, and I began an answer expressing our sympathy. But before I had time, I heard voices and knew Mrs. Atwater and the little girls had come. It was 10:30 and, getting the little ones down as quickly as possible, we then listened to a correct version of the affair.

She said a pounding and yelling began while they were at supper and went on until a large crowd had gathered. Bricks and pieces of tile came flying over the walls into their court, one of which came near killing Celia, another just missed Mr. Atwater's head. During the suspense they could hear blow after blow on their small side gate, which seemed the chief point of attack. There were sounds of chopping going on persistently with the other pounding and yelling, and just as the gate gave way, their cook came and urged them to go out the front way to the *yamen.* To open the front gate in face of hundreds of those come to harm you and to walk boldly among them must have required divine courage. On they went untouched, stumbling over a strange road, through dust, over rough places in the dark, feeling that escaping for life is an experience one need never crave, but Mrs. Atwater was enabled to endure it all only to find themselves shut out of the *yamen* itself when they reached it. They were made to stay in the outer court into which gathered a motley crowd. Mrs. Atwater said that it was good as a play to sit there on a narrow hard bench holding one of the children and watching what went on around. The weird light of flashing lanterns, the loud voices of the excited crowd, the barring and guarding of the door that led into the Kuan's court. There were signs of hurrying to and fro, and the chair of state used by the Kuan was carried out guarded by soldiers but empty as we learned afterward, for the Kuan at the very first notice of the affair had rushed out to the scene of action not even waiting to put on his official robes or for his chair, which he ordered to come after him. We have the greatest admiration for an official who himself went into the thickest of the mob and with his own hands took a man making off with a rug under his arm.

While the Atwaters sat there in the courtyard of the *yamen,* four prisoners were brought in howling in most abject fear. The brave invulnerable "Boxer" met his match in Fen Cho fu's brave official. He dispersed the crowd in a few moments after his arrival, but they had had time to smash windows, stoves, dishes, lamps, etc., which were strewn all over the court. When the Kuan went back to the *yamen,* the Atwaters were sent back with an escort. They walked through the courts over broken pieces of what had been their housekeeping outfit. Chairs, tables, windows, dishes, etc., however, owing to the shortness of time the mob had for its work, were the chief things destroyed. Some other things were stolen. What a home to go back to at ten o'clock at night: two little children tired, excited, and still fearing another mob! They decided to come here. They felt it was running a gauntlet to do so, but it seemed best, and they set off once more in the dark and dust, feeling it a question whether they could reach us alive. The "boys" helped valiantly during the whole disturbance, and we have great reason to be proud of them and their bravery. The necessities were carried over here, and we quieted down about midnight. Mr. Atwater went back and slept in their demoralized home; fortunately there had not been time to get into the bedrooms, and they were in their usual order. Sleep can never be refreshing under such circumstances, and there was still the feeling of doubt as to whether the Kuan would punish the prisoners in anything like an adequate manner. Unless he did, we were only at the mercy of the mob that could gather at any time.

After breakfast yesterday morning our anxieties began afresh, and about half an hour afterward, to add to the horror of our feelings, word came in that a foreigner had been murdered about ten li from the city. We began to go through the dreadful possibilities as to who it could be. Mr. Davis was the first one to come into our minds; then maybe it was Mr. Williams or Mr. Jennings or Mr. Ogren. There were good reasons for serious doubt as to who the murdered man could be, whether it could be a foreigner at all, but we were in a condition of mind to believe the worst. Some foreigner, we could not know who, had evidently been trying to reach us and had lost his life. One could picture details distressing in the extreme and which depressed us greatly in our already strained frame of mind. For hours we were in suspense. Word came that the Kuan had sent out to have the matter investigated. Awful complications presented themselves. Later, the encouraging word came that the Kuan had himself asked Mr. Han, our evangelist, to go with him to help identify the nationality of the man; and we waited in great anxiety. It seems now as though God himself came to the earth to thwart the designs of evil men. This is his story as near as I can tell the details. The Kuan had him put on an official hat, put him in a cart with soldiers on either side, and they set out for the village where the murder occurred. On arrival the Kuan called together the headmen of the village and those of several other villages who had congregated and put them through a set of questions: "Was the man a foreigner? Why was he killed?" "He was found poisoning wells, and we killed him." "Yes, well where is the body?"

They were taken to the place where it had been buried. It was dug up and carried into a temple. The Kuan motioned for Mr. Han to approach it first. He did so in great fear, for at first glance his heart sank as he thought it a foreigner. The body was so hacked and cut up as to scarcely hold together. The face was mutilated, but there was something foreign in his appearance and about his dress which did not seem like the usual dress of the natives. The sleeves were a tighter cut and differed somewhat in detail. Mr. Han carefully examined the external and then opened the outer garment to look at the body inside. At first glance he said, "This is not a foreigner." "What!" cried the Kuan, no doubt in great relief. "No, this is no foreigner. Foreigners are clean. Look at this man's clothes; how dirty they are!" "Yes," said the Kuan excitedly. "Let us look for other things." "Look at the fingernails," said Mr. Han. "The foreigners trim their nails. This man's nails are long. And his hair! This isn't a foreigner's hair. This is a Chinaman's hair!" "Yes," said the Kuan. "And the man is an opium eater. Look at his teeth; how black they are. And the edges of his sleeves are stained with opium too—this man can't be a foreigner." Then, like a flash, he turned on the village elders. "What do you mean by saying this man is a foreigner. This is one of our own men!"

Then followed a scene—raging and storming and raving. During the fray some women came storming up claiming to belong to the invulnerable "Boxers" making their passes and thrusts in the face of the very Kuan himself. There were three of them probably belonging to one family. The Kuan immediately ordered them to kneel, but they refused. In a rage he kicked one of them over and ordered the soldiers to bring the women and those implicated in the murder to the *yamen.* It was a busy day for the poor Kuan. What with the affair of the night before which he had so heroically put an end to; the prisoners, punishments, having proclamations put up on our places, and on top of it all this awful mysterious murder with the insulting acts of the villagers. It must be made a precedent, so he stormed and waved and raged, broke his own teapots and cups— all probably to make an impression on those around as he had done while out in the village when he threw the teapot, contents and all, directly into the face of the village elder.

Late in the morning we heard what punishment had been meted out to the three women. They were dragged all over the city by their hair around the different suburbs, beaten with thorns, 300 blows on their backs, 40 across their mouths, and they were finally glad to kneel and recant. The man found to be the murderer of the unknown man was beaten and pounded with a spade over the head and face until a sight to behold and then was led away to be kept for execution. Four others implicated had each 1,000 blows. The four men arrested at Mr. Atwater's were beaten and fined different sums of money. The one the Kuan himself captured had a wooden collar fastened around his neck, a board two inches thick with a hole in the middle for the neck. The size of the board was about two feet square, and hinged so it closed around the neck and then locked. The culprit wearing this is said to be made to sit in front of Mr. Atwater's place every day so long as the Kuan directs.

....

June 30

In the meantime here we are. So far all safe and well but living in a suspense that cannot be imagined unless by others in like suspense. We are shut in this province with no communication with the coast for weeks. We have no way of knowing what the situation there is. We do not know whether there is war, what nations are implicated if there is war. But we can only live moment by moment, longing for something definite. It gives one the feeling of being caught in a trap with wicked people all about us desiring our extermination, and the feeling will come, in spite of trying to be brave and hopeful, that the Shansi missionaries may need to give their lives for the growth of the Kingdom of God in China. There has been much these days to make us rejoice. The leading men in the church have stood firm and apparently are not "time servers." Mr. Han has been the instrument God has used to work on the mind of the Kuan, influencing him to act so different from what we had reason to suppose. If copious rains would fall and now! Crops could be sown, the idle starving people would have field work, and the prospect of good fall crops would relieve the situation for us here as nothing else could do. Oh, that our merciful Heavenly Father would bless us by adding to what He has so mercifully done for us, this other great blessing.

It is time now for the rainy season to set in—oh, that it might fall in abundance! Daily, for several days, clouds have formed encouragingly but are scattered. We can only live in prayer these days when we know not what an hour may bring forth. An active imagination can picture a chapter of horrors to befall God's children here that keeps one sick. It has been suggested that we dare not have public worship tomorrow; we are advised to stay close by within our own walls. Nights are continual hours of anxious suspense, starting at every sound, and imagining an unruly mob surrounding us and taking our lives in revenge for the way the Kuan has seemingly favored us. The old witch woman, who was one of the three yesterday to receive the greater punishment, told the Kuan to his face that he had received 1,500 taels from the foreigners to act as he did. He has not been a favorite with the worst class of people as he would not allow promiscuous gambling on the street. He too levied an exorbitant tax on the *hsien,* * which enraged

Hsien refers to a county.

the people. Within a few days, however, he has rescinded the tax and is distributing relief to the people. This may counteract the effect of his work yesterday, for the better class of people here, those worth suffering for, realize the good he tries to do. If we are to be murdered, one can but pray that it may come quickly and end our terrible suspense. Our friends at home will have suspense but not such as ours when the heart refuses to act properly and knees and legs shake in spite of all effort to be brave and quiet, trusting in God. We do trust in Him. This is our witness. No matter what comes we are trusting in Him, believing firmly that all this tumult and alarm and real danger, rumors of wars and terrible evil are only working out His infinite purpose for good to come to China. Each day we live, we feel it a deeper truth that man proposes, God disposes. He has made the wrath of even these evil people around us to praise Him. The verses on the Women's Board calendar for yesterday, which was a day of the greatest suspense of our lives, concerned as to the murdered man, as to what the Kuan could do for us, and whether the punishment for all these criminals would be at all adequate was this:

> Thank God, this darkness and earthquake and fire and storm do pass by, and with rapt face and eager soul we listen for the still small voice "Fear not, it is all right. . . . The Lord executeth righteousness and good judgment for all that are oppressed."

If we die we die in peace!

Ever yours lovingly,
(signed) Chas., Eva, Florence

....

July 1

More dreadful news. Miss Whitchurch and Miss Searell in Hsiao-I said to be certainly killed. Dr. Edward's place in Tai Yuen fu destroyed, and the foreigners, we know not whom, killed. It all comes from the wicked Governor who came in here with exaggerated hatred for the foreigners because they were the cause of his being driven out from his former place.

May God keep us in his "Safe Shelter" at the last even as he is now—when we know not what an hour may bring forth. We leave it as a testimony to all who are wavering, who doubt, who deny—the "Grace of God" is sufficient.

Ever yours in dependence and trust in the Savior who saves and the Keeper who keeps.

Lovingly to all,
Eva

....

Of all the many rumors and contradictory accounts of Boxer attacks, the most terrifying was the unconfirmed report that reached Fen Cho fu on the evening of July 17. All of the foreigners at Tai Yuen fu and Shou Yang, the latter the site of a small missionary school, were reported killed. If true, this meant that the dead included the two oldest Atwater daughters, who had been sent to the school in Shou Yang. Since the next few days brought so many contradictory reports to Fen Cho fu, only one thing was certain at the time: foreigners—how many and whom, not known—had been killed at Tai Yuen fu. Only later would the missionaries know that the worst was true.

Events finally began to move in Fen Cho fu on the twentieth of July. The District Magistrate of Fen Cho fu went to a small village two miles west of the city and arrested a small group of Chinese Christians, four of whom were beaten at the Magistrate's office until they renounced their religion. The same day, in a further crackdown on Chinese Christians, the Magistrate ordered all native Christians not members of the Fen Cho fu church to return to their homes. Four guards were assigned by the Magistrate to the missionary compound with orders to prevent the foreigners from going out and to prevent the Chinese Christians from coming in.

A supernatural twist was added to the unfolding events at Fen Cho fu with the arrest in a nearby village of a strange man going door-to-door writing the number "ten." Charles Price wrote in his journal that this man, "a very large man with four rows of teeth . . . was taken to the yamen and beaten 800 stripes which had no effect on him at all." He also wrote about how silly the people were in their superstitions to believe that some calamity would come in ten days.

On July 21, the noose of isolation tightened further around the Fen Cho fu missionaries when all of the Chinese—with four or five exceptions—departed the mission compound. Shockingly, Mr. Han, who had gone with the Magistrate to view the body of the alleged foreigner killed outside Fen Cho fu and who later served as liaison between the missionaries and the Magistrate's office, voluntarily renounced his Christianity. Other converts soon followed and no doubt left the missionaries wondering about the value of their work in China.

Almost a week passed before the situation at Fen Cho fu underwent further change. On July 27, according to a report received by Charles Price, the Fen Cho fu District Magistrate was mortally wounded while attempting to arrest Chinese Catholics at an outlying village. Fear of what the new District Magistrate (who was already on the scene) might do was enough to inspire more Christian converts to recant. Charles Price dismally concluded that "it now seems that our work is to be altogether destroyed."

On July 29, the missionaries at Fen Cho fu were notified that by order of the Emperor they were to be escorted out of Shansi and to the coast. None of the foreigners at Fen Cho fu truly believed that the Governor of Shansi, who two days before had issued a proclamation calling for the extermination of the foreigners, was about to see the missionaries escorted to safety. Therefore, the missionaries made plans to flee into the mountains, and they were helped in their escape preparations by former members of the faith. The escape attempt, which took place on the night of July 31, was aborted when a would-be thief inadvertently brought attention to the open gate through which the missionaries were to flee. Yet in all likelihood the escape would never have succeeded, for bandits and thugs had staked out all potential avenues of flight in hopeful anticipation of a missionary escape attempt.

On the day following the aborted escape, Chinese Christians and former Christians sent a large cartload of necessities toward the mountains in preparation for another try, but the cart was waylaid by thieves. The missionaries gave up all thought of escape.

—R.F.

Fen Cho fu, China
August 1, 1900

Dear, dear Home Folks,

During the past six weeks we have been kept from the manifold dangers around us. Our lives have been threatened and we have lived from day to day expecting it to be our last on earth. Two of our friends, our nearest neighbors, fifteen miles away—Miss Whitchurch and Miss Searell—were brutally killed by a mob who gathered in their court at noon on the twenty-eighth (we think) of June. We dared not go near the place to learn any particulars, nor have we dared stir out of our own courts. All we know we have had to hear through the Chinese.

The whole province has been in a terrible state of unrest, for which the wicked Governor who did so much harm in Shan Tung last year is responsible. He is determined to exterminate the foreigners. In the latter part of June the place in Tai Yuen fu belonging to Dr. Edwards (English) was mobbed and burned. The foreigners fled to another place belonging to the English Baptist mission and on the street defended their lives by using firearms, killing a number of the mob, some say six, others say more. The Governor, who lives in that same city, vowed he would take three lives of foreigners for every Chinese killed. Miss Coombs lost her life at the time of the mob as she did not seem to escape when the others did. She was struck senseless and her body thrown in the burning building. I will enclose letters that will tell of the terrible way in which the Governor carried out his threat to kill foreigners. Thirty-three of our friends, most of whom we know personally and including the two older children of Mr. Atwater of our mission who were in Shou Yang in school, were beheaded in the presence of the Governor on July 8. Among the thirty-three lives were those of twelve children and two pregnant women soon expecting confinement.

The Governor has now issued a proclamation that any foreigners left in the province must leave. We are expecting to go into the mountains unless the Lord shows us the better way. We are having trouble finding anyone to take us, and to walk and carry necessities is almost out of the question. Our lives are worth nothing unless the Lord keeps them. We are all expecting to die and God is giving us grace, and we pray that you at home may too be abundantly blessed by Him. We would not choose to die now, and in any horrible way, but pray without ceasing that God may choose for us and make us glad to go the way He says.

Mr. Atwater's place in this city was mobbed June 26, since which time they have been with us. Mr. and Mrs. Lundgren and Miss Eldred (English) have been with us since the first of June. We are ten in all, counting the three children. Three times when our lives have been in special danger rain has come. It is falling now and we are thankful. The drought has greatly added to our danger. The Magistrate in this city has done what he could to protect us, but now that the Governor has ordered us out he has no strength to resist his order.

If only foreign soldiers could soon come into the province we would probably be saved. We have so longed and prayed they may come in time. We have had no way of hearing what is going on at the coast except the very unreliable rumors through the Chinese. Things to us who have lived in such suspense seem to move oh so slowly!

The Chinese themselves do not dare to travel at such a dangerous time. How does the Governor expect us to get away? He does not expect it, but hopes we will lose our lives in the attempt. Some few of our Chinese friends are doing everything they can to help us. Li Hsien Sheng, Dr. Atwood's helper, risks his life continually to help us and is doing everything he can to save our lives. He has friends here and it may be we will yet be spared. But if we are not, you must think with us that God has done for us and for this poor deluded country that which is for the best. We pray daily to be spared to meet you on earth, but if that be not God's purpose, we will meet you all in our Home where comes no sorrow or shadow of parting.

I must not write more. Were I to write a whole book I could not tell of the dreadful suspense of the past six weeks. We alternate hopes and fears we have all experienced. May God increase our faith and trust, our peace and willingness to do His will.

With a heart full of love to you all from us three, Charles, Eva, and Florence, daughter.

Ever yours lovingly,
Eva Price

....

How Eva Price's letter of August 1, 1900, made its way from Fen Cho fu will always be a bit of a mystery. Eva's letter, together with letters from the other missionaries, was taken through the city gates on August 3, 1900, by Fei Ch'i-hao, a Christian whose loyalty to the missionaries was nothing less than heroic. Since Fei got no further than an inn on the outskirts of Fen Cho fu and returned to the missionary compound three days later, the letters he carried probably continued on their way through a network of Christians and former Christians.

Fei Ch'i-hao's purpose in leaving Fen Cho fu was not to restore postal service. Rather, the situation at Fen Cho fu had become so dangerous that Charles Price urged Fei to escape while he could. The only place left in Shansi province where the Boxers could attack the foreign missionary presence was Fen Cho fu, for on August 2, word reached the Prices that the mission at Taiku, the only surviving Christian mission other than their own, had been wiped out by a combined assault of Boxers and government troops. Fei could escape, although he chose to return; the foreign missionaries could not escape. Two abortive escape attempts and the total inability of foreigners to blend into the local society left the missionaries with only one alternative to waiting sheeplike for the end: self-defense. Initially, Charles Price had rejected the option of resisting the Boxers as contrary to the will of God, but as the danger loomed nearer, and out of concern for Eva and Florence, he reconsidered.

Taking the missionary compound would not have been easy for the Boxers. Charles had experience as a soldier, having fought in the American Civil War, and the missionaries were fairly well armed with two revolvers, a shotgun, and a Winchester with 200 rounds of ammunition left behind by Dr. Atwood. The missionaries, however, made a potentially fatal mistake. Li Yü, the trusted intermediary between the missionaries and the local government, was called to the Magistrate's office, where it was demanded that the foreigners surrender all firearms. Li Yü objected, claiming the weapons were only for self-defense; the Magistrate, in a fit of anger, ordered Li Yü beaten and thrown into jail. Certainly out of concern for Li Yü and less certainly for religious reasons, the missionaries turned in their miniature arsenal.

Most unexpectedly, Fen Cho fu returned to virtual normalcy during the early days of August with very few rumors of impending Boxer activity.

Indeed, Eva Price's life during the troubled days of August was absolutely mundane. Fei Ch'i-hao later told how Eva's life in early August centered totally on her role as a cook, dishwasher, and occasional lifter of sagging spirits. *

Despite his treatment of Li Yü, Fen Cho fu's local Magistrate was not antiforeign, much to the displeasure of his superior, the new District Magistrate. The District Magistrate, a man whose views reflected those of Governor Yü Hsien, bypassed the local Magistrate and took direct control over the foreigners in his district. On August 14, the new District Magistrate notified the missionaries that soldiers would come the following day to escort them to the safety of the coast. This development alarmed the ten foreigners, who sent Fei Ch'i-hao to the local Magistrate with a request for his intervention. The local Magistrate made it very clear that he had nothing to do with the evacuation, and, moreover, that he did not want to meet with the foreigners. The argument that the trip would be too difficult for the pregnant Mrs. Atwater was discounted by the Magistrate's assistant, who pointed out that since the Boxers were quiet at the moment, the trip would be far safer than at any time during the past few months. There was, in any case, no choice since the District Magistrate had vowed that the missionaries would be driven out of the city with whips if need be.

An immediate problem facing the Fen Cho fu missionaries was the need to sell all that they could for travel expenses. The mission buildings had already been confiscated by the government, leaving only the summer residence that Eva called "Peeking Place." The summer property was sold for a pittance—quite possibly to the local Magistrate.

On the evening of August 14, the District Magistrate assigned twenty soldiers to guard the missionary compound from the outside while several others, men from Shan Tung, were assigned to watch from the inside. Word of the impending departure of the missionaries had spread, and the streets outside the compound were jammed with curiosity seekers. Inside the compound, the missionaries, Fei Ch'i-hao, and two other Chinese helpers stayed up till midnight making preparations for the long journey.

On August 15 the sun rose in a clear blue sky. Fei Ch'i-hao had been up before dawn attempting to get the money for "Peeking Place" from the Magistrate's assistant. When Fei finally returned to the missionary com-

*See Appendix A.

pound at eight o'clock, Charles Price took him aside and gave him a small sum of money for travel expenses and a piece of blue cloth on which was written: "This is a trustworthy man; he will tell you of our fate. C. W. Price." Charles insisted that Fei Ch'i-hao promise to escape should the party of travelers run into danger. It was important that the outside world know what happened to the missionaries of Fen Cho fu.

At nine o'clock four carts assigned to carry the missionary party and its baggage were loaded and ready to leave. The Atwaters and Mrs. Lundgren took their places on the first cart, and the Prices, Mr. Lundgren, and Miss Eldred got into the second cart. The two remaining carts carried baggage. Astonishing was the sight that greeted the missionaries as they headed for the city's north gate, for apparently every man, woman, and child in Fen Cho fu had taken to the streets to watch the departing procession.

Once outside the city gates, everyone's spirits rose. For the first time in many weeks they were no longer prisoners in their own compound. The air was fresh with a gentle breeze, and the countryside was alive with vegetation. The troop escort was large enough to deal with any band of Boxers or group of highwaymen. For the first time in weeks the conversation was lighthearted, and the sounds of laughter bubbled through the slow-moving convoy. —R.F.

··

Oberlin, Ohio
September 10, 1900

My dear Clara,*

Is it possible that we must give up hope? I do not want to do so even yet. I do not know what word you may have had, but this is what came to us yesterday in the *Plain Dealer:*

Washington D.C. Sept. 8. The State Department is in receipt of a cablegram from U.S. Consul General Goodnow at Shanghai, dated Sept. 7 reporting the deaths about July 31 at Fen Chou fu and Tai Ku of the following missionaries:

Rev. C. W. Price and wife and
daughter Florence

*Eva Price's niece.

Rev. and Mrs. E. R. Atwater and
    two children
Rev. and Mrs. D. H. Clapp
Rev. George L. Williams
Rev. F. W. Davis
Miss Rowena Bird
Miss Mary L. Partridge

The Fen Chou fu party left the station under a Chinese escort for the coast and were murdered enroute. The Tai Ku party were killed at that station.

The plain facts seem to indicate that it is all true, but some may have escaped. I have thought many times of you all and especially of your aunty's mother, your grandmother. How hard this must be for her. If all is true they are a united happy family on the other shore. Dear Eva seemed to be living in a shadow that some dreadful calamity was to fall upon dear little Florence. It came upon them together, and now they are at rest. Why such loving hands should be called home in this manner is hard for us to say. Some day all will be made plain. What our work will be with all those at rest is hard to even think of, but God knows. He has plans, and we are to follow in his footsteps. I think and pray for you all.

Your loving friend,
Alice M. Williams*

....

The erroneous reports and slipshod journalism that plagued news from China during the Boxer uprising in a small way touched Eva Price. Eva was dead. But the circumstances of her death are noticeably missing from Consul Goodnow's cable of September 7, and he may simply have added the names of the Fen Cho fu missionaries to the list of those killed at Taiku on July 31. Who, then, supplied the information about the death of the Fen Cho fu missionaries under escort? Somewhat surprisingly, the American Board of Commissioners for Foreign Missions had known for over a week the true circumstances surrounding the death of Eva Price and the others

---

*Wife of Reverend George Williams, who was killed at Taiku.

from Fen Cho fu. On August 27, Dr. Atwood, then living in Wisconsin, wrote the Board that he had heard by cable that close friends of Charles and Eva Price, the McConnells, who lived three days to the southwest of Fen Cho fu, had learned that the Fen Cho fu missionaries were killed while under phony escort. The Board, wisely enough, apparently waited for confirmation, and the strongest sort of confirmation available came during the first week of September. In fulfillment of Charles Price's request, Fei Ch'i-hao had escaped and had made his way to Tientsin.

On the morning of August 15, as the Fen Cho fu group journeyed toward presumed safety, Fei Ch'i-hao became increasingly suspicious of the escort. He finally expressed his suspicions to a nearby soldier, who bluntly told him to escape, for the foreigners were about to be killed. Fei, who could do nothing to save his foreign friends, was allowed to flee but only after the escort troops had relieved him of most of his worldly goods. At approximately one o'clock in the afternoon, Fei, who had run with all his might down the road, heard the sound of a rifle. He could only guess at what was happening, but what he suspected was soon confirmed in talks with witnesses.

The missionaries were never aware that they were being "escorted" by forty rather than twenty government soldiers. A second group of soldiers, traveling ahead of the missionaries and their official escort, was commanded by Lü Cheng-san, who was something of an entrepreneur. Lü stopped at each village along the travel route and gave the village elders a choice: either pay a sizable sum to the advance escort or suffer the dubious honor of having the foreigners killed in the village. The inevitable finally happened; the village of Nan-an shih, approximately twenty miles from Fen Cho fu, refused to meet the extortionist's demands, and Lü's troops took up positions in a sorghum field. When the missionaries arrived, Lü's men attacked.

The only resistance to the ambush came from Reverend Atwater, who despite being struck in the forehead with a sword struggled until he was overpowered. The other foreigners were either shot or cut down with swords. The attack, although suspected, was probably a shock when it came; Lü Cheng-san was thought to be a friend of the missionaries. More astonishingly, although he did not use his sword, one of the attackers was reported in contemporary sources to have spent several years as a student of Charles Price.

The corpses were stripped of their clothing and tossed into a roadside ditch. Later, the bodies were collected, placed in rough coffins, and secretly buried in a spot two miles west of Fen Cho fu. A final resting place was achieved the following year, when the missionaries were buried in a large garden a mile east of Taiku.

Eva Price died as she had lived—an ordinary woman who happened to get caught up in extraordinary circumstances. Whether she was a martyr who suffered the ultimate cost in the service of her God or whether she was an agent of imperialist aggression are questions that impute too much to Eva's intentions. Eva was a nineteenth-century woman whose behavior and beliefs were a product of the moment. She did not change history in the way that Mao Zedong and John Kennedy altered the course of human events, but she did change history as ordinary people tend to do, as one element in a larger current for change. Eva may have thought she was bringing Christ to the heathen Chinese (although she was more honest about the evangelizing effort than those more distantly removed from the front lines). And she may have thought she was bringing goodness and civilization to a people suffering a notable lack of both. Eva Price was a good person who would have been repulsed by the thought of wishing, let alone perpetrating, evil on another human being. Yet the Chinese reviled her and killed her. Despite the murder of over 200 of their comrades in 1900, few missionaries ever grasped the ugly possibility that their activities in China may have been truly harmful to the Chinese.

Oberlin College, Charles and Eva Price's alma mater, constructed an arch to the memory of the missionaries martyred in Shansi, but otherwise the memory and grief were remarkably fleeting. When pressed for an official inquiry into the 1900 massacre of missionaries, the English ambassador responded: "The missionary societies have placed their offering upon the altar, and it has been accepted. Let them renew their offering." Although Eva's family lived in Des Moines, Iowa, of the town's two newspapers, one gave her an obituary of two paragraphs, and the other noticed her not at all.

The tragedy of Eva Price was part of a larger tragedy, the great tragedy of an ancient civilization and state tearing apart under the impact of the West. The Boxer uprising destroyed any remaining fantasies about the viability of traditional China and opened the way for a revolutionary China. Eva was a participant and a catalyst in this terrible process of change. China took everything from Eva: her work, her family, her life, and even her final resting place (which was many years later obliterated by the *campus of Shansi Agricultural University). Her memory too belongs to China.—R.F.*

Slain for the Word of God and the
testimony which they held.

Revelation vi:9

In May of 1902 Eva's parents received from Judson Smith, of the American Board of Commissioners for Foreign Missions, urgent letters written to Charles Price by Mr. F. W. Davis, Miss Rowena Bird, and Mr. George Williams that relayed details of the massacre in Tai Yuen fu and Shou Yang. The letters were accompanied by this explanation: "These letters of our friends in Shansi were found by the workmen who are excavating the cellar of Dr. Nobli's house, and I send them on to you at once. They were evidently hidden by Mr. Pitkin in the ashes in the basement. The letters seem like voices from dead. How intensely interesting and pathetic it is to receive these letters almost two years after they were written."

APPENDIX A

The Story of Fei Ch'i-hao:
A Contemporary Account
of the Final Days and Massacre of the
Fen Cho fu Missionaries*

IV

THE GATHERING OF THE STORM

The people of Shansi are naturally timid and gentle, not given to making disturbances, being the most peaceable people in China. So our Shansi Christians were hopeful for themselves, even when the reports from the coast grew more alarming. But there was one thing which caused us deep apprehension, and that was the fact that the wicked, cruel Yü Hsien, the hater of foreigners, was the newly appointed Governor of Shansi. He had previously promoted the Boxer movement in Shantung, and had persuaded the Empress Dowager that the Boxers had supernatural powers and were true patriots.

Early in June my college friend K'ung Hsiang Hsi came back from T'ungchou for his vacation, reporting that the state of affairs there and at Peking was growing worse, that the local officials were powerless against the Boxers, and that the Boxers, armed with swords, were constantly threatening Christians scattered in the country.

*Excerpted from *Two Heroes of Cathay* by Luella Miner (New York: Fleming H. Revell Co., 1903), pp. 63–128. Fei Ch'i-hao was a Chinese convert who assisted at the Prices' school. He later studied at Oberlin College.

From this time we had no communication with Tientsin or Peking. All travellers were searched, and if discovered bearing foreign letters they were killed. So though several times messengers were started out to carry our letters to the coast, they were turned back by the Boxers before they had gone far. It was not long before the Boxers, like a pestilence, had spread all over Shansi. School had not closed yet in Fen Chou Fu, but as the feeling of alarm deepened, fathers came to take their boys home, and school was dismissed before the end of June.

Mr. and Mrs. Lundgren and Miss Eldred of the China Inland Mission had come to Mrs. Price's about the middle of June, and after the Boxer trouble began they were unable to leave. Mr. and Mrs. Lundgren soon heard that their mission at P'ing Yao had been burned.

During the two long months that followed not a word reached us from beyond the mountains. The church in Shansi walked in darkness, not seeing the way before it.

The wicked Governor, Yü Hsien, scattered proclamations broadcast. These stated that the foreign religions overthrew morality and inflamed men to do evil, so now gods and men were stirred up against them, and Heaven's legions had been sent to exterminate the foreign devils. Moreover there were the Boxers, faithful to their sovereign, loyal to their country, determined to unite in wiping out the foreign religion. He also offered a reward to all who killed foreigners, either titles or office or money. When the highest official in the province took such a stand in favor of the Boxers, what could inferior officials do? People and officials bowed to his will, and all who enlisted as Boxers were in high favor. It was a time of license and anarchy, when not only Christians were killed, but hundreds of others against whom individual Boxers had a grudge.

Crowds of people kept passing our mission gate to see what might be happening, for the city was full of rumors. "The foreigners have all fled." "Many foreigners from other places have gathered here." "A great cannon has been mounted at the mission gate." "The foreigners have hired men to poison wells, and to smear gates with blood."

I was staying in the compound with the Prices, inside the west gate of the city, and Mr. and Mrs. Atwater, with their children, Bertha and Celia, lived near the east gate. On the 28th of June all day long a mob of one or two hundred roughs, with crowds of boys, stood at the gate of the Atwater place, shouting:

"Kill the foreigners, loot the houses."

Mr. Atwater came out once and addressed the crowd:

"Friends, don't make this disturbance; whoever would like to come in, I invite to come, and we will talk together."

When the crowd saw Mr. Atwater come out, they all retreated, but when he shut the gate they thronged back again with mad shouts. This happened several times. By six or seven in the evening the crowd had increased and gathered courage. The gate was broken down and they surged in, some shouting, some laying hands on whatever they could find to steal, some throwing stones and brickbats at the windows. As they rushed in, Mr. Atwater and his family walked through their midst and took refuge in the Yamen of the District Magistrate, which was near by. The Magistrate, not even waiting for his official chair, ran at once to the mission and arrested two men with his own hands. His attendants followed close behind him, and the mob scattered. The Magistrate then sent soldiers to stand guard at the mission gate, and the Atwaters came to live with the Prices. We expected the mob to make an attack on us that same night, but we were left in peace.

The next morning a church member hurried in to tell us that it was rumored on the streets that a foreigner had been killed by Boxers, at a village three or four miles east of the city. We sent at once to the Yamen to learn whether this was true, and the messenger returned saying that it was true, for the village authorities had sent a notice to the Magistrate, asking him to come and examine the body. This report made us very anxious. Was this foreigner one of our Tai Ku friends, Mr. Davis, or Mr. Clapp, or Mr. Williams? Or was it someone coming to us from Tai Yuan Fu?

The Magistrate asked that one of our church members go with him to identify the body, and Mr. Han went with the Yamen attendants, wearing the same official garments that they did, as it was feared that there would be a disturbance if it was known that he was a Christian. When the official arrived he found that the body had already been buried, but he commanded that it be disinterred. The Boxers' victim was not a foreigner, but a native, about fifty years old! Probably the Boxers, seeing him hurrying along in the darkness, thought he was a fugitive foreigner, and killed him by mistake.

When the official arrived all of the Boxers had scattered, but there were two women over thirty years old and a girl about seventeen, who walked to and fro, repeating their charms, and called out loudly:

"We are the Heavenly Fairy, the Sacred Mother, come down to earth. We are sisters four."

They did not pay their respects to the official, but feigning madness, talked wildly, while a curious crowd surrounded them. The official feared to arouse opposition by punishing them there, so he persuaded them to get into a cart and accompany him into the city. Arriving at the Yamen he showed great anger, and, sitting at once on his judgment seat, summoned the women before him, first ordering that these "sacred mothers" be beaten two hundred strokes. When the beating began they still kept calling out that they were gods, but after twenty strokes they abandoned their claims and cried for mercy. The official was still angry, and after the beating was over, he asked:

"Do you still dare by your spooky words to mislead men?"

They knocked their heads on the ground, saying, "We will do so no more, we are truly penitent."

The Magistrate then commanded that they be led through the streets of the city as a warning to others. I saw them as they were led past our mission, crying as they went.

The Magistrate also issued a proclamation prohibiting Boxer drill, and the "Red Lanterns," a women's auxiliary. But alas! only a few days later the proclamations of the Governor commanding Boxer drill and ordering that the church be exterminated were received, and our Magistrate was obliged to take down his own proclamation and post those of the Governor.

Ten miles southeast of Fen Chou Fu, in the city of Hsiao-I, were two ladies of the China Inland Mission, Miss Whitchurch and Miss Searell, who were very earnest workers and much beloved.

On June 30 the missionaries at Fen Chou Fu sent a church member to see whether they were safe. He found that their door had been bricked up, and fragments of foreign books and other rubbish lay in the streets, while red-turbaned Boxers, with drawn swords, stood on guard. By inquiring elsewhere he learned that the two ladies had been cruelly killed the day before. A few days later we heard the sad story of their lingering death, as, hand in hand, kneeling in prayer, blows from the fists of the mob and brutal kicks rained down on their poor bodies. These were the first martyrs among the missionaries of Shansi, and like Jesus they died praying for their murderers. We all wept when these details and many others were told us, for we knew and loved these noble missionaries. Their sufferings were over, but our danger was greater, day by day. But still we were not hopeless, for our Magistrate was doing his utmost to protect us, and had sent four Yamen soldiers to guard our gate.

We heard from our Tai Ku mission that Mr. Davis and Miss Partridge had come to the city for greater safety, and that all had gathered in one place, where they were in great danger, as mobs constantly congregated on the street by the mission.

Gathered with the missionaries at Fen Chou Fu were about twenty Chinese. We helped the missionaries to patrol the compound by day and night, and resolved with the few weapons which we could muster to defend our lives as long as possible. At first the missionaries had decided to offer no resistance to the mob which came to kill them, for though they could easily kill several, in the end their lives would be lost. The three ladies said:

"If our enemies come, by no means fire your guns. Let them do as they will."

So the missionaries buried their guns and ammunition, but afterward they thought, "If we offer no resistance, perhaps we men will be killed first, then a worse fate may befall the women. It will be better to resist as long as we can, then our enemies, in confusion and anger, will be likely to kill us all quickly." So they took their guns out again.

Mr. Atwater's two oldest girls, ten and eight years of age, were studying in a little school in Mr. Pigott's mission in Shou Yang. Before the middle of July rumors began to reach us that all of the missionaries there had been carried to Tai Yuan Fu, and that later there had been a terrible massacre of all the missionaries gathered there. But the rumors were so conflicting that we still hoped against hope until the sad news was confirmed. Thirty-three Protestant missionaries, men, women, and little children, had been beheaded on the 9th of July, and Chinese Christians with them. Ernestine and Mary Atwater were with that company of martyrs. There was not one of our little Fen Chou Fu company who did not weep with Mr. and Mrs. Atwater that sad night when these tidings came.

One evening after the massacre at Tai Yuan Fu, just before sunset, a man hurried in to tell us that several hundred soldiers had come from Tai Yuan Fu and were now outside the city, ready to kill the missionaries that very night. This word greatly alarmed us, but the missionaries had no way to turn: they could only wait death. Mr. Price urged all of the Chinese to leave at once and flee for their lives. As they were going he gave each one a little money, and his horse to a servant. They parted with many tears.

After all the rest had gone I paced up and down the school court irresolute. It was already dark, and clouds were gathering for a storm. The court was silent as I walked there alone.

Just then Mr. Price came searching for me, and asked: "Where are you going?"

"I am not thinking of going anywhere," was my reply.

"You must escape now," said Mr. Price, "and save your life. We foreigners would be recognized wherever we might go, so it is useless for us to flee. If there were hope, we would run too. There is hope that you might escape, and you cannot save us by remaining here."

When he had finished speaking he gave me a cash bill amounting to several dollars and urged me to leave at once. Still irresolute, I took the bill with bowed head and tears streaming from my eyes. Again Mr. Price tried to hasten my steps, saying:

"I know you love us, but you cannot help us by dying with us."

So picking up a quilt I grasped Mr. Price's hand in farewell and left. As I passed out through the compound gate I saw the Yamen soldiers with lighted lanterns guarding it, and feared that they would stop me, but one simply remarked, "Are you leaving too?" and with a groan I went on my way.

While I was talking with Mr. Price rain began to fall from the darkening clouds, and it poured down as I left the gate. As I walked out into the night I knew not where to go, for I had been in Fen Chou Fu only five or six months, and my duties as teacher had left me little time for getting acquainted or forming friendships.

I started to retrace my steps. The rain had ceased, but it was pitch-dark, and my shoes were full of mud when I reached the mission. It was about nine o'clock. The gate was shut, but not locked, and pushing it open I went to my own room in the school court. The lamp was still burning as I had left it on my hasty departure. After resting a few minutes I went to Mr. Price's court. He and Mr. Lundgren stood there, each holding a gun. Seeing me, Mr. Price was both startled and pleased, and stepping up he held my hand and asked:

"Why have you come back?"

I told him my story, adding, "I truly have no place to go. I want to stay with you."

That night was a time of great unrest. We were not afraid of death, but standing thus at death's door, our thoughts flew back over the past and forward into the future, so no one slept except the three children. Midnight passed, and all was quiet. Perhaps no one was coming that night to kill us. The three ladies went to their rooms to rest, and Mr. Atwater and Mr. Lundgren went into the house. Mr. Price urged me to go and rest, but there was so much in my heart that I knew I could not sleep, so I replied, "I am not sleepy."

He said, "If you do not wish to rest, come, let us take a walk."

So I went with him to a court at the back which was filled with flowers and a few small trees which Mr. Price had planted himself. The flowers were luxuriant and fragrant in their midsummer beauty, and carrying our guns we paced back and forth for an hour talking confidentially. Mr. Price first said:

"It is past midnight. I do not think anyone is coming to harm us tonight."

Then he asked me if I had been happy during my two years in Shansi, and if I felt that I had grown in my religious life. After we had conversed a long time he said:

"Though I know that we are now in the greatest danger, and

that there is little hope that our lives will be saved, I am glad that God has used me in His holy work here. I am not sorry that I came as a missionary to China." Then he added:

"Though no one is likely to come tonight we cannot tell how soon we shall be in peril. I fervently hope that God will save your life, and use you in carrying on His work, and I hope also that you can tell others the story of our life during these days." Later Mr. Price said:

"Last night I buried eighty taels of silver and two boxes of valuables. After our death, if you can escape and return in peace, you can excavate them and use them."

When he had finished speaking, he led me to the spot where the boxes were buried.

Grief and joy mingled in my heart that night, grief that the friends whom I loved were in such extremity and I was powerless to help them; joy that Mr. Price could love me so much, look on me as a member of his own family, and tell me the secret thoughts of his heart. It made me love him more than ever to be treated thus. Gladly would I die with him.

A few days later I knew the origin of the report that several hundred soldiers had come from Tai Yuan Fu expressly to kill the foreigners. Several hundred were really passing Fen Chou Fu on their way to another place, where there was danger of a riot.

On the morning of July 20 the Magistrate, with ten soldiers and underlings, went through the west gate of the city to the village of Shih T'a, two miles away. There he arrested our little Christian community, between ten and twenty men, women, and children, and while they were being led into the city, a mob looted their homes. They were brought before the Magistrate, but had no trial. He simply commanded that each man in the company be beaten three hundred strokes. Then while the blood was streaming down their limbs, the Magistrate said:

"There is an edict commanding you to recant and leave the foreigners. If you do not recant, your lives are in danger. I have beaten you today because I want to save your lives."

He then commanded that all be led to one of the city temples to worship the gods, after which they were to return to the Yamen and pledge themselves under seal to leave the church and cease all intercourse with foreigners.

For two or three weeks proclamations had been out ordering Christians to recant, and that same day one was posted in our gateway. Christians were also ordered to leave the missionaries and go to their homes. Then four Yamen men stationed at the gate were ordered to prevent the missionaries from passing out and in, also to shut out Chinese who attempted to see the missionaries. The next day all of the Christians left the compound except myself and five others, two of whom were servants.

Several other Christians were taken to the Yamen and beaten. A man named Han, who had been a helper in the church for three or four years, was so alarmed at this that he went himself to the Yamen and asked the privilege of recanting. The official gave him a card to show in proof that he had renounced his religion, and he wore this constantly, and went about telling people that he had recanted, hoping thus to escape the Boxers. He was the first of the Protestants and Catholics in Fen Chou Fu to renounce his faith, and his example was soon followed by many others. This is not strange, for they had been in the church only a few years, and the government had commanded them to recant, but it brought to the missionaries keener sorrow than all the danger and trouble of the Boxer persecutions.

In this time of desertion and sorrow, the devotion of Li Yü (Hei Kou) was a great comfort to the missionaries. He had joined us July 6, coming from Tai Ku because he felt that he was more needed in Fen Chou Fu. He had been Dr. Atwood's medical assistant, and was well known in the city, where he had made friends with officials and men in business, so that in this time of stress his aid was invaluable to the missionaries.

Words cannot describe the longing of our hearts to penetrate the darkness that shut us in like a pall. With the exception of those at Tai Ku all of the missionaries within two hundred miles were either dead or fugitives, and every mission building was in ruins. For two months we had received no trustworthy news from Peking or Tientsin, and did not know whether the foreigners there were dead or alive. Had a foreign army come to deliver them? Did they know of the bitter suffering through which the Shansi church was passing? Fruitless efforts had been made to send messages to the coast. The ominous silence was so hard to bear; we would try again.

Our regular messengers, who were so well known on the road, could not go. Li Yü found one outsider who demanded forty taels (about thirty dollars) before he would start out on the journey to Tientsin, and Mr. Price promised him much more if he brought a return message. We could ill spare this money from our scanty hoard, but perhaps he could carry to Tientsin the news of the desperate straits of Tai Ku and Fen Chou Fu, left like little islands in an ocean of destruction, and deliverance might yet come before it was too late. Day and night we hoped and prayed that God would protect this messenger, that he might go and come in peace, and bring good tidings to comfort our burdened hearts. So twenty days passed, and the messenger returned. He said that he had gone as far as Pao Ting Fu, but beyond all was in confusion and he was obliged to turn back. He said that the foreigners had all left Pao Ting Fu, and gave us other information, so like the rumors current in Fen Chou Fu that we doubted a little, but his face was bronzed as if by travelling. Perhaps he had really been to Pao Ting Fu. A few days later we were told that he had not even started toward Tientsin, but had gone into the mountains to work in the opium fields, returning in due time to tell his plausible lies.

Late in July a proclamation of the Governor was posted in the city in which occurred the words, "Exterminate foreigners, kill devils." Native Christians must leave the church or pay the penalty with their lives. Li Yü and I talked long and earnestly over plans for saving the lives of our beloved missionaries. "You must not stay here waiting for death," we said. Yet we realized how difficult it would be to escape. Foreigners with light hair and fair faces are not easily disguised. Then where could they go? Eastward toward the coast all was in tumult. Perhaps the provinces to the south were just as bad. Our best way would be to find a place of concealment in the mountains. Li Yü and I thought that the chances of escape would be better if the missionaries divided into two companies; they must carry food, clothing, and bedding, and the large company would surely attract attention. Moreover, if they were in two parties, and one was killed, the other might escape. So Li Yü and I went to talk the matter over with Mr. Han, the former helper, and a Deacon Wang. Both of these men had recanted, but they still loved their foreign friends. Deacon Wang, who lived in a village over ten miles from Fen Chou Fu, wished to conceal Mr. and Mrs. Price and little Florence in his home for a day or two, and then take them very secretly to a broken-down temple in the mountains. Li Yü said to me:

"If you can escape with Mr. and Mrs. Price to the mountains, I will try to take the Atwaters, Mr. and Mrs. Lundgren, and Miss Eldred to another place in the mountains."

But when I proposed this plan to Mr. and Mrs. Price, they said:

"We missionaries do not wish to be separated. We must be in one place, and if we die we want to die together."

When I spoke to them again about going, they said:

"Thank you for your love, but we do not want to desert the other missionaries."

"You will not be deserting them," I pleaded. "If you decide to flee with me, Mr. Li will do his best to escape with the others."

Then I brought forward all my arguments to persuade them. Again all consulted together, and decided to go. I think this was the last day of July—the very day of the Tai Ku tragedy. Mr. and Mrs. Price made up two bundles of baggage and gave them to Mr. Han, to be carried secretly to Deacon Wang's home. Mr. Han paid a large price for a covered cart to wait for us secretly at ten o'clock in the evening at the gate of an old temple north of the mission. We were to walk to the cart, as it would attract attention if the cart stopped near the mission. We could not leave by the front gate, for the four Yamen men were guarding it; and patrolling the streets in front by day and night were twenty soldiers, ostensibly protecting us, but, as we surmised, stationed there to prevent the escape of the foreigners. I went privately to the back of the compound and unlocked an unused gate, removing also a stone which helped to keep it shut. I had already made up a bundle to carry with me, and asked Mr. Jen, a Christian inquirer, to take care of it while I was helping Mr. and Mrs. Price to get ready. After I had opened the gate I asked

Mr. Jen to wait there until I went into the south court to call the Prices.

Man proposes, but God disposes. A Mr. Wang who had often come to the mission knew that we were planning to escape that night and saw me give my bundle to Mr. Jen. Thinking that it must contain some valuable things belonging to the Prices, an evil thought entered his heart. He watched when Mr. Jen laid the bundle in a small empty room close by the gate, and after he came out, Mr. Wang went into the room. Mr. Jen thought nothing of this, supposing that Mr. Wang was a friend. But in a minute he saw Mr. Wang rush out of the room, leap over the wall, and run away. Going at once into the room and not finding the bundle, he lost his head completely, and set up a loud wail. His one thought was that he had been faithless to his trust, and sitting down in the back gate which I had opened so secretly, he cried at the top of his voice, thus bringing to naught our carefully laid plans to escape. Up ran the four Yamen men and the soldiers from the street. Everyone in the compound appeared on the scene. When I heard his outcry I thought that he had received some serious injury. All gathered about him asking his trouble, but overcome with emotion he jumped up and down, slapping his legs and crying lustily. Finally he managed to say through his tears, "Mr. Fay [Fei], Mr. Wang has stolen the things which you gave me."

When I heard this I could neither laugh nor cry nor storm at him. The Yamen men and soldiers at once picked up their lanterns and began to search. When they saw that the back gate had been unlocked and the stone removed, not knowing that I had done it, they began to scold and mutter:

"These things! How contemptible they are! When did they open this gate in order to steal the foreigners' things?"

As they muttered they locked the gate and replaced the stone, then left two men to guard it.

It was after midnight when this commotion was over, and every gate was guarded. Mr. Price and I saw that it would be impossible to get out that night. Even if we could leave the compound, we could not reach Deacon Wang's before daylight. If we attempted it, the Prices would not be saved, and Deacon Wang's whole family would be endangered.

So I went alone outside the compound to tell Mr. Han to dismiss the cart. As soon as he saw me, he said quickly:

"It is indeed well that the Prices have not come. I just came across several thieves, and was mistaken for one of their company. One of them said to me, 'If you get anything, you must divide with me.' If the Prices had come out, I fear they would have been killed."

The next day we consulted again about flight. Li Yü said:

"Let us flee all together to the mountains from thirty to sixty miles away."

So we hired a large cart and loaded it with food and other necessities, and sent it ahead of us into the mountains. Two Christian inquirers went with the cart to guard it. When it had entered the mountains about seven miles from the city, suddenly a man ran up and said to the inquirers:

"Run quick for your lives! Your mission in the city is burning, and the foreigners have all been killed."

As soon as they had jumped down from the cart and run away, rascals came up and stole all that was on the cart.

When we heard this we gave up all hope of escape, especially as we were told that bad men in the city had heard of our intention, and were hiding outside the city day and night ready to kill and rob the foreigners if they should appear. So we talked no more of fleeing, but committed our lives into the hands of our Heavenly Father, to do as seemed to Him best. We had little hope that we would be saved. Still we kept guard every night, Mr. Atwater and Mr. Lundgren being on duty the first half of the night, and Mr. Price and I the last half. At that time all of the servants had left us, and Mrs. Price did all the cooking, Mrs. Lundgren and Miss Eldred helping her. It was the hottest time in summer, and Mrs. Price stood over the stove with flushed face wet with perspiration. Li Yü and I were so sorry for her, and wanted to help her, but alas! neither of us knew how to cook foreign food, so we could only wash the dishes and help to wash the clothes.

Li Yü was so helpful those days. He alone went outside the compound to see the Magistrate, to transact business, to purchase food, and every day to get the news.

August had come, and we were still alive. Could it be that God, wishing to show His mighty power, would out of that whole province of Shansi save the missionaries at Fen Chou Fu and Tai Ku?

The second day of August, a little after noon, a man came into our compound with the saddest story that our ears had heard during those sad summer days. He was Mrs. Clapp's cook, and two days before, in the afternoon, he had fled from the Tai Ku compound when flame and sword and rifle were doing their murderous work. As he fled he saw Mr. Clapp, Mr. Williams, and Mr. Davis making a last vain effort to keep back the mob of hundreds of soldiers and Boxers, and saw Mrs. Clapp, Miss Partridge, Miss Bird, and Ruth taking refuge in a little court in the back of the compound. Miss Bird had said to him as he ran:

"Be quick! be quick!"

Over the compound wall, then the city wall, he had taken shelter in a field of grain, where he still heard the howling of the mob and saw the heavens gray with smoke from the burning buildings. He hid in the grain until morning broke, then started on his journey to Fen Chou Fu.

So to our little company waiting so long in the valley of the shadow of death, came the tidings that our Tai Ku missionaries had crossed the river. Several native Christians who counted not their lives dear unto themselves, had gone with the martyr band. Eagerly I asked about my sister, her husband* and child. The messenger did not know whether they were living or dead—only that they had been staying in the mission buildings outside the city. Two days later full accounts of the massacre reached us, and I knew that they were among the slain.

Bitter were the tears which we shed together that afternoon. It seemed as if my heart was breaking as I thought of the cruel death of those whom I loved so much, and whom I should never again see on earth. What words can tell my grief? I could not sleep that night, nor for many nights following. I thought how lovingly Mr. and Mrs. Clapp had nursed me through my long illness. I wept for Miss Bird, who had sympathized with me and helped me. "My dear ones, my dear ones, who loved and helped me as if I were your very

*The Prices' beloved Mr. Liu.

flesh and blood, who brought so much joy and peace to the lonely one far from his home, who worked so earnestly for God, who pitied and helped the suffering and poor, would that I could have died for you! Could my death have saved one of you, gladly would I have laid down my life."

The Tai Ku missionaries were gone, the Christians were killed or scattered, the buildings were all burned. We of Fen Chou Fu alone were left. We all thought that our day was at hand, but God still kept us for nearly two weeks. And now I want to tell you the story of those remaining days.

V

LAST DAYS AT FEN CHOU FU

The next day after we heard of the Tai Ku tragedy a man ran in to tell us that several hundred Boxers were coming from the east. They were those who had killed the missionaries at Tai Ku, and now they were resting in a village outside the east gate, prepared to attack our mission that afternoon. We all believed this report, for we were hourly expecting death. There was nothing the foreigners could do but to wait for the end. Mr. Price urged me to leave them at once and flee. Mr. Price, Mrs. Atwater, Mrs. Lundgren, and Miss Eldred all gave me letters to home friends. All of my foreign friends shook hands with me at parting, and Mrs. Atwater said, with tears in her eyes:

"May the Lord preserve your life, and enable you to tell our story to others."

Miss Eldred had prepared for herself a belt into which was stitched forty taels of silver. She thought that she was standing at the gate of death and would have no use for money, so she gave it to me for my travelling expenses. Mrs. Price gave me her gold watch and an envelope on which an address was written, and asked me to take the watch to Tientsin and find someone who would sent it to her father. Before I went out of the I gate I saw Mrs. Price holding her little daughter to her heart, kissing her through her tears, and heard her say:

"If the Boxers come today, I want my little Florence to go before I do."

My heart was pierced with grief as I saw the sad plight of my friends, but I could do nothing for them. Had I died with them it could not have helped them. So we parted with many tears.

While I was away the Magistrate had sent for Li Yü and demanded that all the firearms of the foreigners be given up to him. Li Yü replied, "I know the missionaries will use their weapons only in self-defense."

The Magistrate was very angry, and ordered that Li Yü be beaten three hundred blows, with eighty additional blows on his lips because he had used the word "I" in speaking to the Magistrate, instead of the humble "little one" which was customary. Li Yü was then locked in the jail, and the Magistrate sent men to the mission to demand the firearms. The missionaries could not refuse to comply, so their two shotguns and two revolvers were given up.

In this time of need two Christians named Chang and Tien came to help the missionaries. They worked for Mrs. Price to the last. The sufferings of the missionaries were indeed sore. Their patience and perfect trust in God greatly moved my heart. In the summer heat Mrs. Price three times a day hung over the stove preparing food for her family of ten, yet I never heard a word of complaint. Her face was always peaceful, and often she sang as she went about her work.

One evening when we were all standing in the yard together Mrs. Price said to me:

"These days my thoughts are much on 'the things above.' Sometimes when I think of the sufferings through which my loved friends passed it seems as if a voice from heaven said to me, 'Dear sister, see how happy we are now; all of earth's sufferings are over, and if our sorrows on earth are compared with our bliss in heaven, they are nothing, nothing."

Miss Eldred was very young, and had come from England only a year or two before, so she could speak little Chinese. The expression of her gentle face moved one to pity. When she was not helping Mrs. Price, she played outdoors with the three children, and gave Mrs. Price's little daughter music lessons.

We still patrolled the place at night, I continuing to take my turn with Mr. Price in the last half of the night. So I had an opportunity for forming a most intimate friendship with Mr. Price. He told me many things during those long hours, sometimes relating his own experiences when a soldier during the American Civil War.

Every day at sunset I played with Florence Price and Celia and Bertha Atwater. Ever since I had come to Fen Chou Fu I had played an hour with Florence. This had been good for both of us, for me because I learned English by talking with her, and for Florence because she had no children for companions and was very lonely. If there was a day when something prevented my going to her as usual, she would come or send for me. When Mr. Atwater moved to the same place his two little girls were very fond of romping with me too. I often carried the children on my shoulder, and they loved me very much. At seven o'clock, when their mothers called them to go to bed, all three would kiss me, saying: "Good-night, Mr. Fay, good-night. Pleasant dreams, pleasant dreams." So it was until the day when they left the earth.

At this time it seemed as if the Boxer trouble might be over. There were few rumors on the streets, and there had never been organized Boxer bands in Fen Chou Fu. So our hearts were more peaceful. Perhaps it was God's will after all to save our little band. Still no word reached us from the outside world. We walked on in the darkness. It was because of the friendliness of the Fen Chou Fu Magistrate that the little Christian community there was preserved so long after the floods of destruction had swept over every other mission in the province. His superior officer, the Prefect, a weak old man, died July 27. Upon the character of his successor might depend the life or death of the missionaries.

On August 12 the new Prefect appointed by the Governor arrived from Tai Yuan Fu. He was a man of great learning but little practical ability, the tool of the Governor, who had sent him expressly to murder the foreigners. So he made their extermination his first business on reaching Fen Chou Fu. It was the 13th when he took the seals of office, and that same day he went to the Magistrate and upbraided him for his remissness in the work of massacre. "In this whole province of Shansi the foreigners are killed and expelled, only those in Fen Chou Fu still live in peace." The Magistrate replied: "The foreigners here are all good men. In all the years they have lived here they have been at peace with the people, and have never caused a disturbance."

The Prefect uttered an ejaculation of anger, returned to his sedan chair in a rage, and was carried back to his own Yamen. Almost immediately the Magistrate called on him, but the Prefect refused to see him. The Prefect then summoned Lü Cheng San, who commanded the local soldiery, and the two were closeted together for a long time plotting the massacre of the foreigners. So fearful were they that their words might be overheard, that they communicated in writing.

At noon on the 14th of August the Prefect sent word to the mission that a band of soldiers would be sent next day to escort the foreigners on their way toward Tientsin. The missionaries were very reluctant to go, as they knew that great danger and suffering awaited them on the journey. Moreover, the time for Mrs. Atwater's confinement was not far distant. So they sent me to the Yamen of our old friend, the Magistrate, to inquire the reason for the Order, and to ask him to intercede with the Prefect in their behalf, beseeching him to permit them to remain until peace was restored. When I reached the Yamen I first saw an under official named Li Wan Chung and asked him to present my request to the Magistrate. He returned saying that the Magistrate had no authority in the matter, as the Prefect had made the plan. When I gave the missionaries this answer they said:

"We want to go to the Magistrate ourselves, and tell him our sore straits. Perhaps he will pity us, and contrive some way so that we can remain here."

So taking Mr. Price's card I returned to the Yamen, and sent the card in to the Magistrate by Li Wan Chung. Li came back saying:

"It won't do! It won't do! Don't you know that all the people on the street are saying that the Magistrate has been bribed by the foreigners? He has already incurred the displeasure of the Prefect, and really does not dare to see the foreigners."

I entreated most earnestly for my friends, and asked if there was not some way to prevent their being sent away. Li replied:

"There is no help for it. The Prefect says that if you don't go you will be driven out of the city with whips. There is no way but for you to prepare for the journey."

He added deceptive words, trying to convince me that the Prefect had no evil intention, but meant to send us in peace to Tientsin. In conclusion he said:

"The journey will be much less dangerous than it would have been two months ago, for the Boxers are quiet now."

There was reason in what he said, and he showed me the despatch in regard to escorting the foreigners to Tientsin. There was nothing objectionable in it. It stated that since war had broken out with foreign countries it was the will of the Empress Dowager that all foreigners should be escorted safely out of the country.

When I returned to the mission with a report of this interview the missionaries resigned themselves to the inevitable, and commenced their preparations for leaving the next day. All that afternoon we were very busy collecting and packing the things which we must use on the long journey of five hundred miles, which would take two or three weeks. The missionaries counted all the money in their possession, and found that it amounted to only a little over a hundred taels. This little hoard would have been spent long before had they not observed the strictest economy, for no money had been received from Tientsin for three or four months. How could more than ten people take the journey to Tientsin unless more money could be obtained? So Mr. Price sent me back to the Yamen to ask the Magistrate if he would give us the needed silver and take our two mission compounds in Fen Chou Fu as security. Li Wan Chung reported after interviewing the Magistrate that the mission buildings had already been confiscated, so the missionaries had no control over them. And the Magistrate had no money to lend to foreigners. Earnestly I entreated, saying:

"How can ten or more people make that journey without money? I beseech you, see the Magistrate again in our behalf."

I then mentioned the fact that the missionaries owned a place six miles from the city where they sometimes went in the summer. It was worth two thousand taels, and I entreated Li Wan Chung to let the missionaries sell this property to get money for travelling expenses. He consented on condition that I give him several taels if the property was sold.

That same evening a man came from the Yamen saying that the Magistrate had received an offer of one hundred and fifty taels for the place. Everyone knew that the missionaries were compelled to sell, so no more would be given. So the papers were made out, and it was arranged that I should go to the Yamen early the next morning to get the money.

In the afternoon of this same day, when in the Magistrate's Yamen, I went to the jail to bid Li Yü good-bye. He had heard that the missionaries were to be escorted away the next day. Tears came to his eyes when he saw me, and he said:

"Brother, I have asked a friend, Li Ching Fang, to care for you. He lives not far from the city and has promised to hide you and preserve your life. Or if you want to go to the home of my brother's father-in-law outside the North Gate, he will certainly help you to hide. A myriad times I beseech you not to go with the missionaries, for I have been told that all of them are to be killed before they reach P'ing Yao (a city twenty-seven miles away). If you go with them, you can't help them, and you will probably lose your life. You must flee tonight to one of the places which I have mentioned."

This made little impression on me, for I had been hardened to hearing such rumors. For two or three months there had not been a day when men had not been saying on the street: "Today the foreigners will be killed," or "Tomorrow the houses will be burned."

So although Li Yü told me so plainly that the foreigners would never reach P'ing Yao alive, I did not lay it to heart, but answered:

"If I do not go with them, I am afraid their difficulties on the journey will be still greater. Perhaps I can help them a little. Then the Boxers have subsided and the Prefect will send twenty soldiers as an escort; so though there will be dangers by the way, I hope we may still reach Tientsin. I have determined, whatever may happen, to go with the missionaries."

Seeing that further words were of no use, Li Yü said, "May you and the missionaries reach Tientsin in safety."

Already the rumor was afloat in the city that the foreigners were to be sent out of the province, and when I returned to the mission I found the street packed with people who had come to see what might happen.

At sunset a man interested in Christianity, who had a printing establishment in the city, came to see me. This Mr. Kuo had been a friend of my brother-in-law, and had been very kind to me since I came to Fen Chou Fu. At great personal risk he came to the mission, and, when he saw me, said:

"Find a quiet place; I have something to say to you."

I led him to a vacant space in the back court near the wall. He said, "On the street all are saying that the Prefect is going to escort the foreigners away from the province. Is it true?"

"It is true," I answered. "Word has come from the Yamen."

"What is your intention?"

"I shall go with the missionaries."

With many words he exhorted me, "A myriad times, don't go with them. I know that you will certainly meet danger on the way. Your brother-in-law is already dead. You must not be obstinate about this."

Long we talked about it, and at last I said, "Thank you much for your kind intention, but I have decided positively to go with the missionaries."

So he could only bid me good-bye, and leave the dangerous place to which he had come because of his love for me.

That evening Mr. Price said to me, "We must go tomorrow; there is no help for it, though I know that we shall meet danger by the way. We can only entrust ourselves to the care of the Almighty Lord, to do as He wills. But I do not know what you think about yourself. If you want to go with us, you will be of great assistance to us on the journey, but you will share our danger. If you wish to flee alone, I will give you a little silver for your travelling expenses and tomorrow after we are gone you can escape for your life. I want you to decide for yourself."

I answered, "I have already decided, no matter what comes, to go with you."

When he heard this Mr. Price was both glad and fearful—glad

for my help on the journey, fearful because of the danger which I would incur. Mr. Chang and Mr. Tien, who had been helping at the mission for several days, also decided to accompany them to Tientsin.

We were busy until midnight with preparations for the journey, and I went out to purchase a pair of boots for travelling.

That evening the Prefect sent twenty soldiers to keep strict watch about the mission, and also sent several Shantung men who were with him to keep watch inside the compound. All had rifles. We did not close our eyes in sleep that night, for we were very apprehensive.

Before the sun rose the next morning I was in the Yamen waiting at the door of Li Wan Chung for the hundred and fifty taels. He was not yet up, and I waited more than an hour outside his window, until the sun was high in the heavens and my heart was uneasy lest there be some trouble about the matter. Still I did not dare to disturb him.

When at last I saw him he refused to give me the money, saying gruffly, "Go back to the mission, and I will see that it is sent to you before you leave."

I suspected that we would never get the money, but it was now eight o'clock and I could wait no longer, so I returned to the mission with a very anxious heart.

Mr. Price called me aside and said, "Although we are glad that you have decided to go with us, still I want you to promise me one thing: that when danger comes, if there is a chance for you to escape, you will make every effort to save your life, so that, afterward, you can tell our story to others." I promised this and then Mr. Price gave me seven or eight taels of silver, saying, "Carry this on your person, so that if you escape you will have it for travelling expenses."

He also gave me a piece of blue cloth, about three inches long and two wide, on which he had written, *"This is a trustworthy man; he will tell you of our fate. C. W. Price."* It was sure death to be caught by the Boxers carrying a foreign letter, but this little piece of cloth could easily be concealed. Mr. Price said:

"Hide this on your person, and if you get through to Tientsin, give it to any foreigner whom you may find. I do not know whether our missionaries there are living or dead."

He also instructed me to be careful if I met any foreign soldiers, and to halt as soon as they commanded me to. "Then give them the little piece of cloth, and they will take you to an American official." Mr. Price was indeed my loving friend, taking forethought for me in all things.

Mr. Lundgren said, "If we can all reach Tientsin in peace, it will be well, but if we cannot, I hope that you will not perish with us. May God preserve your life, and may you tell our friends of our fate. I want to give you my white horse. You can ride it on the way."

Mr. Price then led me into his room and selected several garments which would be suitable for me to wear on the journey, and I prepared a bundle also of my own things.

Four long carts were already waiting for us at the gate, two of them with awnings and two open carts for our baggage. The soldiers and Yamen men gathered about and helped us load our things into the carts.

Just then Li Wan Chung came from the Yamen with the one hundred and fifty taels. This truly was unexpected. But before he could hand over the silver Mr. Atwater was surrounded by a crowd demanding money, and Li himself was making demands. The Yamen men wanted money, the leader of the soldiers wanted money, the carters wanted money, this one spoke and that one shouted, and there was nothing to do but give it to them. This one snatched a piece and that one grabbed a piece, so though Mr. Atwater did his best to resist them several tens of taels disappeared.

It was nine o'clock, so the leader of the soldiers hurried us off. We all went to the north court, where the four carts were standing. Mr. and Mrs. Atwater, their two girls, and Mrs. Lundgren took their places in the first cart, while Mr. and Mrs. Price, Florence, Mr. Lundgren, and Miss Eldred rode in the second cart. The two men who had been helping us, Chang and Tien, rode behind in one of the baggage carts. My horse was already saddled, and I led it out of the stable.

Just as I was about to mount, a young soldier strode up and demanded the horse, saying, "Our officer wants it to ride."

Knowing that I would never get the horse again if I let it go, I refused, but the soldier was determined to have it. Several others came up together and seized the bridle. I still clung to it, but I was no match for them, so the horse was soon in their hands. The missionaries tried to intercede for me, but the soldiers answered fiercely that the officer wanted the horse, so there was nothing for us but to submit. I then got into the first cart with Mr. Atwater.

VI

OUTSIDE THE CITY WALL

It was a clear, beautiful day, with a gentle wind blowing, a bright sun shining, and not a cloud within sight. As we drove out of the gate we saw the streets packed with a dense crowd of spectators. From the mission to the North Gate of the city they seemed a solid mass, while house roofs and walls swarmed with men and women eager for a sight of us. There were tens of thousands, and when we left the city gate behind, many flocked after us and stood watching until we were out of sight. So we left Fen Chou Fu on that fateful morning, August 15.

We had been imprisoned within walls for two or three months, and our hearts had all the time been burdened and anxious. Now suddenly we were outside the city in the pure, bracing air, in the midst of flowers and trees, luxuriant in summer beauty, riding through fields ripe for the harvest. It was all so beautiful and peaceful and strength-giving. So as soon as we were out in the country air our spirits rose and fresh life and joy came to us.

In the front of our cart sat Mr. Atwater with the carter, behind him were Mrs. Atwater and Mrs. Lundgren, and I sat in the back of the cart with the two little girls. On both sides, before and behind, walked the twenty soldiers, while in front of all, mounted on my white horse, with chin held high and a very self-satisfied manner, rode the leader. After ten o'clock the sun's rays grew warmer, and Mrs. Lundgren handed her umbrella to a soldier, asking him to offer it to the leader to shield him from the heat.

We talked as we rode along. Mrs. Lundgren remarked: "What a beautiful day it is!"

Mrs. Atwater said, "Who would have thought that when we left Fen Chou Fu we would have such an escort?"

"See the soldiers' uniforms, gay with red and green trimmings," said Mrs. Lundgren.

So the light conversation went on. Mrs. Atwater said to me, "I'm afraid they'll not give your horse back to you at P'ing Yao."

"I'm afraid not," I replied.

Then the two ladies turned and talked in English with Mr. Atwater, and I talked and laughed with the two children close beside me. We played a finger game, and they prattled ceaselessly.

"Mr. Fay, please tell us where we are going," they said.

After a while little Bertha grew sleepy, and nestled to rest in her mother's arms.

When we left Fen Chou Fu we thought that we might meet Boxers or robbers by the way, but we said, "If any danger comes, these soldiers will protect us with all their might."

Little did we dream that these very soldiers were to murder us.

We passed through several villages, and every man, woman, and child was out to stare at us. Then we came to a large village. It was nearly noon and very hot, so we stopped to rest a while, and the carters watered their mules. A man happened to be there peddling little sweet melons. We were all thirsty, so we bought some, and as Mr. Atwater had no change handy I paid for them with the cash in my bag. We passed some back to those in the other cart, and Mrs. Lundgren took out a package of nice foreign candy and passed some to us. After a few minutes we were on our way again.

As we travelled the young soldier who had taken my horse away walked close behind my cart, never taking his eyes off me. I thought that he was angry because I had objected to giving him the horse, so I gave little attention to it. Then I noticed something strange in his way of looking at me, as if there was something he wished to say to me.

After we had gone on a little farther with the soldier walking behind the cart, still keeping his eyes on me, he heaved a great sigh, and said:

"Alas for you—so very young!"

The soldier walking at the side looked sternly at the speaker, and said something to him which I could not hear, but I heard the reply:

"This is our own countryman, and not a foreigner."

When I saw the expression on their faces and heard these words, suddenly it flashed across me that they had some deep meaning, and I asked the young soldier what was up.

"I don't know," he replied.

"If anything is going to happen," I said, "please tell me."

He hung his head and said nothing, but followed still closer to the cart, and after a while said to me plainly:

"You ought to escape at once, for only a short distance ahead we are to kill the foreigners."

I jumped down from the cart, but another soldier came up, saying, "Don't go away."

Then I began to think it was true that the foreigners were to be killed, and wanted to get farther away from the cart, but the soldier who had first talked with me, said:

"You can't go yet; you must first leave your money with us."

I said, "I have only a little, barely enough for my journey."

But I knew that they would not let me off without money, so I gave my watch to the soldier who had taken my horse. Another soldier demanded money, saying:

"If you have no money you may give me your boots."

So I took off my newly purchased boots and gave them to him, putting on the well-worn shoes which he gave me in exchange. Another soldier took away my straw hat and the whip which I carried in my hand. It happened that at just this point a little path branched off from the main road through a field of sorghum higher than my head. I started off on the path. While I had been talking with the soldiers Mr. Atwater had conversed with the two ladies, and had not noticed our words. As I left my friends I took a last look at them, saying in my heart:

"I fear that I shall never again on earth see your faces."

I had no chance to speak to them, for the village where they were to be killed was only a quarter of a mile away, the carts had not stopped, and many people were following close behind. A crowd was also coming out from the village which they were approaching.

I had walked only a short distance on the little path when I heard footsteps following, and looking back saw that it was the two soldiers hastening after me. My heart stood still, for I thought that they were coming to prevent my escape and kill me. I did not dare to run, for they had rifles in their hands. Soon they overtook me, one seizing my queue and another my arm, and saying:

"You must have some money; we'll only let you escape with your life; your money must be given to us."

Before I had time to answer, the soldier snatched from my purse all the silver which Mr. Price had given me. I made an effort to get it back, but the soldier said:

"If we kill you, nothing will be yours. If we let you escape with your life, should not your silver be given to us?"

There was some reason in their talk, so I only entreated them to leave me a little money, for I had many hundred miles to travel before I would reach my home. The soldiers had a little conscience, for dividing the silver between them they took out a small piece amounting to about a tael, and gave it to me.

The young soldier who had first talked with me said:

"Don't go far away yet. Wait until you see whether we kill the foreigners or not. If we don't do it, hunt me up and I'll give you your watch and all of your silver. If we kill them consider that we did not take your money without cause."

They then hurried back to the road.

When I had gone on a little farther I heard a loud rifle report. By that time I was almost convinced that they were indeed going to kill the foreigners. So I ran with all my might. It was about one o'clock and the sun beat down fiercely. After I had gone several miles I felt very weary, and though I was not afraid, my heart still fluttered and my flesh crept.

The sun was sinking westward, and I looked up to the sky with a sigh. The atmosphere was clear, wind and light were fair, and I asked myself:

"Can the great Lord who rules heaven and earth permit evil

men under this bright heaven, in this clear light of day, to murder these innocent men and women, these little children? It cannot be. Perhaps I can still reach P'ing Yao, and look in the faces of those whom I love."

Then I thought that if the soldiers had really killed them in that village, as they said they would, they were no longer on the earth, but were happy with God. When this thought came I lifted my face toward heaven, saying:

"My beloved Mr. and Mrs. Price and other dear friends, if you are truly in heaven now, do you see my trouble and distress?"

So I walked on, my heart now in heaven, now on earth, a thousand thoughts entangling themselves in my bewildered mind.

I was weary and would walk a mile or two, then rest. I came to the bank of the Fen River, five miles from P'ing Yao, and waited some time at the ferry to hear what men were saying; for if the foreigners had not been killed they must certainly cross by this ferry, and everyone would be talking about it. But though I stood there a long time I heard no one mention the subject, and the dread that my friends had been killed took full possession of my heart. Then I crossed on the ferry with others, and strange to say the ferryman did not ask me for money.

Once across the river I reached a small inn outside the wall of P'ing Yao. I had walked twenty miles that day—the longest walk I had ever taken, and I threw myself down to sleep without eating anything. Often I awoke with a start and turned my aching body, asking myself, "Where am I? How came I here? Are my Western friends indeed killed? I must be dreaming."

But I was so tired that sleep would soon overcome me again.

The sun had risen when I opened my eyes in the morning. I forced myself to rise, washed my face, and asked for a little food, but could not get it down. Sitting down I heard loud talking and laughter among the guests. The topic of conversation was the massacre of foreigners the day before! One said:

"There were ten ocean men killed, three men, four women, and three little devils."

Another added, "Lü Cheng San yesterday morning came ahead with twenty soldiers and waited in the village. When the foreigners with their soldier escort arrived a gun was fired for a signal, and all the soldiers set to work at once."

Then one after another added gruesome details, how the cruel swords had slashed, how the baggage had been stolen, how the very clothing had been stripped from the poor bodies, and how they had then been flung into a wayside pit.

"Are there still foreigners in Fen Chou Fu?" I asked.

"No, they were all killed yesterday."

"Where were they killed?"

"In that village ahead—less than two miles from here," he said, pointing as he spoke. "Yesterday about this time they were all killed."

"How many were there?" I asked.

He stretched out the fingers of his two hands for an answer.

"Were there none of our people?"

"No, they were all foreigners."

My heart was leaden as I rode on the cart, with my face turned toward Fen Chou Fu. It was eight when the carter drove up to an inn in the east suburb of Fen Chou Fu, and I walked on into the city. Fortunately it was growing dark, and no one saw my face plainly, as, avoiding the main street, I made my way through alleys to the home of a Mr. Shih, a Christian who lived near the mission. When I knocked and entered Mr. Shih and his brother started up in terror and amazement, saying:

"How could you get here?"

We three went in quickly, barring the gate, and when we were seated in the house I told my sad story. Sighing, Mr. Shih said:

"We knew when the foreigners left yesterday that death awaited them on the road. Not long after you had gone the Prefect and the Magistrate rode in their chairs to the gate of the mission, took a look inside without entering, and then sealed up the gate."

Mr. Shih told me also how the Prefect, as soon as he had returned to his Yamen, had ordered Li Yü brought before him, and inflicted more cruel blows on his bruised body. Then he told details of the massacre. There was one young soldier named Li who had studied several years in the mission school, and whose sword took no part in the carnage. When the leader knew this he beat him from head to foot with his great horsewhip. The poor remains of the missionaries would have been left on the village street had not the village leaders begged that they be taken away. So the soldiers dragged them to a pit outside the city, where they found a common grave.

APPENDIX B

Eva Jane Price's Family Tree

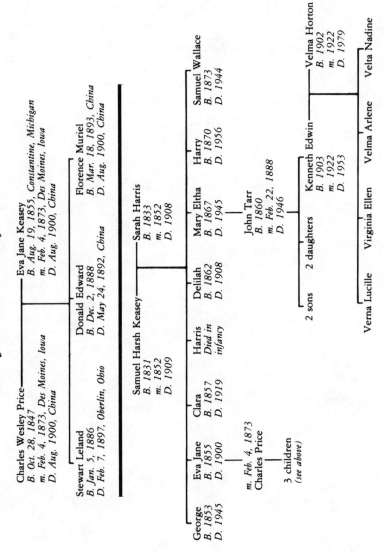

Charles Wesley Price
B. Oct. 28, 1847
m. Feb. 4, 1873, Des Moines, Iowa
D. Aug. 1900, China

Eva Jane Keasey
B. Aug. 19, 1855, Constantine, Michigan
m. Feb. 4, 1873, Des Moines, Iowa
D. Aug. 1900, China

Stewart Leland
B. Jan. 5, 1886
D. Feb. 7, 1897, Oberlin, Ohio

Donald Edward
B. Dec. 2, 1888
D. May 24, 1892, China

Florence Muriel
B. Mar. 18, 1893, China
D. Aug. 1900, China

Samuel Harsh Keasey
B. 1831
m. 1852
D. 1909

Sarah Harris
B. 1833
m. 1852
D. 1908

George
B. 1853
D. 1945

Eva Jane
B. 1855
D. 1900

Clara
B. 1857
D. 1919

Harris
Died in
infancy

Delilah
B. 1862
D. 1908

Mary Eltha
B. 1867
D. 1945

Harry
B. 1870
D. 1956

Samuel Wallace
B. 1873
D. 1944

m. Feb. 4, 1873
Charles Price

3 children
(*see above*)

John Tarr
B. 1860
m. Feb. 22, 1888
D. 1946

Kenneth Edwin
B. 1903
m. 1922
D. 1953

Velma Horton
B. 1902
m. 1922
D. 1979

2 sons   2 daughters

Verna Lucille   Virginia Ellen   Velma Arlene   Velta Nadine

APPENDIX C

A Partial List of Missionaries Who Served in China with the Prices *

Irenaeus J. Atwood	1882–1887 1890–1899 1901–1909
Annette Williams Atwood	1882–1887 1890–1899 1904–1909
Francis Marion Price (Charles's brother)	1883–1884 1887–1890
Sarah Jane Freeborn Price	1883–1884 1887–1890
Dwight H. Clapp	1885–1894 1895–1900
Mary Jane Rowland Clapp	1885–1894 1895–1900
James Brettle Thompson	1885–1896 1897–1899
Tinnie DeEtta Hewett Thompson	1890–1896 1897–1899
Francis Ward Davis	1889–1897 1899–1900
Lydia Lord Davis	1889–1897
James Goldsbury Mary Grace Fisher Goldsbury	1889–1893 1889–1893
Susan Rowena Bird	1890–1897 1898–1900

Ernest Richmond Atwater	1892–1900
Jennie Evelyn Pond Atwater	1892–1896
Elizabeth Graham Atwater (2nd wife) (She was married in 1898, but she was in Shansi earlier as a teacher.)	1898–1900
George Lewis Williams	1892–1900
Mary Alice Moon Williams	1892–1899 1909–1912
Mary L. Partridge	1893–1900
William L. Hall	1894–1898
Lou Alberta Wear Hall	1894–1898

*List compiled from information in *Oberlin in Asia: The First Hundred Years,* by Ellsworth C. Carlson, Oberlin Shansi Memorial Association, Oberlin, Ohio, 1982.

APPENDIX D

A Word on the Transliteration of Chinese Words

Chinese is a language without an alphabet, and the representation of Chinese with the Roman alphabet presents unique problems. Over the decades, the search for a transliteration system that accurately represents Chinese pronunciation has spawned a variety of romanization schemes, none of which is without flaws. The letters that comprise this journal used at least three different romanization schemes, but the dominant scheme is one that has been unused for many years. Most affected by this archaic romanization are place names. Since many of the places named in this journal may be unrecognizable to all but China specialists, the following list transliterates the place names most frequently encountered in the text into their modern-day romanized equivalents.

JOURNAL PLACE NAME	WADE-GILES ROMANIZATION	PINYIN ROMANIZATION
Chihli	Chih-li	Zhili
Fen Cho fu	Fen-chou fu	Fenzhou
Foo Chow	Fu-chou	Fuzhou
Hsiao-I	Hsiao-I	Xiaoyi
Jen Tsun	Jen-ts'un	Rencun
Paoting fu	Pao-ting fu	Baoding
Peking	Pei-ching	Beijing
Shan Tung	Shan-tung	Shandong
Shansi	Shan-hsi	Shanxi
Shensi	Shen-hsi	Shaanxi
Shou Yang	Shou-yang	Shouyang
Tai Ku	Tai-ku	Taigu
Tai Yuen fu	T'ai-yüan fu	Taiyuan
Tientsin	T'ien-chin	Tianjin

INDEX

Index